rebuilding the foundation

Effective Reading Instruction for 21st Century Literacy

Solution Tree | Press

a division of

Solution Tree

555 North Morton Street
Bloomington, IN 47404
800.733.6786 (toll free) / 812.336.7700
FAX: 812.336.7790
email: info@solution-tree.com
solution-tree.com
Printed in the United States of America

15 14 13 12 11   1 2 3 4 5

Library of Congress Cataloging-in-Publication Data

Rebuilding the foundation : effective reading instruction for 21st cen-
tury literacy / Timothy V. Rasinski (ed.) ; Peter Afflerbach ... [et al.].
    p. cm.
  Includes bibliographical references and index.
  ISBN 978-1-935542-00-1 (hardcover : alk. paper)
  1. Reading. 2. Literacy. 3. Curriculum planning. I. Rasinski,
Timothy V. II. Afflerbach, Peter.
  LB1573.R297 2011
  428.4071--dc22
                                    2010046304

Solution Tree
Jeffrey C. Jones, CEO & President
Solution Tree Press
President: Douglas M. Rife
Publisher: Robert D. Clouse
Vice President of Production: Gretchen Knapp
Managing Production Editor: Caroline Wise
Senior Production Editor: Suzanne Kraszewski
Proofreader: David Eisnitz
Cover Designer: Orlando Angel

Table of Contents

About the Editor

Timothy V. Rasinski

 Timothy V. Rasinski, PhD, is a professor of literacy education at Kent State University. He has written numerous articles and chapters and has authored, coauthored, or edited more than forty books and curriculum programs on reading education. He is author of the best-selling book *The Fluent Reader*, now in its second edition. His scholarly interests include reading fluency and word study, and readers who struggle. His research on reading has been cited by the National Reading Panel and has been published in journals such as *Reading Research Quarterly*, *The Reading Teacher*, *Reading Psychology*, and the *Journal of Educational Research*. Rasinski is the coauthor of the fluency chapter for Volume IV of the *Handbook of Reading Research*.

Rasinski recently served a three-year term on the board of directors of the International Reading Association and has served as coeditor of *The Reading Teacher*, the world's most widely read journal of literacy education, and the *Journal of Literacy Research*. Rasinski is past president of the College Reading Association and winner of the A.B. Herr and Laureate Awards from the College Reading Association for his scholarly contributions to literacy education. In 2010, he was elected to the Reading Hall of Fame.

Rasinski received his doctorate from The Ohio State University. He taught at the University of Georgia and as an elementary and middle school classroom and intervention teacher in Nebraska.

Introduction

Timothy V. Rasinski

Literacy is the key to success in life; we've heard these words so often from politicians, the media, researchers, school officials, and community members that they have almost become a cliché. Yet there is great truth in this statement. The ability to read underlies our potential—our ability to find personal success and satisfaction in life and to make a substantive and positive difference in the world. Although we have statistics galore to support the importance of reading, it should be self-evident that the ability to read is important.

Despite our acknowledgement of the importance of reading, as well as enormous sums of stimulus money from federal, state, and local governmental and philanthropic agencies aimed at helping all students acquire the ability to read, we have not made much progress toward this goal. Since 1992, reading achievement trends for fourth- and eighth-grade students in the United States have remained largely flat (National Assessment of Educational Progress, 2009). Moreover, reading achievement levels for certain groups of students have remained substantially and significantly below the national norms during this period.

And against this backdrop of little, if any, substantive progress, we have seen numerous initiatives at the national, state, and local levels aimed specifically at improving literacy levels among elementary, middle, and secondary students. Why have these quite significant efforts had such a minimal impact on student achievement? Of course, there are a number of reasons we can point to, from a lack of scientific rigor in designing and implementing appropriate reading curricula and instruction, to a lack of fidelity of implementation of instructional programs, to a lack of parental and family involvement, and so on. Although we often look for quick fixes and easy ways to add on to the existing approaches to reading instruction, I believe that it may be time to reconsider the full reading curriculum—how reading instruction is conceptualized and what must be done to make it work for all students. Hence, this book is less about building onto or altering existing models of reading education and more about how reading educators and policymakers might think about rebuilding and reconceptualizing, perhaps from the ground up, what it means to provide effective instruction in reading to all students at all levels—reading instruction that truly does work!

> Although we often look for quick fixes and easy ways to add on to the existing approaches to reading instruction, I believe that it may be time to reconsider the full reading curriculum—how reading instruction is conceptualized and what must be done to make it work for all students.

In my own considered opinion, I feel that one of the most important reasons for the lack of progress in reading achievement across the United States has been the level at which we have aimed our improvement efforts. Most efforts at literacy reform have been aimed at the classroom or school level. What can teachers and school administrators do in their classrooms and schools to improve student achievement in reading? This thinking led the National Reading Panel (2000) to examine research into effective reading instruction at the classroom and school levels. The panel identified phonemic awareness, phonics or word recognition, reading fluency, vocabulary, reading comprehension, and teacher professional development as key components of effective literacy instruction for students in classrooms and skills. Thus, President George W. Bush's national reading initiative Reading First mandated that schools and primary-grade classrooms obtaining financial resources from this program commit themselves to integrating these elements into their classroom and school literacy programs.

While the results of Reading First have been somewhat checkered, I feel that the program did have a positive impact on the way literacy and literacy education is viewed at the primary-grade classroom levels. Yet throughout the implementation of Reading First, I could not help but wonder how Reading First might impact classrooms beyond the primary-grade levels as well as entire school districts and clusters of schools. How are district reading supervisors, curriculum directors, directors of instruction, and even superintendents viewing literacy and literacy instruction in their school districts? My guess is that Reading First, as well as other literacy initiatives, had minimal impact on these upper-level decision makers in schools and the reading-related policies they implemented. If anything, these initiatives simply led upper-level decision makers to commercial reading programs their school district could purchase that would satisfy the requirements of the initiative. Little in the way of substantive change was made at the district (or even school or classroom) level, aside from the new program preapproved by the granting agency. No wonder improvement in student literacy achievement has been so slow in coming across the United States. Change is needed at the classroom and school level for sure. But change is also needed at the district, state, and national levels. With this volume, I hope that we might start new conversations about reforming reading instruction at all levels—from classroom to district and beyond.

> This book is less about building onto or altering existing models of reading education and more about how reading educators and policymakers might think about rebuilding and reconceptualizing, perhaps from the ground up, what it means to provide effective instruction in reading to all students at all levels— reading instruction that truly does work!

Why This Book?

This volume is an attempt to break the literacy logjam that has developed in the United States. This volume brings together some of the best minds in the area of literacy instruction. The contributors write about their own areas of specialty to a wider audience—teachers, principals, educational administrators beyond the individual school level, and school policymakers at all levels.

In chapter 1, P. David Pearson and James V. Hoffman set the stage by challenging us to think more broadly about what constitutes effective teaching and effective teachers of reading. It is more— much more—than teaching phonics. Effective teaching does involve instruction in key competencies related to reading success, but it goes considerably deeper.

In chapter 2, Linda B. Gambrell reminds us that reading is not only a matter of cognition. Reading and learning to read also have social and affective dimensions that teachers and schools need to consider. It is not enough to teach students how to read; we must work to instill in them an internal desire or motivation to read.

Literacy involves literature. In chapter 3, Junko Yokota and William H. Teale explore the role of materials in the reading curriculum—materials not just for teaching the skill of reading, but also for helping students develop an appreciation for the written word and the wide variety of formats available to them.

Clearly, success in learning to read is most likely when children experience success in reading instruction in the earliest moments of their school careers. In chapter 4, Lesley Mandel Morrow shares her insights on creating effective reading curricula for beginning and primary-grade readers.

The momentum developed in the primary grades needs to carry through into the intermediate and middle grades. In current models of reading instruction, these grade levels are often neglected. In chapter 5, Timothy Shanahan identifies what must be done to make reading instruction successful in these grades.

What sort of reading instruction should we provide to students who struggle in learning to read? Current models of instruction often mandate new curricula, new materials, and new methods to meet the needs of these students. In chapter 6, Richard L. Allington and Patricia M. Cunningham challenge this notion and suggest that we should look at the instruction given to successful readers as the starting point for conceptualizing instruction for struggling readers.

Chapters 7 through 10 examine key competencies that empirical research has found to be associated with high achievement in reading. In chapter 7, word-study experts Shane Templeton and Donald R. Bear propose that learning to read words is a developmental process and that a greater understanding of the process that children go through in learning to decode and spell (encode) words can help teachers provide instruction that more closely meets the instructional needs of their students.

After years of neglect, reading fluency has finally been recognized as an important competency in reading. However, reading fluency has been defined by some experts as teaching students to read fast. In chapter 8, I argue that reading fluency is more than reading fast—it is a critical link from word recognition to comprehension—and it can be taught in ways that are authentic, engaging, and effective.

It's not enough to be able to read words accurately and fluently; students also need to understand the meanings of the words they encounter in texts. Camille L. Z. Blachowicz, Peter J. Fisher, and Susan Watts-Taffe tell us in chapter 9 that effective vocabulary instruction is much more than learning (and memorizing) the definitions of selected words. Vocabulary instruction that works aims at developing in students a "word consciousness," an awareness that words are important, that they make a difference, and that they are worth exploring.

Reading comprehension is the essential and ultimate goal of reading instruction. Moreover, comprehension does not simply happen by reading the words in a text fluently and understanding what the words mean. And comprehension is not simply the ability to remember or recall the basic facts from a text. There are strategies that successful readers employ to gain deep meaning from text. In chapter 10, Maureen McLaughlin shares an instructional model for moving students to those deeper levels of meaning-making.

Reading and writing clearly are connected. Writing and instruction in writing can have a powerful and positive effect on a student's reading development. Chapter 11 focuses on writing. Ruth Culhum explores how key characteristics or traits in writing can facilitate students' growth in reading, or as she describes it, "learning how to read with the writer's eye."

Reading and learning in the content areas are also integrally connected. In chapter 12, Richard T. Vacca and Maryann Mraz share workable and engaging strategies that teachers at all levels and in all content areas can use to help students make meaning in discipline-specific texts.

Schools have certainly become more consumed by testing, and this test orientation has caused a great deal of anxiety in students and teachers. Assessment is important. Instruction in reading is only effective to the extent to which growth can be measured. However, the best assessments not only measure growth, but also guide instruction and learning. In chapter 13, Peter Afflerbach helps us consider the purpose and nature of effective assessment and how it might be woven seamlessly into the school reading curriculum.

The final chapter in this volume changes the focus on what needs to be taught (and assessed) in reading from the student and the teacher to the person behind the instruction—the reading coach who provides leadership and professional development within the school setting. The role of the reading coach is relatively new and not fully understood in many schools. Rita M. Bean helps to clarify the nature and role of the reading coach. Teaching can be a lonely job. The knowledge that there is someone in the school to support teachers and provide assistance in improving instruction can make all the difference between reading instruction that is mediocre to instruction that is state of the art and effective for all students.

Effective Reading Instruction for All Students

This book is not offered as a prescription for designing reading programs, nor is it presented as an antidote to the various troubles that schools face in developing and implementing reading curricula that meet the needs of all students. Rather, my best hope for this book is that it leads its readers—preservice teachers, inservice teachers, reading coaches, reading specialists, school administrators, and school policymakers at all levels—to engage in a deeper and more thoughtful professional conversation about what is meant by effective reading instruction for all students. Teaching reading is indeed a complex task. There is no simple formula for developing good instruction in reading. What really matters, when it comes down to it, are well-meaning and knowledgeable literacy professionals at all levels willing to engage in deep and thoughtful analyses and discussions about what it means to be a reader, what it means to be

> Teaching reading is indeed a complex task. There is no simple formula for developing good instruction in reading.

an effective teacher of reading, and what it means to be a school and school system that provides reading instruction that works for all its students. I hope you find this volume valuable, and I hope it leads you into that deeper discussion.

References

National Assessment of Educational Progress. (2009). *The Nation's Report Card.* Washington DC: U.S. Department of Education, Institute of Educational Sciences. Accessed at http://nationsreportcard.gov/reading_2009/ on September 21, 2010.

National Reading Panel. (2000). *Report of the National Reading Panel: Teaching children to read. Report of the subgroups.* Washington, DC: U.S. Department of Health and Human Services, National Institutes of Health.

P. David Pearson

P. David Pearson, PhD, is a faculty member in the Language, Literacy, and Culture program in the Graduate School of Education at University of California, Berkeley, where he also served as dean from 2001–2009. His current research focuses on issues of reading instruction and reading assessment policies and practices. Pearson has served as editor of *Reading Research Quarterly* and the *National Reading Conference Yearbook*, as president of the National Reading Conference, as a member of the International Reading Association board of directors, and as the founding editor of the *Handbook of Reading Research*. He is currently on the board of directors for the National Writing Project and a member of the National Academy of Education. He has received the IRA's William S. Gray Citation of Merit and Albert Harris Award, NRC's Oscar Causey Award, NCTE's Alan Purves Award, the University of Minnesota's Outstanding Alumni Award, and AERA's Distinguished Contributions to Research in Education Award. Before coming to UC Berkeley, Pearson served on the reading education faculties at Minnesota, Illinois, and Michigan State. He began his education career as a fifth-grade teacher in Porterville, CA.

James V. Hoffman

James V. Hoffman, PhD, is a professor of Language and Literacy Studies at the University of Texas at Austin. In addition to his graduate teaching responsibilities, he directs the undergraduate teacher education program in the area of reading. His research interests focus on reading acquisition, reading instruction, reading texts, and teacher education. He is the author of more than one hundred scholarly articles, chapters, monographs, and books. He is a former editor of *Reading Research Quarterly* and the *National Reading Conference Yearbook* and former director of the Research in Teacher Education program at the Research and Development Center for Teacher Education at the University of Texas. Hoffman is a past president of the National Reading Conference. He served on the board of directors of the International Reading Association and as director of the IRA Commission on Excellence in the preparation of preservice teachers in the area of reading. He was elected to the Reading Hall of Fame and just completed a term as president of this organization. He has been active in numerous literacy projects in the developing world. He has worked with International Reading Association's international division on projects in Belize, Thailand, Tanzania, Kenya, and South Africa.

In this chapter, Pearson and Hoffman present two sets of principles of practice: ten for teaching in general and ten for teaching reading in particular.

Chapter 1

Principles of Practice for the Teaching of Reading

P. David Pearson and James V. Hoffman

Attorneys practice law. Physicians practice medicine. Teachers, however, practice *to get ready to* teach. Teachers are more like hockey players in the way they practice than they are like attorneys, doctors, and other major service professionals. This positioning of teaching as technical and not professional arises as much from a self-imposed view found in the discourse that surrounds teaching as it does from comments made by those outside of education. Educators typically speak of teaching practices (even best practices) as tied to teaching behaviors and not to the kinds of thought processes, dispositions, and passions that research has demonstrated as critical to effective teaching. Whether the omission of these professional dimensions of teaching practices is intentional or not, the consequences are the same: teaching is "doing," and effective teaching is reduced to "doing the right thing." Nothing, we believe, could be further from the truth.

Our goal in writing this chapter is to elevate the notion of practice in teaching to the status of other service professions. We will argue for a concept of professional practice in teaching as a context for simultaneously acting, serving, and learning, and for a conception of professional practice that is grounded in a philosophy of pragmatism that gives shape to a personal practical theory of teaching. We will further argue for a conception of the teaching of reading that promotes synergy between the practice of teaching and the practice of literacy.

We present two sets of principles of practice: ten for teaching in general and ten for teaching reading in particular. These principles are the product of our own experiences as classroom teachers and literacy educators. They reflect the intersection of our own personal practical theories. We hope that they provoke conversations around the practical teaching of literacy, help reframe the ways in which teachers approach (examine and reflect upon) their own practice, and become part of the larger discourse surrounding teaching and literacy practices.

> We present two sets of principles of practice: ten for teaching in general and ten for teaching reading in particular.

Our Pragmatic Roots

According to Kurt Lewin (1951), "There is nothing as practical as a good theory" (p. 169). This widely quoted assertion is open to interpretation. Perhaps he is suggesting that practice should be guided by theory. Perhaps he is suggesting that theory should be guided by practice. Or perhaps, as we believe, he means that every action is guided by theory, whether the actor is aware of it or not. An examination of Lewin's academic career as a gestalt theorist, a pioneer in the field of social psychology, and as the initiator of the action-research movement suggests that he would champion all three interpretations. Lewin was a pragmatist and believed that to truly understand something you needed to examine it in the context of change, and like most of his contemporary pragmatists, he abided by the principle that if you truly want to understand something, try to change it.

Pragmatism, as a philosophical movement, arose in the late nineteenth century and is best represented in the writing of William James (1907/1979) and Charles Pierce (see Turisi, 1997).[1] The essence

---

[1] In pragmatism, we find alignment with other important movements in the late nineteenth and early twentieth century: Darwinism, Marxism, and the scientific method. Indeed, the marginalized view of learning and development as represented in the work of Vygotsky and Piaget is aligned with the view that experience is tested and constructed (really transformed) into knowledge within the individual (with a heavy dose of social mediation).

of *pragmatism* is found in the argument that the truth of a proposition (or action) can only be discovered in the examination of the consequences. A *theory of practice* is constructed around problems experienced in a particular context. In pragmatism, we find truth by attending to the practical consequences of ideas. We construct truth in the process of successful living in the world: truth is in no sense absolute. Beliefs are considered to be true if and only if they are useful and can be practically applied. The truth may change as contexts change (as they always will), but the path leading to the discovery of the truth is always the same. The pragmatist proceeds from the basic premise that the human capability of theorizing is integral to intelligent practice. Theory and practice are not separate spheres; rather, theories are tools or maps for finding our way around and engaging with the world or for understanding the pathways we have followed—intentional or not—in traversing that world.

For the pragmatist, learning is practical in the sense that it grows out of and is tested through experience. John Dewey was one of the leading figures in applying the philosophy of pragmatism to education (see Hickman & Alexander, 1998). For Dewey, the philosophy of pragmatism formed the crucial link between his interests in truth, democracy, and education. For Dewey, there was no question of theory versus practice, but rather a question of intelligent practice versus uninformed, stupid practice. For Dewey, pragmatism provided the guiding framework for a personal life and a social order. Pragmatism is much more than "whatever works" or "anything goes" or "be practical"; in fact, it really is none of those. *Pragmatism* is an approach to understanding experience—critically and methodically analyzed—unfettered by ideologies and driven by examining the good, the right, the just, and even the beautiful that follow from our actions, including the words we speak.

> *Pragmatism* is an approach to understanding experience—critically and methodically analyzed—unfettered by ideologies and driven by examining the good, the right, the just, and even the beautiful that follow from our actions, including the words we speak.

Personal Practical Theories

In the *Third Handbook of Research in Teaching*, Lee Shulman (1986) described *teacher knowledge* as the missing paradigm in research in teaching. Of course there had been earlier research focused on teacher thinking (such as Clark & Yinger, 1977), but Shulman's chapter seemed to be a watershed moment for a shift in focus for research in teaching away from teacher behaviors toward teacher thinking. While much of the research that responded to Shulman's challenge focused on the identification of different types of teacher knowledge (such as teacher pedagodical knowledge), a powerful line of research emerged that examined the nature of and important role of the practical knowledge that reflects and guides teachers. Elbaz (1981) proposed the term *practical knowledge* as the key to understanding teacher thought processes. He defined five sources of teachers' practical knowledge: situational, personal, social, experiential, and theoretical. Clandinin (1985) and Connelly and Clandinin (1984; 1985) extended this work by offering the framework of personal practical knowledge. They described this knowledge as personal in the sense that it grows out of circumstances, actions, and undergoings that have affective meaning for the individual. This personal practical knowledge includes a body of convictions that may be conscious or unconscious. While there was some early criticism of this construct for the extreme focus on the individual and not the social and institutional forces that might give shape to this knowledge, this line of research has continued to evolve. Most of this research continues to reveal the important role that narratives, images, and metaphor play in shaping the construction of this knowledge. A highly reflective process known as *personal theorizing* (Cornett, Yeotis, & Terwilliger, 1990) allows teachers to identify and make explicit their personal practical knowledge by transforming it into personal practical theories (for a discussion of this process as it relates to thoughtfully adaptive teachers, see Fairbanks et al., 2010). This construct has been described elsewhere (such as in Cervetti & Pearson, 2005) in terms of situated knowledge to capture the idea that this is knowledge used to shape practice in particular settings (such as classrooms).

Elbaz (1981) suggested such a theoretical structure for personal practical knowledge when he stated, "But a sense of order and a structure inherent in practical knowledge is also required." Elbaz proposed three terms intended to reflect varying degrees of generality in teachers' knowledge. These terms are *rules of practice, image,* and *practical principles*. The *rules of practice* may be thought of as routines that are followed methodically (if not automatically). The *images* are tied to intuitive ways of teaching. The *practical principles* are framing constructs used reflectively to guide, inspect, and transform the known into the new.

Practical Principles of Teaching

We lean on Elbaz's framework for teacher knowledge and in particular on the notion of practical principles as the organizer for the two sections that follow. Without apology, we frame these principles in terms of the *practicing* teacher. We have struggled in settling on an adjective to describe our ideal teacher. We started with *thoughtful* teacher, but found it a bit ethereal. We toyed with *effective* teacher, but found it too behavioral. We considered *pragmatic* teacher (to capture the close relationship between theory and practice), but found it a bit obscure. We also considered *reflective* teacher, but thought that phrase was overused in the teacher education literature. So *practicing* teacher was all that was left. We like it because of its focus on practice; at that same time we fear that it might not convey enough of a sense of how theory and practice are wedded in enacting practice. So when you read *practicing teacher*, think thoughtful, effective, pragmatic, reflective, practicing teacher!

The first set of ten principles are related to general principles of teaching.

Ten General Principles to Guide the Practicing Teacher

1. The Principle of Praxis
2. The Principle of Purpose
3. The Principle of Serendipity
4. The Principle of Exploration
5. The Principle of Reflection
6. The Principle of Community
7. The Principle of Service
8. The Principle of Flexibility
9. The Principle of Caring
10. The Principle of Reward

The Principle of Praxis

The practicing teacher understands and acts on the understanding that education has the power to transform individuals and society (for the better, or sometimes for the worse).

According to Paulo Freire, *praxis* is "reflection and action upon the world in order to transform it" (1970, p. 36). Like Dewey, Freire was a pragmatist who believed in the power of democracy and a curriculum grounded in experience. According to Glass (2001), Dewey's and Freire's views on teaching and learning are quite parallel. Dewey's views are framed in terms of a biological-organic conception of human existence and growth with emphasis on intelligent adaptation to the environment through problem solving. Dewey argued that the conditions that "maximize this evolutionary adaptive potential are precisely those linked to the formation of the ideal society: full participation, open communication with minimal barriers, critical experimental practice aimed at overcoming problems, and close attention to the consequences of actions" (Glass, 2001, p. 17). Freire situates his philosophy in the context of social structures and in the ways in which societies can potentially oppress some while privileging others. Freire warned that a system of education that is not critically minded may fall into the trap of perpetuating inequality rather that promoting opportunity. For Freire, education should be directed toward promoting freedom of thought and action for the individual and for the society through critical self-reflection and action. In the end, education must be directed toward something, and if not freedom of thought and action, what else? In assuming the role of teacher, the individual has taken on a responsibility to his or her students and to his or her society that is far beyond that of an individual citizen.

> In assuming the role of teacher, the individual has taken on a responsibility to his or her students and to his or her society that is far beyond that of an individual citizen.

The Principle of Purpose

The practicing teacher always operates in the moment with a clear understanding of purpose.

While the principle of praxis operates at the broadest level of a practicing teacher's professional life, the principle of purpose operates at the most specific level of daily teaching. Teachers are, at any given moment, forced to make choices. Practicing teachers make these choices based on their learners' knowledge and their own knowledge of the important intermediate and long-term learning goals they hold for their students. A pragmatic philosophy focuses attention on the relationship between actions (the results of these choices) and outcomes (what students know, sense, or feel as a consequence of pedagogy and experience). The teacher's critical examination of teaching events in relation to purpose is at the very heart of learning through practice. Whether the teacher engages in cooperative learning, inquiry learning, or direct instruction, there is always purpose.

In particular, teacher clarity on the outcomes for teaching optimizes the critical examination of the action/outcome relationship that shapes teacher learning. A shared understanding of these purposes and outcomes that both teacher and learner can articulate enhances the possibilities for both teacher and student learning. When teacher and learner have co-constructed and jointly committed to the learning outcomes, learning for both is enhanced even more. Learners in classrooms are offered choices. Learners make these choices, supported by a practicing teacher, through a careful consideration of and conversation around the desired outcomes, potential obstacles along the path, and strategies for working around these. One way to think about the student role in settings where purposes and outcomes are tightly linked is that when students are given both voice and choice in the process, they are likely to be more motivated participants in the learning process.

> When students are given both voice and choice in the process, they are likely to be more motivated participants in the learning process.

The Principle of Serendipity

The practicing teacher, aware of the dangers of routine, is open to opportunities of the moment.

Teaching can become so bound up in comfortable routines (as in Elbaz's rules of practice) that there is hardly space left for the unexpected. As important as it is in everyday learning, purpose and routine can become the enemy of learning. It is the unexpected that opens doors to transformative learning opportunities. James

_____

It is the unexpected that
opens doors to transformative
learning opportunities.

_____

Marshall was inspired by a drop of green paint that had fallen in the wrong place to create the characters George and Martha and the story of split pea soup. William Herschel was looking for comets and initially identified the planet Uranus as a comet until he noticed the circularity of its orbit and its distance suggested that it was indeed a planet. Percy Spencer invented the microwave oven while testing a magnetron for radar sets. He noticed that a peanut candy bar in his pocket had melted when exposed to radar waves. A child's question that, on first glance, may seem out of left field (or at least off the lesson focus) may be the catalyst for much more powerful learning. At even a more critical level, the principle of serendipity relates to the permeable curriculum connecting the classroom to the world. What teacher in the United States in 2005 did not use hurricane Katrina as an opportunity to explore important concepts in science and social studies, regardless of grade level?

The Principle of Exploration

The practicing teacher is always in the process of changing his or her practices based on the exploration of possibilities in his or her classroom.

Dewey, as a pragmatist, believed in the importance of problem solving for productive teaching/learning environments. For Dewey, the struggle to recognize, engage, and solve problems was the core of all learning. The experiential curriculum relies on activity that engages the learner in educative experiences rooted in goals and aspirations. Learners are motivated to explore the unknown to gain control over it. Teachers are no different. While respecting Dewey's emphasis on the term *experience*, we have chosen to use the term *exploration* in the framing of this principle. We opt for exploration for two reasons. First, exploration encompasses Dewey's requirements for educative experiences and continuity of experiences. Second, exploration promotes the view of the learner (the teacher or the student) as active. There is less emphasis on experiences as things that are provided and more emphasis on the need to construct meaning through exploration.

Exploration as a scientific endeavor privileges another feature of quality instruction: authenticity of purpose and action. Exploration occurs in the natural world largely for purposes of learning about what makes that natural world around us tick; we are constantly trying to unearth the fundamental processes that shape our very existence in that world. Exploration is thus inherently authentic; we study the real world around us, not some specially constructed world that some of us created. The metaphor of authenticity is powerful in its application to teaching and learning in school settings; we want school tasks, texts, and even tests to possess an air of authenticity—to look as much as possible like tasks, texts, and assessments that would occur outside of school settings, such as in the workplace, the home, and the community. The danger in creating special tasks and texts for purposes of specific instructional goals is that we end up reifying (making real what is not) those texts and tasks, thus giving them a life of their own and preventing students from learning how to apply cognitive skills and strategies to the texts and tasks of the world outside of school. The exploration of authentic tasks (with inherent ambiguity and risk qualities) is the preferred path for a curriculum.

> The exploration of authentic tasks (with inherent ambiguity and risk qualities) is the preferred path for a curriculum.

The Principle of Reflection

The practicing teacher engages in reflection through and following teaching activity as a tool of problem solving and goal setting.

Dewey recognized the important role of reflection in learning through experience. While Dewey identified five stages in reflection, he essentially regarded the act of reflection as holistic and an "active, persistent and careful consideration of any belief or supposed form of knowledge in the light of the grounds that support it and the further conclusion to which it tends" (Dewey, 1933, p. 9). He distinguished between primary and secondary experiences and believed that reflection was the secondary experience, beginning when the primary experience fails to meet the needs of the learner (Miettinen, 2000). Tools of reflection range from a teacher's journal to the exercise cycle—practically any space that provides an opportunity to engage deeply with the second experience.

Donald Schon (1983) has helped us understand that the reflection process may operate in a double-loop cycle. Practicing teachers do not limit their reflection to the teaching experience (reflection in action); they also critically examine the perceived governing variables that surround the act of teaching (reflection on action). Attention to governing variables in the reflection process in the current scene is likely to include the press of standards, mandates, consequential assessments, and scripted curriculum on teaching. At the same time, as practicing teachers use reflection for their own learning, they begin to find ways for students in their classrooms to use reflection as a learning tool. Both Dewey and Schon agree that reflection must always lead to changes in practice; indeed, without the action that leads to change, it isn't reflection, but rather some sort of random mental exercise.

> Reflection must always lead to changes in practice; indeed, without the action that leads to change, it isn't reflection, but rather some sort of random mental exercise.

The Principle of Community

The practicing teacher engages in discussions around experience within and across multiple communities with the purpose of growing personally and giving back professionally.

In the history of the human race, social communities arose, at least in part, in response to the need to accomplish tasks (survival, production, and even education) that an individual could not perform alone or could perform much better with others. Only recently have we come to appreciate the important role that community and social life play in the development of our language, our thinking, and our identities—even as we engage in those activities as individuals. The view of the classroom where rules for getting along are essential to maintain the order that permits learning has given way to a view of the classroom as a community of learners that includes the teacher and the students. Teachers, in their professional lives, must rely on communities to support learning. These communities may not always be those formalized by the structure of schools (for example, grade-level teams or an assigned mentor–new teacher partnership) but may be communities that arise informally. Some examples include a small group of teachers getting together to explore an alternative approach to informal assessment in the classroom writing program; a group of teachers from different schools coming together around the study of social justice and the development of a peace curriculum; a group of university-based teacher educators coming together with a group of teachers in a school to explore possible partnerships in preservice teacher preparation; and a group of community leaders partnering with a group of teachers to explore the possibility of service learning opportunities for students in the community surrounding the school. These kinds of activities reflect the creation of flexible, often mission-driven, learning communities that break down the isolation of the self-contained teacher and classroom and create new possibilities for learning.

Part of the responsibility in being a professional is learning how to belong to many communities—and to respect and do justice to each. Part of the responsibility of being a teacher is to introduce each and every student to the benefits and responsibilities of being a part of a community, for each student will have many opportunities to accept or reject community membership and responsibility throughout his or her life. From the pragmatic perspective, these layers of communities open up new challenges and new opportunities to address outcomes important to learners in the moment and in their lives as adults. Within all of these communities, language and thinking expand. An old saying about teaching is that teaching is what happens when you *close* the classroom door. Nothing could be further from the truth—teaching, in this communitarian framework, is what happens when you *open* the classroom door.

> An old saying about teaching is that teaching is what happens when you *close* the classroom door. Nothing could be further from the truth—teaching . . . is what happens when you *open* the classroom door.

The Principle of Service

The practicing teacher serves the learners in his or her classroom and their parents.

Within a pragmatic philosophy, the ethic of responsibility argues that individuals are responsible for the consequences of their actions. Teaching, as a service profession, is client oriented. Teachers work for those they serve—the children in their classrooms and their parents.

Teachers are like medical doctors and nurses who serve their patients, and attorneys and (the best of our) politicians who serve their clients and constituents. Professionals do not serve institutions. It is only an accident that teachers happen to be housed in institutions. The ethical and moral responsibility for the student falls on the teacher. In a perfect world, schools would be organized to support the teacher at the point of delivery. In this world, principals would serve teachers. Superintendents would serve principals. Accountability would be bottom up, with the client (the student and his or her family) ultimately in charge. But that is not the reality of our world. The reality is just the opposite as different levels of policymakers, such as the federal government, states, districts, and schools, have conspired, intentionally or not, to use mandates that constrain rather than inform teaching, and they do it from the top down. Too often our conversations tend to focus more on raising test scores than on ensuring that our students and teachers are engaging in important work in classrooms. Too often today our conversations are limited to the academic (in particular on what is tested) and not on a critical examination of the personal, social, cultural, and moral consequences of teaching and learning.

> Too often our conversations are limited to the academic (in particular on what is tested) and not on a critical examination of the personal, social, cultural, and moral consequences of teaching and learning.

The Principle of Flexibility

The practicing teacher expects challenges and is strategic in finding alternative approaches without compromising on his or her goals.

Flexibility in teaching is well documented as a quality of effective practice. Seldom do lessons unfold as planned. Teachers must be nimble, so that they can adapt within a lesson to unanticipated events or responses in ways that make learning possible. To be a "practicing" teacher is to recognize the reality of the moment and respond. For a teacher to simply carry on down a planned path ignoring the reality of current circumstances is a recipe for failure. Flexibility involves adjusting the strategies we use to achieve a particular goal; it is intentional. We would argue that teachers who are particularly effective are transparent in the adaptations they make during teaching. They are explicit in sharing with their students why and how they are adjusting a plan. The teacher's stance of flexibility in teaching is an important model for students so that they become flexible in the ways in which they approach problem solving and in the challenges they face.

The teacher's stance of flexibility in teaching is an important model for students so that they become flexible in the ways in which they approach problem solving and in the challenges they face.

Flexibility, though, is not a principle manifested only in the context of lessons or interactions with students. This is particularly the case for practicing teachers who challenge the status quo of how schools work and expectations for students. These teachers often face pressures to engage in ways that they see as inconsistent with the needs of students. Prescriptive curriculum mandates, assessment demands, and peer pressure to conform may present a greater challenge than the teacher faces inside of the lesson. Long ago, Postman and Weingartner (1969) wrote about the need for teachers to assume a "subversive" stance to push back on a context that constrains. A direct, confrontational approach seldom works. Rather, teachers learn to be flexible in adjusting the path they take without losing sight of the goals. Some teachers may use a strategy of creative compliance, adhering to the letter of the law (mandate) while ensuring no compromise to their teaching principles. Some teachers may follow the "easier to ask forgiveness than ask for permission" strategy when innovating in the classroom.

The Principle of Caring

A practicing teacher acts on the understanding that caring is necessary to build the core relationships essential to the teaching and learning transaction.

Nell Noddings has articulated a compelling vision of the caring teacher extended into a view of the caring classroom and the caring curriculum. The trusting relationships that grow in a caring classroom are critical to learning. Keith (1999) argues that Nodding's view of caring is rooted in a philosophy of pragmatism with an added dimension of feminist theory. Keith points in particular to the writing of George Herbert Mead—a colleague of Dewey at the

University of Chicago. Mead examined the development of the social self through interactions with others. Ethical behavior emerges out of practice, not out of principle. Ethical caring grows out of the natural caring as found in a mother's care for a child. Ethical caring is intentional and active. Caring relationships begin to grow through an exploration of how we are alike, moving to the appreciation of how we are different, moving to the bonds that grow out of successful collaborative activity. The establishment of caring relationships supports the risk taking essential to learning activity.

We find strong connections between this ethic of care at the interpersonal level and the commitment in South Africa to an envisioned society through the practice of *ubuntu*. *Ubuntu* is a Nguni word from South Africa that addresses our interconnectedness, our common humanity, and the responsibility to each other that grows from our connection. *Ubuntu* roughly translates into "humanity or fellow feeling" or "I am because you are." "A human being can only be a human being through other human beings," and "People live through the help of others." Variations on the theme of ubuntu are found throughout Africa. Nussbaum (2003, p. 4) offers typical Shona greetings (from Zimbabwe) as reflecting this spirit of ubuntu:

Mangwani, marara sei? (Good morning, did you sleep well?)

Ndarara, kana mararawo (I slept well, if you slept well.)

And at lunchtime:

Marara sei? (How has your day been?)

Ndarara, kana mararawo? (My day has been good, if your day has been good.)

The spirit of ubuntu has become a critical part of the social transformation of South Africa from apartheid to reconciliation. The principle of ubuntu is mentioned in the preamble to the new South African constitution. It is educational policy in South Africa that every lesson taught regardless of subject area or the ages of the learners embody the spirit of ubuntu. We cannot underestimate the importance of this caring and relational dimension to the practice of teaching. The caring classroom finds order and flow through a purpose that goes beyond being productive and in ways that can be carried forward in life outside of the classroom.

The caring classroom finds order and flow through a purpose that goes beyond being productive and in ways that can be carried forward in life outside of the classroom.

The Principle of Reward

The practicing teacher finds satisfaction—even happiness—in what he does for others, not in what is done for him.

No one would deny that teachers are underpaid. But to believe that the goal of attracting and retaining quality teachers in classrooms can be solved by just increasing pay or tying compensation to student achievement growth or offering the annual "teacher of the year" award is naive if not patently wrong. The pragmatist would ask, What is it that sustains the best teachers to put forward incredible levels of effort day after day, year after year? We believe the kinds of things Philip Jackson discovered over forty years ago regarding the rewards of teaching are as true today as ever (Jackson, 1968):

- Great teachers value the spontaneity of classroom life.

- Great teachers value the immediacy of the classroom and the learning they are part of.

- Great teachers value the autonomy of making decisions around curriculum and instructional approaches.

It would seem that current trends in education, designed as they are to guarantee curricular standards by reducing teacher prerogative in the classroom, are at odds with what is fundamentally rewarding in teaching. The greatest professional sustenance accrues to teachers who stop looking "out" or "up" for recognition but instead look within various learning communities for validation, affirmation, and professional identity. Practicing teachers begin by re-examining classroom culture wherein the manipulation of rewards (mainly the distribution of praise) is used as the primary tool for motivating student engagement and performance. Practicing teachers begin to focus on

It would seem that current trends in education, designed as they are to guarantee curricular standards by reducing teacher prerogative in the classroom, are at odds with what is fundamentally rewarding in teaching.

learning achievements in the classroom in ways that help learners examine, assess, and appreciate their own progress. In such an environment, students learn to rely less on external and more on internal cuing systems to gauge their own learning. Practicing teachers apply this same principle to the various learning communities in which they participate. Satisfaction and perseverance are the results of progress recognized toward goals and purposes.

Principles of Practice Specific to the Teaching of Reading

Our emphasis on the meaning of *practice* in the professional life of teachers, as informed by a philosophy of pragmatics, stands in close parallel with recent efforts to frame reading as a social practice. But an older, more popular notion of practice in the teaching of reading comes from a more behaviorally oriented image of practice as drill: activities such as reading sight words on flashcards to build automaticity or rereading texts to build fluency. This kind of practice situates reading as a school activity, quite apart from "real reading." This view of practice fits well within autonomous models (the highly text-driven technical models that focus on what happens inside the head of an individual during reading) of the reading process and reading acquisition (Street, 1995). In contrast, the social-practice perspective of literacy focuses on engagement with a text in some social context with some purpose in mind. The meanings surrounding these experiences with texts are socially constructed and interpreted. The social-practice perspective requires attention to cognitions and motivations that surround activity. From a pedagogical perspective, the social-practice perspective requires teachers to deliberately consider ways of connecting reading activity that occurs inside the classroom with the kinds of reading activity that occur outside the classroom.

With this socially grounded view of practice and our ten general principles of teaching firmly in mind, we turn our attention to ten principles of effective reading pedagogy that are triply aligned (1) with a social-practice perspective on reading, (2) with our general principles, and (3) with what we know about the process of learning to read (see the feature box on page 25). We provide answers to the following questions:

- What are the explicit and implicit principles that practicing teachers of reading use to organize and guide activity?

- What guides teachers' practice as they work to ensure that all students are becoming more effective readers?

We offer a set of principles grounded in the belief that practicing teachers are action oriented and thoughtfully adaptive in their efforts to support growth in literacy. Each of the specific principles is practice oriented and, as with the general principles, framed in terms of the practicing teacher.

Ten Specific Principles to Guide the Practicing Teacher of Reading

1. The Principle of Reading in a Literate Environment
2. The Principle of Reading as Meaning Making
3. The Principle of Reading as Social Practice
4. The Principle of Reading as a Developmental Process
5. The Principle of Reading as Balance
6. The Principle of Reading as a Strategic Process
7. The Principle of Scaffolding Reading Processes
8. The Principle of Reading Assessment as Consequential
9. The Principle of Adaptability in Teaching Reading
10. The Principle of Teaching Reading as a Tool

The Principle of Reading in a Literate Environment

The practicing teacher of reading works with his or her students to create a literate environment that continually reinforces the utility, practicality, and joy of reading.

Extending the general principle of community into the effective teaching of reading in the classroom context, these teachers understand classrooms as spaces that can be used to support students as they link their literate lives in the classroom to their social spaces outside the classroom. These are classroom environments in which students witness and participate in the ways in which reading, along with writing and language study, is used as a tool for the development of learning, enjoyment, insight, reflection, and self-fulfillment.

Students who daily interact with print, read what others have written, and write to, with, and for others develop conceptual understandings about the value of reading as a transformative tool for the remainder of their life. The classroom literate environment is part physical, part social, and part psychological. The literate environment is physical in the sense of the variety of texts, both commercial and locally constructed, and the organization of these texts. The literate environment is social in the sense that these texts are actively engaged with and interpreted in the context of teaching and learning with peers and teachers. The literate environment is psychological in the sense that the classroom is a safe place to explore, take risks, and learn. The classroom environment serves as both a window and a mirror of literate lives. The window ensures that the literate lives of students outside of school can find a path into the classroom and that the literate lives of students inside the classroom can readily flow into daily life outside of school. The mirror dimension of the literate environment offers a critical space for the teacher and students to carefully inspect their own practices and set priorities and goals for growth.

> Classrooms are spaces that can be used to support students as they link their literate lives in the classroom to their social spaces outside the classroom.

The Principle of Reading as Meaning Making

The practicing teacher of reading acts on the understanding that reading instruction provides students opportunities to construct meaning through the texts they read.

Extending the general principle of exploration into effective classroom teaching, these teachers situate reading activity in the context of problem spaces, questions, or interests that are important to the learner. Practicing teachers teach enabling skills (they enable understanding but they themselves are not understanding) that allow readers to unlock words and their meanings, process syntax (both simple and complex), and clarify misunderstandings on the way to making meaning. Practicing teachers know that in asking students to construct meaning, they will need to teach students how to engage all the resources at their disposal as students activate their background knowledge, discover new information, and construct new understandings. For optimum learning to occur, these teachers know that their students should think about what they already know about a topic, gather new information from the text (and, if appropriate, from experience), and gradually come to understand the topic at hand. Students who do not receive help in learning the strategies used in these three areas (activating prior knowledge, reading for information, and constructing their own models of text meaning) usually have trouble with difficult reading material and, consequently, learn less—both in any given lesson and cumulatively across a year or a school career.

The Principle of Reading as Social Practice

The practicing teacher of reading acts on the understanding that every act of reading *and* every act of teaching reading are inherently social and interactive—they require readers and teachers to engage in reciprocal negotiation processes.

Extending the general principle of community into the effective teaching of reading, these teachers emphasize the social nature of reading and reading pedagogy. The meanings students create for the texts they read are complex negotiations involving an unseen author, the traces of meaning the author left for them to decipher in the text, a practicing teacher to serve as a guide, and an interpretive community of peers with whom to share and revise provisional meanings. Practicing teachers help students discover how this negotiation process works.

In the same way, practicing teachers of reading act on the understanding that reading instruction is an inherently interactive, social, and reciprocal negotiation process. Just as students learn to read literary and informational texts, so they learn to read pedagogical texts (the texts teachers create inside the classroom). The meanings students develop about their instructional situations involve similarly complex negotiations among self, teacher, peers, and the situation itself. Teachers and students provide one another with demonstrations of how to build, share, and revise models of meaning, both of the texts they read and the instruction they are trying to render sensible. This is nothing more or less than an extension of Paulo Freire's (1970) admonition/observation that as human beings we

It is useful for all teachers to realize that students are trying as hard to make sense of *them* as teachers as they are the *texts* to which we hold them accountable.

learn to read the word (written texts) and the world (the broad panoply of experience that life presents to us). It is useful for all teachers to realize that students are trying as hard to make sense of *them* as teachers as they are the *texts* to which we hold them accountable.

The Principle of Reading as a Developmental Process

The practicing teacher of reading acts on the understanding that reading develops as a process of emerging expertise.

Reading is not best learned, if ever learned, through the acquisition of a set of isolated skills picked up one by one along an assembly line offered by the teacher and the commercial (or state or district-mandated) reading program. Instead, a single central goal—building meaning—carries the teacher and his or her students from one situation to the next. Extending the general principles of purpose and exploration into the effective teaching of reading, the teacher focuses on what is important for the students at that moment. *Need* in a developmental perspective is not tied to the kind of deficit thinking so prominent in teaching today (as in, "What is missing here that the student needs to know that I must teach?"). Rather, need in a developmental perspective is based on the assumption that the student is an active learner. Thus, a teacher who is responsive to a student's reading interest or curiosity is adapting the curriculum to the needs of the student. The practicing teacher follows the lead of the student into the learning she is exploring. This perspective positions the learner as active and building knowledge and gaining control over processes.

This perspective positions the learner as active and building knowledge and gaining control over processes.

What changes over time is the students' level of reading expertise and topical knowledge, along with the amount and type of conceptual and contextual scaffolding teachers need to provide to ensure that all of their students are successful. Teachers would be better off to regard their role not as the source and purveyor of knowledge and wisdom, but as a tour guide leading knowledgeable and purposeful apprentices on a journey toward increasing mastery of the secrets of reading and the acquisition of knowledge about the world they are trying so hard to make sense of.

The Principle of Reading as Balance

The practicing teacher of reading embraces a framework of balance in conceptualizing and delivering curriculum.

It is commonplace for reading curriculum theorists to construct a curriculum beginning with the basics of specific skill orientations/processes (letter knowledge, phonemic awareness, phonics) and then moving on to higher processes of oral language development, fluency, vocabulary, comprehension, and critical reading. *Balance* is viewed here as something that exists in the curriculum (even to the distribution of time devoted to particular reading activity). We understand and accept that curricular perspective on balance (see Pearson, Raphael, Benson, & Madda, 2007 for an elaborated treatment of curricular balance), and we believe that balance across atomistic skills and global processes is essential. But there is more to be said about balance.

There is an alternative perspective on balance, one that conceptualizes balance as a characteristic of the reader rather than of the curriculum. Teachers guide students toward becoming competent readers with elaborate skill infrastructures, high motivation to read and learn, and strong habits of mind. Attention to balance helps to create flexibility in the reader through simultaneous attention to all. Extending the general principle of flexibility into the effective teaching of reading, we see the need both for the reader to become flexible in balancing processes and the teacher to be flexible in responding to the needs of the learner. The most well-elaborated approach to balance comes from a delightfully simple metaphor popularized by Freebody and Luke (1990) in the four resources model, which suggests that readers need the skill and flexibility to move freely among four stances toward reading:

1. **Reader as decoder**—In this stance, the reader focuses on getting the message the author left on the page. (So what is the author trying to say here?)

2. **Reader as meaning maker**—In this stance, the reader focuses on using his or her personal resources (for example, knowledge and strategic skill) to create a coherent model of meaning for a text. (What did you learn from this text that you didn't already know?)

3. **Reader as text user**—In this stance, the reader focuses on understanding the form-function relationships in text by analyzing how writers use particular words, structures, and genres to achieve particular effects on readers. (How does the author's choice of words shape our understanding of the main character?)

4. **Reader as text critic**—In this stance, the reader moves from understanding of form-function relations to an evaluation of authorial motives and intentions. (What is the author trying to persuade us of in this essay? Why?)

In adopting a balanced approach of the sort we are describing, a teacher would be embracing general teaching principles of purpose, exploration, and reflection. The exploration comes in the form of leading students on a journey across the landscape defined by this range of stances. We want readers who change their stances between texts and even within a given text. The purpose is transparent: we change our stance depending on our purpose. And the reflection is embedded in the very process of figuring out why different approaches are needed to serve different situations, texts, and purposes.

The Principle of Reading as a Strategic Process

The practicing teacher of reading acts on the understanding that reading instruction must promote strategies.

The general principles of purpose, flexibility, and serendipity drive this specific principle of reading pedagogy. Teachers begin instruction with some intentions, usually curricular goals—understandings about what reading is and how it works—that they want students to achieve and some teaching strategies for helping students achieve them. But they realize that they have to adapt their goals and their strategies just as soon as they start teaching, in response to students' understanding of the goals and strategies they use as teachers. And adaptation always entails reflection on what we are doing (in other words, the activity itself) and whether that activity is suiting our purposes.

Practicing teachers of reading apply this same tension between intention and adaptation to the strategies and understandings they are trying to help students develop. They know that, like their own instruction, *reading strategies are as adaptable as they are intentional*. Reading strategies begin as conscious plans that readers use to make sense of text. They are intentional; readers have a few predetermined ideas about how to go about building meaning. But reading strategies are also adaptable; they

> Reading strategies are as adaptable as they are intentional.

can and should change quickly and easily depending on how readers size up the situation at hand. Good readers change what they do depending on their perceptions about the text (How hard is it?), the task (What do I have to do to achieve my goal or satisfy the teachers' goal?), their knowledge resources (What do I know that will help me understand this text?), their own purpose (Why am I doing this? What could I gain from it?), and the consequences of reading (What will happen to me if I do or do not succeed?).

Practicing teachers of reading help students develop understandings and related strategic processes through careful inspection of literate activity and literacy products. The general principle of reflection is applied here to reading instruction. This principle requires that teachers of reading bring students inside the act of reading in order to develop their understanding of reading both as a global process and a more specific set of processes that tell us how, when, and where to use different strategies and skills. Developing both types of understandings simultaneously is extremely difficult. The process is something like the creation of a tapestry, where specific patterns must be understood in order to understand and create the whole design. As we help students create this tapestry of reading, we know that they must understand the specific patterns that make it up (including the functions they serve for the entire tapestry), but in the end, it is the full tapestry that we enjoy, understand, and use. The smaller patterns become a vehicle for making the whole tapestry accessible. While this duality is difficult to achieve in reading instruction (it is based on holding this tension between the whole and the parts in a delicate balance), it is necessary if students are to develop appropriate understandings of reading as a cognitive, aesthetic, and cultural practice. It is the hardest—but most reward-ing—part of teaching reading.

The Principle of Scaffolding Reading Processes

The practicing teacher of reading carefully scaffolds learning in a way that allows students to use and gradually gain control of a skill, strategy, or tool before they fully understand it.

This business of scaffolding, particularly scaffolding that is sen-sitive to individual differences among students and the situation at hand is at once both the most elusive and the most beautiful (and satisfying) aspect of teaching reading. Scaffolding is what teaching is all about, and in delivering just-in-time individualized scaffolding, a teacher embraces most of the general principles we have described. Scaffolding is inherently exploratory and serendipitous because it requires that teachers be sensitive to the moment-by-moment enact-ment of learning in the classroom environment—and that sensitivity makes it inherently reflective, too. It is clearly communitarian because it is enacted within the context of a classroom community of learners. And providing scaffolding, especially individualized scaffolding, is the ultimate hallmark of teaching as a service to the teacher's number-one clientele—the students who enter his or her classroom hoping to finally get the help they need to become real readers.

By using analogies, explanations, explicit cues, redirecting metaphors, elaborations, and modeling (in short, anything they can find to make what must seem opaque to students more transpar-ent), teachers can create a form of assistance that allows students to complete a task (like summarizing a test or figuring out the pronunciation and meaning of an obscure word) before they cog-nitively understand how and when to use it. This form of assistance is highly productive as long as the scaffolding is gradually removed as students gain control of the task. Teachers who teach reading in this way are using what we have come to call the *gradual release of responsibility* (from teacher to student) for helping readers become independent and self-sufficient readers—readers who know when and whether they have understood a text, and, if they haven't, what to do to fix things up.

The Principle of Reading Assessment as Consequential

The practicing teacher acts on an understanding that the contexts of accountability in high-stakes testing must be negotiated with the need for students to take responsibility for their own learning as they develop the independence they need to become lifelong learners.

This principle extends the general principles of exploration and reflection. Assessment tools are seen as critical to inform responsive teaching and independent learning. The problem with assessment in our current accountability milieu is that we regard assessment as something someone else does to us, not as something we do to and for ourselves. We forget a fundamental principle of any and all assessment systems—that the student is the number-one client of the assessment system (IRA/NCTE, 2010). The only reason that we as teachers have the right to assess students today is so that they can assess themselves tomorrow. If we kept that idea in our minds as we constructed, administered, and interpreted assessments, we would have more valid, more transparent, and more service-oriented assessments. These assessments would go beyond categorizing kids to actually helping them and their teachers craft curricular activities to promote growth along a pathway to more skilled reading.

Assessments must distinguish clearly between mastery constructs and growth constructs. *Mastery constructs* are the enabling skills of the curriculum—letter sounds, word identification, vocabulary meaning, clarifying; they are all the bits and pieces on the pathway to real reading, but they are *not* real reading. *Growth constructs* are the goals of reading instruction, constructs like comprehension and critical reading; they are the very reason we bother to teach reading in the first place. We celebrate when the mastery constructs are under control so we can get on with real reading. And we always make sure that the growth constructs guide our assessment of student competence and our plans for future curricular activity. Reading for understanding begins the minute students step into the kindergarten classroom, and it is the ultimate justification for each and every moment of instruction devoted to enabling skills.

This understanding of accountability may be at odds with the dominant forms of assessment (high-stakes tests) that are shaping curriculum in classrooms across the United States and in an increasing number of countries around the world. The practicing teacher finds ways to negotiate the spaces between the external demands for accountability and the need for students to be aware of their own learning and growth processes.

> The practicing teacher finds ways to negotiate the spaces between the external demands for accountability and the need for students to be aware of their own learning and growth processes.

The Principle of Adaptability in Teaching Reading

The practicing teacher of reading negotiates the space around specific mandates for curriculum and teaching.

This principle is a direct extension of the flexibility principle. For example, currently most reading curricula, both commercial programs and state or district standards-driven curricula, contain too many skills to teach. Pressured by so much to cover in so little time, teachers quickly gloss over everything, which leaves no time to teach anything very well. Everyone involved—teachers, students, and parents—would benefit from a leaner, meaner curriculum composed of a handful of key processes taught well and frequently applied to lots of authentic texts. In this regard, we are encouraged by the conceptualization of reading we see in the 2010 Common Core Standards (CCSSO/NGA, 2010). They seem to have managed not to let the reading curriculum explode into a cascade of ever-expanding standards that prevent teachers (and students) from engaging in the kind of thoughtful exploration of ideas and processes that characterizes reading at its best.

The Principle of Teaching Reading as a Tool

The practicing teacher of reading understands that just as enabling skills (like phonics and word identification) are a means to an end (comprehension and critique), so reading is not an end unto itself, but rather a tool to enable individuals to accomplish other goals—learning, insight, enjoyment, and participation.

We don't read for the sake of engaging in the reading process. We read to accomplish specific goals in our lives—to learn something more about outer space, to gain insight into our own motivations, to experience the aesthetic joy by losing oneself in a well-written piece of literature, to gain entry into a book club, or to participate in civic discourse about our collective future. Reading, like writing and language, are better situated as means of achieving these broader goals rather than ends unto themselves. When we situate reading (or writing or language) as an end unto itself, we run the risk of taking pride in promoting readers who *can* read rather than nurturing readers who *do* read. There is a mounting body of evidence that this utilitarian (call it pragmatic, if you will, because of the emphasis on the consequences of reading) view of reading pays dividends not only in helping students acquire a portfolio of useful tools but also in promoting better test scores on both subject-matter and reading assessments (Goldschmidt, 2009).

> When we situate reading . . . as an end unto itself, we run the risk of taking pride in promoting readers who *can* read rather than nurturing readers who *do* read.

Conclusion

> *One cannot understand the history of education in the United States during the twentieth century unless one realizes that Edward L. Thorndike won and John Dewey lost.*
>
> —Ellen Condliffe Lagemann

The progressive movement in education, so closely tied to pragmatism and John Dewey, has become something of a footnote in the history of education. The progressive movement was simultaneously too idealistic and too pragmatic for the times. But as we have come to think about the principles that could and should guide the teaching of reading in these challenging times, we find ourselves drawing inspiration and insight from the "loser" (John Dewey) and the philosophy of pragmatism. Even so, there are many reasons why we align ourselves with Dewey:

- Because we are optimists. Because we believe that the 21st century may lead to a different understanding than the twentieth. And the Common Core Standards, even though they are externally imposed standards, are more encouraging than what we have seen since 1990.

- Because we believe Dewey was mostly right in what he argued for and was not always interpreted as he would have hoped.

- Because we believe that the struggle to improve teaching and schools is difficult but worth the effort. Our use of Dewey is tied less to his advocacy for progressive schooling than it is on the philosophy of pragmatism (and the key role accorded to experience and consequences of one's actions) that is core to his thinking.

- Because we believe that through engagement with principles of practice like those we have put forward, we can begin to push back against those who would dismiss teacher education as irrelevant, as the last three U.S. Secretaries of Education (Page, Spellings, and Duncan) have, or argue for "teacher training" rather than teacher education (see Hoffman & Pearson, 2000), as is implicit in most of the current models of mandated reform.

- Because we believe that through engagement with principles of practice, we can push back against those who see successful reform from schools emanating from some combination of mandated standards or high-stakes testing.

- Because we would like to see reform driven by a broader, more uplifting vision of the possible and the practical.

- Because we believe that through engagement with principles of practice, we can push back on the popular notion that research should reveal "best practices" narrowly construed as a set of behaviors, not as ways of doing, thinking, and valuing that will never be "best" but always contextualized in the moment and always evolving.

- Because we are pragmatists.

- Because we are practicing teachers.

References and Resources

Cervetti, G., & Pearson, P. D. (2005). A model of professional growth in reading education. In C. Snow, M. Griffin, & S. Burns (Eds.), *Knowledge to support the teaching of reading: Preparing teachers for a changing world* (pp. 201–224). San Francisco: Jossey-Bass.

Clandinin, D. J. (1985). Personal practical knowledge: A study of teachers' classroom images. In *Curriculum Inquiry* 15(4), 361-385.

Clark, C. M., & Yinger, R. J. (1977). Research on teacher thinking. *Curriculum Inquiry, 7*(4), 279–304.

Connelly, F. M., & Clandinin, D. J. (1984). Teachers' personal practical knowledge. In R. Halkaes & J. K. Olson (Eds.), *Teacher thinking: A new perspective on (persistent problems in) education.* Heirewig, Holland: Swets Publishing Service.

Connelly, F. M. & Clandinin, D. J. (1985). Personal practical knowledge and the modes of knowing. *Review of Research in Education* 16(3), 56.

Cornett, J., Yeotis, C., & Terwilliger, L. (1990). Teacher personal practical theories and their influence upon teacher curricular and instructional actions: A case study of a secondary science teacher. *Science Education, 74*(5), 517–529.

Council of Chief State School Officers/National Governors Association. (2010). *Common core standards.* Washington, DC: Author.

Dewey, J. (1933). *How we think: A restatement of the relation of reflective thinking to the educative process.* Boston: D.C. Heath.

Elbaz, F. (1981). The teacher's "practical knowledge": Report of a case study. *Curriculum Inquiry, 11*(1), 43–71.

Fairbanks, C., Duffy, G. G., Faircloth, B. S., He, Y., Levin, B., Rohr, J., & Stein, C. (2010). Beyond knowledge: Exploring why some teachers are more thoughtfully adaptive than others. *Journal of Teacher Education, 61*(1–2), 161–171.

Freebody, P., & Luke, A. (1990). Literacies programs: Debates and demands in cultural context. *Prospect: Australian Journal of TESOL, 5*(7), 7–16.

Freire, P. (1970). *Pedagogy of the oppressed.* New York: Seabury.

Glass, R. D. (2001). On Paulo Freire's philosophy of praxis and the foundations of liberation education. *Educational Researcher, 30*(2), 15–25.

Goldschmidt, P. (2009). *Evaluation of seeds of science/roots of reading: Effective tools for developing literacy through science in the early grades.* Los Angeles: National Center for Research on Evaluation, Standards, and Student Testing. Accessed at http://seedsofscience.org/PDFs/CRESST_Evaluation_LightEnergy.pdf.

Hickman, L. A., & Alexander, T. M. (1998). *The Essential Dewey, Vol. 2: Pragmatism, education, democracy.* Bloomington: Indiana University Press.

Hoffman, J., & Pearson, P. D. (2000). Reading teacher education: What your grandmother's teacher didn't know that your granddaughter's teacher should know. *Reading Research Quarterly, 35*(1), 28–45.

International Reading Association/National Council of Teachers of English. (2010). *Standards for the assessment of reading and writing* (Rev. ed.). Newark, DE: International Reading Association.

Jackson, P. W. (1968). *Life in classrooms*. New York: Holt, Rinehart and Winston.

James, W. (1979). *Pragmatism*. Cambridge, MA: Harvard University Press.

Keith, H. (1999). Feminism and pragmatism: George Herbert Mead's ethics of care. *Transactions of the Charles S. Peirce Society, 35*(2), 328–344.

Lewin, K. (1951). *Field theory in social science; selected theoretical papers*. D. Cartwright (Ed.). New York: Harper & Row.

Miettinen, R. (2000). The concept of experiential learning and John Dewey's theory of reflective thought and action. *International Journal of Lifelong Education, 19*(1), 54–72.

Morris, C. W. (1934). *George Herbert Mead, mind, self and society: From the standpoint of social behaviorist*. Chicago: University of Chicago Press.

Nussbaum, B. (2003). African culture and Ubuntu. *Perspectives, 17*(1), 1–16.

Noddings, N. (1984). *A feminine approach to ethics and moral education*. Berkeley: University of California Press.

Pearson, P. D., Raphael, T. E., Benson, V. L., & Madda, C. L. (2007). Balance in comprehensive literacy instruction: Then and now. In L. B. Gambrell, L. M. Morrow, & M. Pressley, *Best practices in literacy instruction* (3rd ed.) (pp. 30–54). New York: Guilford Press.

Postman, N., & Weingartner, C. (1969). *Teaching as a subversive activity*. New York: Dell.

Schon, D. (1983). *The reflective practitioner: How professionals think in action*. London: Temple Smith.

Shulman, L. S. (1986). Paradigms and research programs in the study of teaching. In M. C. Wittrock (Ed.), *Handbook of research on teaching*. New York: Macmillan.

Street, B. (1995). *Social literacies*. London: Longman.

Turisi, P. A. (1997). *Pragmatism as a principle and method of right thinking: The 1903 Harvard lectures on pragmatism/Charles Sanders Peirce*. Albany: State University of New York Press.

Linda B. Gambrell

Linda B. Gambrell, PhD, is Distinguished Professor of Education in the Eugene T. Moore School of Education at Clemson University, where she teaches graduate and undergraduate literacy courses. She is former director of the School of Education at Clemson University.

Prior to coming to Clemson University in 1999, she was Associate Dean for Research in the College of Education at University of Maryland. She began her career as an elementary classroom teacher and reading specialist in Prince George's County, Maryland. From 1992–1997, she was a principal investigator at the National Reading Research Center at the University of Maryland, where she directed the Literacy Motivation Project. She has served as president of the three leading professional organizations for reading: the International Reading Association, National Reading Conference, and College Reading Association.

Her major research areas are comprehension and cognitive processing, literacy motivation, and the role of discussion in teaching and learning. Her research has been published in major scholarly journals including *Reading Research Quarterly, Educational Psychologist,* and *Journal of Educational Research.*

Gambrell has received professional honors and awards including the College Reading Association A.B. Herr Award for Outstanding Contributions to the Field of Reading, the International Reading Association Outstanding Teacher Educator in Reading Award, the National Reading Conference Albert J. Kingston Award, and the College Reading Association Laureate Award. She is a member of the Reading Hall of Fame.

In this chapter, Gambrell presents theories of motivation and their implications for the school curriculum before discussing nine classroom features and practices that nurture and enhance students' reading motivation and achievement.

Chapter 2

Motivation in the School Reading Curriculum

Linda B. Gambrell

It is not enough to teach children to become readers and writers; we want children to leave our schools with the continuing desire to read, write, and learn. Our task is to pursue this vision so that it becomes a reality.

—Carol Minnick Santa

In a perfect world, all our students would be highly motivated to read for pleasure and to acquire information; their motivation and excitement for learning to read as kindergarteners and first graders would continue throughout their lives. Unfortunately, this is not the world we live in. Data from the 2005 National Assessment of Educational Progress (NAEP) report revealed that 65 percent of fourth graders did not have reading as a favorite activity, 73 percent did not read frequently for enjoyment, and 59 percent did not believe they learned very much when reading books (Perie, Grigg, & Donahue, 2005). Perhaps more important, the NAEP data revealed that students' intrinsic motivation to read decreased from 2002 to 2005. According to Guthrie, McRae, and Klauda (2007), "These statistics indicate that a substantial majority of grade four students are not intrinsically motivated to read" (p. 237).

The Importance of Motivation in the School Reading Curriculum

The construct of motivation has been widely researched by psychologists and educators. Although motivation in general has been studied extensively, only in recent decades has attention focused on the role of motivation in reading development. Motivating students to read is a practical concern and a demanding task for both classroom teachers and parents alike. Consequently, there is great interest in exploring motivational factors that are specifically associated with reading development so that we can create more motivating classroom, school, and home contexts for literacy learning. One of the primary reasons motivation is so central to the school reading curriculum is the simple but profound understanding that the more one reads, the better reader one becomes (Cunningham & Stanovich, 1997; Gambrell, 2009). While all students deserve high-quality reading instruction in the areas of phonemic awareness, phonics, vocabulary, fluency, and comprehension, it is clear that if our students are not motivated to read, they will never reach their full literacy potential (Gambrell, 1996).

Motivation to read can be defined as the likelihood of engaging in reading or choosing to read. This definition has been used for decades in research conducted by behavioral, humanistic, cognitive, and social-cognitive psychologists. Students who are highly motivated to read will pursue reading, make time for reading, and develop the reading habit. Unfortunately, there is no single formula for motivating students to read. Not all students are motivated by the same needs, desires, or values. One student's background knowledge, interest, ability, and efficacy for a particular reading task will likely be quite different than that of nearly every other student in the classroom. Therefore, researchers and educators have cautioned against viewing motivation as a general phenomenon.

> One of the primary reasons motivation is so central to the school reading curriculum is the simple but profound understanding that the more one reads, the better reader one becomes.

Theories of Motivation: Implications for the School Reading Curriculum

Theories of motivation deal with the "whys" of behavior: the choices individuals make about whether to engage in an activity or not, their persistence at the task, and the amount of effort they expend as they engage in the activity (Eccles, Wigfield, & Schiefele, 1998; Wigfield, 1997). The history of motivation theory demonstrates the complexity of the construct of motivation. Early theories suggested that an individual is motivated to act if consequences seem pleasant, and unmotivated if he or she perceives the consequences to be unpleasant. While these early theories accounted for much human behavior, theorists and researchers recognized they failed to explain an individual's response in a situation that was completely unfamiliar. For example, how would an individual be expected to act if the consequences are unclear or unknown? Researchers then began to explore behaviorist theories of motivation in terms of an individual's response to external stimuli (Phillips & Soltis, 1991). Learning, in this view, takes place as we become conditioned to certain stimuli—in other words, individuals are motivated to act depending on how the behavior or task has been rewarded or punished previously. The glaring flaw in behaviorist theory is that it fails to explain an individual's response in a novel situation or a situation involving new information with no reinforcement.

Social learning theory soon emerged with an emphasis on the role of experience and imitation (Bandura, 1986; Thomas, 1985). Social theorists began to emphasize *self-efficacy*, the belief that feelings of competence influence human motivation. This theory suggests the importance of students developing positive self-concepts as readers. Students need to experience success with reading materials that are within their ability range, and they need to experience success with increasingly challenging texts so that they view themselves as competent and successful readers. This theory has clear implications for the classroom, as it suggests that students need to see and hear their teachers reading aloud with enjoyment and appreciation.

Learning theorists then turned to cognitively based theories to more fully explain motivation to learn. Cognitive theorists are concerned with issues that are difficult to observe, such as perception, memory, and attention (Bruner, 1966; Piaget & Inhelder, 1969). In contrast to behaviorists, cognitive theorists believe observable behaviors are not simply responses to external stimuli. Rather, these behaviors represent the active structuring and organization of knowledge in the mind. Cognitive theorists do not view motivation solely in terms of how past reinforcement affects behavior or how an action might feel to an individual; instead, they see it as a process of thoughts and decision making. Cognitive theorists believe people do not passively respond to the environment—they believe people actively make choices, attend to salient factors, and organize information in an effort to understand or to seek a goal. However, cognitive models of reading do not adequately account for all behavior. For example, a purely cognitive theory of reading would not explain why some students do not choose to read even though they are very skilled and proficient readers.

The social cognitive theory, primarily developed by Bandura (1986, 1997), integrates constructs of both social and cognitive theories of learning. This theory emphasizes that cognition is central to learning and that individuals learn by interpreting the behavior of others. In other words, learners don't thoughtlessly imitate others. The practice of teacher modeling of reading and writing processes during instruction is grounded in social cognitive theory. Social cognitive theory also emphasizes the role of self-efficacy in learning. In keeping with this theory, students with positive self-concepts as readers are more likely to put forth more effort, read more, and sustain their engagement with text for longer periods of time than students with negative self-concepts.

A theory that draws on social cognitive theory and has strong implications for the reading curriculum is the expectancy-value theory of motivation (Fishbein, 1967, 1968; Wigfield & Eccles, 2000). This theory draws on earlier theories, particularly the social cognitive theory. According to the expectancy-value theory, the motivation to engage in a behavior is the product of the degree to which students (1) expect to be able to perform the given task successfully (self-concept), and (2) value the process of engaging in the task. Students' motivation to read, then, is a result of their self-perception of their capability or competence as readers (expectancy) as well as their appreciation of reading engagement (value). If a student's expectancy or value is low, then there is a decreased likelihood that he or she will be motivated to engage in reading. On the other hand, if a student has a strong self-concept as a reader and values reading, there is an increased likelihood that he or she will be highly motivated to read.

A newer theory that integrates expectancy-value and social cognitive theories with strong implications for the reading curriculum is based on the engagement perspective (Guthrie & Humenick, 2004; Guthrie & Wigfield, 2000; Tracey & Morrow, 2006). The engagement theory articulates the differences between engaged and disengaged readers and focuses on the characteristics of the engaged reader. In keeping with this theory, engaged readers are intrinsically motivated to read for a variety of personal goals, strategic in their reading behaviors, knowledgeable in their construction of new understandings from text, and socially interactive about the reading of text.

Guthrie (2004) notes that data from the 1998 NAEP report revealed that the correlation between engaged reading and reading comprehension achievement was higher than the correlation between reading comprehension and other demographic characteristics, such as gender, income, or ethnicity. Also, nine-year-olds from low-income and low-education family backgrounds, but who were highly engaged readers, substantially outscored students who came from high-education and high-income family backgrounds, but were less engaged readers. According to Guthrie, these findings suggest the "stunning conclusion that engaged reading can overcome traditional barriers to reading achievement, including gender, parental education and income" (p. 5).

Instructional practices based on the principles of engagement theory include the characteristics of relevance, choice, success, and collaboration. A review of research on the effects of reading instruction based on these principles revealed that students demonstrated increased intrinsic motivation for reading, increased use of strategic reading behaviors, and increased gains in conceptual knowledge (Guthrie et al., 2007). Engagement theory provides clear implications on how to support students in becoming more motivated and proficient readers.

Motivation Is Multidimensional

Motivation theorists make a distinction between extrinsic and intrinsic motivation (Deci, 1972; Lepper & Green, 1978). *Extrinsic motivation* refers to forces that are external to an individual that influence his or her inclination to engage in a behavior. Behavior that is motivated by internal needs or feelings is considered *intrinsic*. Students who behave appropriately because doing so provides them with a sense of pride would be said to be intrinsically motivated. Students who engage in reading for its own sake, because they find it enjoyable or because they want find out how to put together a model airplane, would be intrinsically motivated. On the other hand, students who engage in reading for an incentive or reward, such as good grades or prizes, would be extrinsically motivated (Guthrie et al., 2007; Ryan & Deci, 2000).

According to Deci (1992), intrinsic motivation has two components: experience and disposition. The experience component involves excitement, curiosity, interest, and enjoyment in participating in the task or activity, while the disposition component involves the desire to interact with the task or activity.

A number of studies have demonstrated that intrinsic motivation is associated with achievement. Gottfried (1990) reports correlations of intrinsic motivation with reading comprehension for students in the upper elementary grades. Wigfield and Guthrie (1997) found that intrinsic motivation is positively associated with standardized reading comprehension test scores. Intrinsic goals for reading have also been shown to increase conceptual learning from text to a greater extent than extrinsic goals (Guthrie, Wigfield, & Von Secker, 2000; Vansteenkiste, Simons, Lens, Sheldon, & Deci, 2004). A number of studies have concluded that intrinsically motivated students have higher achievement and more positive classroom attitudes than extrinsically motivated students (Deci & Ryan, 1992; Deci, Vallerand, Pelletier, & Ryan, 1991; Guthrie et al., 2007).

Researchers and theorists agree that motivation is multidimensional and have identified at least nine components of motivation (Baker & Wigfield, 1999; Wigfield & Guthrie, 1997):

1. Curiosity/interest

2. Preference for challenge

3. Task involvement

4. Self-efficacy

5. Competition

6. Recognition

7. Grades

8. Social interaction

9. Work avoidance

Some of these components are intrinsic reasons for reading, such as curiosity and task involvement, while others are extrinsic reasons for reading, such as earning recognition and grades. Research suggests that instructional intervention supporting intrinsic motivation for reading increases students' curiosity, involvement, and preferences for challenge (Wigfield, Guthrie, Tonks, & Perencevich, 2004). Of particular importance is the finding that intrinsic motivation for reading (reading for its own sake, reading for enjoyment) is associated with reading achievement (Gottfried, 1990; Guthrie et al., 2004; Sweet, Guthrie, & Ng, 1998). Guthrie et al. (2007) assert that "the association of intrinsic motivation to achievement lends it a decisive urgency" (p. 238).

Classroom Practices Associated With Intrinsic Motivation to Read

Research and descriptions of best practice suggest that certain aspects of the classroom environment and teachers' instructional practices can support and encourage reading motivation (Guthrie et al., 2007; Guthrie & Wigfield, 2000; Malloy, Gambrell, & Williams, 2006; Malloy, Marinak, & Gambrell, 2010; Wigfield et al., 2004). The following classroom features and practices have been identified as those that nurture and enhance students' reading motivation and achievement:

1. Access to a range of reading materials

2. Opportunities for students to choose what they read

3. Adequate time for students to engage in sustained reading

4. Opportunities for success with challenging texts

5. Opportunities for social interactions about text

6. Opportunities to engage in reading tasks that have relevance

7. Incentives that reflect the value of reading and learning

(Allington & McGill-Franzen, 1993; Anderman & Midgley, 1992; Gambrell, Hughes, Calvert, Malloy, & Igo, 2009; Gambrell & Marinak, 1997; Guthrie et al., 2007; Turner & Paris, 1995)

Access to a Range of Reading Materials

Classrooms that provide easy access to an abundant array of interesting reading materials support students' development of intrinsic motivation to read and their engagement with reading. Research suggests student motivation to read increases (Allington & McGill-Franzen, 1993; Guthrie et al., 2007; Morrow, 1992) and reading achievement increases (Kim, 2004, 2006; Neuman & Celano, 2001) when the classroom environment is rich in reading materials and includes books from a variety of genres and text types, magazines, access to the Internet, resource materials, and real-life documents. Providing a variety of reading materials that reflect authentic forms of text communicates to students that reading is a worthwhile and valuable activity and sets the stage for students to develop the reading habit. According to Vellutino (2003), instruction that focuses on students' interests and "surrounds them with high-interest reading materials at their level of proficiency is more effective than instruction that does less" (p. 77).

It stands to reason that increasing the number of books and other reading materials in the classroom will have a positive effect on the amount and quality of students' reading experiences.

Researchers have made recommendations about the number of books needed in the classroom library. Reutzel and Cooter (2004) recommend a minimum of three books for each student in the classroom, while the International Reading Association recommends seven books per student. It stands to reason that increasing the number of books and other reading materials in the classroom will have a positive effect on the amount and quality of students' reading experiences.

It is worth noting, however, that researchers and educators caution that access to books is not sufficient for improving reading motivation or achievement (Byrnes, 2000; Kim & White, 2008). While access to books sets the stage, there are a number of factors that need to be coupled with book access to promote reading motivation and achievement, including time to read and teacher-directed reading instruction.

Opportunities for Students to Choose What They Read

Choice is a powerful force that allows students to take ownership and responsibility for their learning (Rettig & Hendricks, 2000). Research indicates that intrinsic motivation is increased when students have opportunities to choose what they want to read and believe that they have some autonomy or control over their own learning (Deci et al., 1991; Skinner & Belmont, 1993). According to Sweet et al. (1998), perceived autonomy in the form of liking to make choices in reading is associated with higher academic grades in reading.

Guthrie et al. (2007) explored fourth-grade students' motivation and reading comprehension growth and reported that allowing students to select their own books supports their autonomy, as compared to teachers or other adults choosing books for them. Students' autonomy was further supported when they acquired strategies for choosing books to read.

Many students, especially struggling readers, often choose books that are far too easy or too difficult; therefore, it seems important to provide students with opportunities to make choices and guidance in how to make appropriate choices about texts and literacy activities (Carver & Leibert, 1995; Kim & White, 2008). Antonio and Guthrie (2008) suggest that teachers consider the following guidelines for scaffolding student choice:

1. Offer simple choices at first.

2. Help students practice making good choices.

3. Provide feedback about student choices.

4. Have students make team choices.

5. Offer feedback that clarifies good choices.

6. Provide choice within a task. (For example, allow students to choose the sequence of text materials to read or the questions they answer after reading a text).

Studies have found that the books students find most interesting and enjoyable to read are those they have selected for their own reasons and purposes (Gambrell, 1996; Schiefele, 1991; Spaulding, 1992). It appears that students who are allowed to choose their own reading materials are more motivated to read, expend more effort, and gain better understanding of the text.

Adequate Time for Students to Engage in Sustained Reading

Hiebert (2009) argues that time to read, or opportunity to read, is a critical but neglected area in the school reading curriculum. Classroom cultures that support motivation to read and provide sufficient amounts of time to read create the necessary foundation that is essential for supporting students in becoming proficient readers. Research studies have documented that time spent reading is associated with reading achievement and the development of intrinsic motivation to read. Observational and interview studies conducted by Heathington (1979), Midgley (1993), and Mizelle (1997) concluded that increased amounts of time for free reading in the classroom were associated with increased motivation to read.

Reading practice, or time spent reading, is vital to becoming not only a proficient reader, but a motivated and engaged reader who chooses to read for pleasure and information. Research studies have explored the amount of time that students read during instructional, self-selected reading time, both throughout the school day and outside of school. A study conducted by Brenner, Hiebert, and Tompkins (2009) revealed that students in classrooms where ninety minutes or more was devoted to

> Reading practice, or time spent reading, is vital to becoming not only a proficient reader, but a motivated and engaged reader who chooses to read for pleasure and information.

reading/language arts instruction spent an average of only eighteen minutes actually engaged in the sustained reading of text. During the ninety-minute reading/language arts period, the teachers talked to the students about reading strategies and skills, and students later practiced aspects of reading; however, their time engaged in sustained reading was very limited.

A study by Foorman et al. (2006) examined time allocation during reading instruction. Observations of first and second graders and their 107 teachers revealed that the amount of time allocated to text reading was positively associated with growth in reading proficiency. Only time devoted to text reading significantly explained gains on posttest measures, including word reading, decoding, and passage comprehension. No other time-allocation factors, including time spent on word, alphabetic, or phonemic awareness instruction, contributed to reading growth.

Studies have also investigated the effects of students reading in school and outside of school on reading achievement. In a study by Taylor, Frye, and Maruyama (1990), time spent reading in school was highly correlated with reading achievement, while the correlation between reading outside of school and reading proficiency was much lower. More important, when differences in students' prior knowledge, reading ability, and time allowed for reading at school were controlled, in-school reading time was a significant factor in reading growth. In a subsequent study, Guthrie, Wigfield, Metsala, and Cox (1999) reported that the amount of time spent reading in and outside of school predicted reading comprehension. Given the evidence that time is strongly associated with reading proficiency, it is surprising that the time students spend in sustained reading of text in the classroom has not increased substantially over the years (Hiebert, 2009).

The school reading curriculum should include ample opportunities for students to read—both at home and during the school day. Encouraging students to take books home to read for pleasure is a simple but effective way to encourage reading at home. It is critically important that sufficient time during the school day be devoted to the sustained reading of books and other reading materials of interest to the student. In addition to reading instruction time in the classroom, devoting time to self-selected reading, or independent reading, during the school day demonstrates the value of reading and allows for the reading practice necessary for the development of proficient reading.

Opportunities for Success With Challenging Texts

According to Turner (1995), a hallmark of good reading instruction is offering reading tasks and activities that advance, rather than overwhelm, the reader. If activities are too complex or confusing, the reader is more likely to choose not to continue engaging in the reading task. On the other hand, if the reading tasks and activities are too easy, the reader is more likely to become bored with the task. The most motivating reading tasks and activities are moderately challenging, where the student must put forth some effort. Success with challenging tasks provides the student with evidence of accomplishment, resulting in an increase in self-concept or self-efficacy (Schunk, 1989; Schunk & Zimmerman, 1997). Accomplishing a challenging task has been shown to enhance students' intrinsic motivation (Guthrie et al., 2007; Weiner, 1992).

Motivated readers are constantly extending their skills to meet new challenges. As Turner (1995) notes:

> These elements are cyclical: individuals improve skills to meet challenges, and then, equipped with greater skills, they seek new challenges. The result is synchrony between the demands of the activity and the individual's ability to respond. When challenges and skills are out of balance, students may feel either frustration or boredom—familiar motivation problems in the classrooms. (p. 187)

The research clearly indicates that students who believe that they are capable and competent readers are more likely to outperform those who do not hold such beliefs (Paris & Oka, 1986; Schunk, 1989; Schunk & Zimmerman, 1997).

Opportunities for Social Interactions About Text

Social interaction is defined as communicating with other individuals or groups, through writing and discussion, about what has been read (Applebee, Langer, Nystrand, & Gamoran, 2003). In a study conducted by Guthrie et al. (2000), social interaction included talking about books with others, reading together with others, borrowing and sharing books with others, talking about books with peers in class, and sharing writing about books with others. Instruction that incorporates social interaction about texts has been found to increase students' perceived social support for reading as well as their reading comprehension achievement (Ng et al., 1998). Guthrie et al. (2007) concluded that instruction that incorporates social interaction increases intrinsic motivation.

Turner and Paris (1995) suggest several ways in which social interaction supports motivation to read. First, peer comments can pique students' curiosity. Second, students' observations of their peers' progress may increase their confidence in their own ability to succeed. Third, working with others promotes student engagement in work. Literacy tasks and activities that encourage collaboration and social interaction provide opportunities for students to develop competence and efficacy as readers and writers. Intrinsic motivation to learn is enhanced in classrooms where students can join groups of students with the same reading interests.

Opportunities to Engage in Relevant Reading Tasks

Students who perceive reading as valuable and important and who have personally relevant reasons for reading will engage in reading in a more planful and effortful manner (Ames & Archer, 1988; Guthrie et al., 2007). Relevant or "authentic" reasons for reading are reflected in tasks in which the goal of reading is to comprehend the text well enough to use the acquired information for real purposes, such as engaging in a book discussion, putting together a toy airplane, or finding out what to feed a pet gerbil. Instructional practices that focus on connections between school reading and authentic, real-life reading enhance student motivation. In a study of authentic instruction, Purcell-Gates, Duke, and Martineau (2007) found that the most effective instruction combined reading for real-world purposes, interesting texts, and student choice.

A number of studies provide evidence that involving students in authentic reading tasks and activities accelerates reading motivation and achievement (Assor, Kaplan, & Roth, 2002; Gambrell et al., 2009; Knapp, 1995; Purcell-Gates et al., 2007). Gambrell and her colleagues conducted a study of authentic literacy tasks in which elementary students engaged in reading books, exchanging letters with an adult pen pal, and participating in peer-led discussions about both the books and the pen-pal letters. The results revealed statistically significant increases in literacy motivation on a pre- and post-assessment and provided evidence that the discussions about the books and pen-pal letters engaged students in critical thinking. Purcell-Gates et al. (2007) explored student growth in reading and writing informational text genres and the degree of authenticity of literacy activities in elementary classrooms. They defined authentic literacy activities as those serving a communicative purpose outside of a learning-to-read-and-write context and purpose (for example, reading to complete a task and writing a thank-you letter). The results of the study indicated that classrooms with more authentic reading and writing tasks increased in reading and writing proficiency at a faster rate than those with exposure to less authentic literacy tasks. Literacy tasks that are authentic and have relevance to real-life are supportive of intrinsic motivation because they enable students to see the connections between school reading and real-life, out-of-school reading.

> Literacy tasks that are authentic and have relevance to real-life are supportive of intrinsic motivation because they enable students to see the connections between school reading and real-life, out-of-school reading.

Incentives That Reflect the Value of Reading and Learning

Many teachers and administrators believe that extrinsic rewards or incentives spark students' reading motivation (Marinak & Gambrell, 2009). Moore and Fawson (1992) surveyed five diverse public school districts and found that 95 percent of elementary teachers used some form of incentive program to encourage students to read. These teachers reported that the main reason they used an incentive program was to develop students' intrinsic motivation to read.

Theories of extrinsic motivation maintain that behaviors, such as reading, are performed for external incentives or consequences. Numerous studies have investigated the effects of both nontangible (verbal praise and feedback) and tangible incentives on learning. These studies suggest that not all extrinsic incentives have the same effect on motivation and achievement. Some external incentives appear to support motivation and learning, while others have a diminishing or undermining effect.

Nontangible incentives. Nontangible extrinsic incentives such as teacher praise and feedback have been shown to positively influence students' intrinsic motivation and achievement (Cameron & Pierce, 1994; Deci, 1971). Lepper and Cordova (1992) conducted a study with upper elementary students on the effects of teacher praise and feedback on student performance. The results revealed that teacher praise provides verbal scaffolding, support, and direction to the students and leads to increased student motivation to learn. In addition, the study revealed that elaborated or embellished teacher praise is more motivational than tangible incentives (prizes).

According to Brophy (1981), effective teacher praise is given contingent on the student's effort and achievement, specifies the particulars of the student's accomplishment, attributes success to the student's effort, orients the student toward a better appreciation of his or her own work, and fosters appreciation of task-relevant strategies. However, teacher praise is not always effective. If students perceive teacher praise to be dishonest or undeserved, motivation may decline because the students may feel that they are being manipulated (Guthrie & Wigfield, 2000). When teachers give praise and students interpret it as recognition of achievement, it can increase students' feelings of competence and motivation (Fink, Boggiano, Main, Barrett, & Katz, 1992; Gambrell & Marinak, 1997; Guthrie & Wigfield, 2000).

Tangible incentives. Research is less clear about the effects of tangible incentives on student motivation and performance. Giving tangible incentives such as gold stars, points, candy, or other prizes is paradoxical: tangible rewards can increase short-term attention on specific activities, but in general they have been found to undermine the development of intrinsic motivation (Deci & Ryan, 1992). Clear and replicable research findings on the effects of rewards reveal that offering students tangible rewards for performing an intrinsically motivating activity leads to a decrease in intrinsic motivation for engaging in the activity (Deci, 1971, 1972, 1975; Lepper & Green, 1978).

A number of studies by Deci (1971, 1972, 1975, 1992) investigated the effects of rewarding students with money and other tangible incentives for engaging in a task that was already intrinsically interesting. Students who engaged in a task in one session and were then paid during a second session tended to show less intrinsic motivation toward the task than did the comparison group that was not paid. These studies suggest that offering students prizes, money, or other tangible rewards results in a decrease in their interest in engaging in a task they already find interesting. Thus, Deci (1992) concluded that tangible rewards undermine intrinsic motivation.

The reward proximity hypothesis. One notable feature of both teacher praise and teacher feedback is that they are always closely linked to the desired student behavior, while tangible incentives (such as gold stars and stickers) are usually unrelated to the desired behavior. Drawing on this discrepancy, the reward proximity hypothesis (Gambrell, 1996) posits that intrinsic motivation is enhanced when the incentive or reward is linked to the desired behavior. Teachers foster students' intrinsic motivation in an activity when the incentive not only rewards the desired behavior, but also reflects the value of and encourages future engagement in the behavior. For example, to develop intrinsic motivation to read, students would get appropriate incentives that are clearly linked to the desired behavior of reading, including books, bookmarks, extra time for pleasure reading, and extra teacher read-aloud time.

Marinak and Gambrell (2008) examined the reward proximity hypothesis and the conditions under which rewards influenced reading motivation. They assessed intrinsic motivation using a series of task-persistence measures: choosing to read, time spent reading, and number of words read. The major finding was that students who were given a book as a reward (proximal reward) and students who received no reward were more motivated to engage in subsequent reading than students who received prizes other than books as rewards. This finding is in keeping with Deci's (1971, 1972, 1975, 1992) work indicating that tangible rewards undermine motivation.

However, the findings of Marinak and Gambrell suggest that when a tangible reward is related or proximal to the desired behavior, such as a book reward for reading, reading motivation is not undermined. This study suggests that if incentives are used in the classroom, the proximity of the reward to the desired behavior of reading is a particularly salient factor in supporting motivation to read.

We should carefully consider the use of rewards and incentives to promote reading motivation in the classroom. Our students know that rewards and incentives, by definition, are usually things that are regarded as having high value, whether it is teacher praise or a pizza. If we want our students to value reading and academics, we have to be clever enough to create classrooms where the message is clear that reading and learning are the best reward. Some examples of reading incentives that are related to reading and support reading engagement include additional time for teacher read aloud, opportunities to read aloud to younger students, or even the option to choose which homework assignment to complete (for example, either page 9 or page 10 from the textbook).

> If we want our students to value reading and academics, we have to be clever enough to create classrooms where the message is clear that reading and learning are the best reward.

Research suggests that nontangible incentives, such as teacher praise and teacher feedback, can increase student motivation. When teachers give frequent, positive, and honest feedback about student reading performance, it supports students' belief that they can read well and increases their motivation to read. With respect to tangible incentives offered for reading, research suggests that the incentives should be a natural extension of the desired reading behavior, such as books and extra time for reading.

A Critical and Necessary Foundation

While the National Reading Panel (National Institute of Child Health and Human Development, 2000) encourages schools to focus on quality instruction in the five research-based instructional areas of phonemic awareness, phonics, vocabulary, fluency, and comprehension, it is also incumbent upon principals, teachers, and other educational leaders to promote and support classroom cultures that encourage and nurture motivation to read. Classroom cultures that support students' motivation to read provide a critical and necessary foundation for lifelong learning.

An understanding of the dimensions of motivation as they relate to instructional practices can assist teachers and administrators in developing a school reading curriculum that fosters a love of reading and supports students in developing the reading habit. The following seven questions will guide teachers, principals, and other educators in assessing the motivation-to-read climate of their classrooms:

1. Is the classroom rich in reading materials?

2. Are students provided with opportunities to choose the books they read?

3. Are students supported in learning how to choose appropriate-level books for independent reading?

4. Is adequate time allotted during the school day for independent reading?

5. Is time devoted to student book sharing and discussion?

6. To what extent do reading tasks and activities reflect real-life reading?

7. If incentives are given, do they reflect the value of reading and learning?

These questions address the essentials of classrooms that reflect a high value of reading and the expectation that all students can become independent, proficient readers. Answers to these questions can provide information that is needed to make recommendations about resources and best practices for creating highly motivating classroom climates where students develop both a love of reading and a "need to read."

The research is clear: motivating classroom climates support reading achievement and the development of the reading habit. We all want students who are eager to read and who read for pleasure and information. We all want students who get excited about stories they read and new information they have discovered. We all want students who enjoy sharing book experiences and want to read increasingly challenging materials. Simply put, we want our students to want to read.

The most basic goal of any school reading curriculum is the development of readers who can read and who choose to read. Instruction in the most essential reading skills is necessary, but not sufficient, to reach this goal. If our students are not motivated to read, they will never reach their full literacy potential.

References

Allington, R. L., & McGill-Franzen, A. (1993). What are they to read? Not all children, Mr. Riley, have easy access to books. *Education Week, 13*(6), 26.

Ames, C., & Archer, J. (1988). Achievement goals in the classroom: Students' learning strategies and motivational processes. *Journal of Educational Psychology, 80*(3), 260–267.

Anderman, E. M., & Midgley, C. (1992). Changes in achievement goal orientations, perceived academic competence, and grades across the transition to middle-level schools. *Contemporary Educational Psychology, 22*(3), 269–298.

Antonio, D., & Guthrie, J. T. (2008). Reading is social: Bringing peer interaction to the text. In J. T. Guthrie (Ed.), *Engaging adolescents in reading* (pp. 49–63). Thousand Oaks, CA: Corwin Press.

Applebee, A., Langer, J., Nystrand, M., & Gamoran, A. (2003). Discussion-based approaches to developing understanding: Classroom instruction and student performance in middle and high school English. *American Educational Research Journal, 40*(3), 685–730.

Assor, A., Kaplan, H., & Roth, G. (2002). Choice is good, but relevance is excellent: Autonomy-enhancing and suppressing teacher behaviours predicting students' engagement in schoolwork. *British Journal of Educational Psychology, 72*, 261–278.

Baker, L., & Wigfield, A. (1999). Dimensions of children's motivation for reading and their relations to reading activity and reading achievement. *Reading Research Quarterly, 34*, 452–477.

Bandura, A. (1986). *Social foundations of thought and action: A social cognitive theory.* Englewood Cliffs, NY: Prentice Hall.

Bandura, A. (1997). *Self-efficacy: The exercise of control.* New York: Freeman.

Brenner, D., Hiebert, E. H., & Tompkins, R. (2009). How much and what are third graders reading? Reading in core programs. In E. H. Hiebert (Ed.), *Reading more, reading better* (pp. 118–140). New York: Guilford Press.

Brophy, J. (1981). Teacher praise: A functional analysis. *Review of Educational Research, 51*(1), 5–32.

Bruner, J. (1966). *Studies in cognitive growth: A collaboration at the Center for Cognitive Studies.* New York: Wiley.

Byrnes, J. P. (2000). Using instructional time effectively. In L. Baker, M. J. Dreher, & J. T. Guthrie (Eds.), *Engaging young readers* (pp. 188–208). New York: Guilford Press.

Cameron, J., & Pierce, W. D. (1994). Reinforcement, reward, and intrinsic motivation: A meta-analysis. *Review of Educational Research, 64*(3), 363–424.

Carver, R. P., & Leibert, R. E. (1995). The effect of reading library books at different levels of difficulty upon gain in reading ability. *Reading Research Quarterly, 30*(1), 26–48.

Cunningham, A. E., & Stanovich, K. E. (1997). Early reading acquisition and its relation to reading experience and ability ten years later. *Developmental Psychology, 33*(6), 934–945.

Deci, E. L. (1971). Effects of externally mediated rewards on intrinsic motivation. *Journal of Personality and Social Psychology, 18,* 105–115.

Deci, E. L. (1972). Intrinsic motivation, extrinsic reinforcement, and inequity. *Journal of Personality and Social Psychology, 22,* 113–120.

Deci, E. L. (1975). *Intrinsic motivation.* New York: Plenum.

Deci, E. L. (1992). The relation of interest to the motivation of behavior: A self-determination theory perspective. In A. Renninger, S. Hidi, & A. Krapp (Eds.), *The role of interest in learning and development* (pp. 43–70). Hillsdale, NJ: Erlbaum.

Deci, E. L., & Ryan, R. M. (1992). The initiation and regulation of intrinsically motivated learning and achievement. In A. K. Boggiano & T. S. Pittman (Eds.), *Achievement and motivation: A social developmental perspective* (pp. 3–36).Cambridge, England: Cambridge University.

Deci, E. L., Vallerand, R. M., Pelletier, L. G., & Ryan, R. M. (1991). Motivation and education: The self-determination perspective. *Educational Psychologist, 26,* 325–346.

Eccles, J. S., Wigfield, A., & Schiefele, U. (1998). Motivation to succeed. In W. Damon (Series Ed.) & N. Eisenberg (Ed.), *Handbook of child psychology: Vol. 3. Social, emotional, and personality development* (5th ed., pp. 1017–1095). New York: Wiley.

Fink, C., Boggiano, A. K., Main, D. S., Barrett, M., & Katz, P. A. (1992). Children's achievement-related behaviors: The role of extrinsic and intrinsic motivational orientations. In A. K. Boggiano & T. S. Pittman (Eds.), *Achievement and motivation: A social-developmental perspective* (pp. 189–214). New York: Cambridge University Press.

Fishbein, M. (1967). Attitude and the prediction of behavior. In M. Fishbein (Ed.), *Readings in attitude theory and measurement* (pp. 477–492). New York: Wiley.

Fishbein, M. (1968). An investigation of relationships between beliefs about an object and the attitude towards that object. *Human Relationships, 16,* 233–240.

Foorman, B. R., Schatschneider, C., Eakin, M. N., Fletcher, J. M., Moats, L. C., et al. (2006). The impact of instructional practices in grades 1 and 2 on reading and spelling achievement in high poverty schools. *Contemporary Educational Psychology, 31*(1), 1–29.

Gambrell, L. B. (1996). Creating classroom cultures that foster reading motivation. *The Reading Teacher, 50*(1), 14–25.

Gambrell, L. B. (2009). Creating opportunities to read more so that students read better. In E. Hiebert (Ed.), *Reading more, reading better* (pp. 251–266). New York: Guilford Press.

Gambrell, L. B., Hughes, E., Calvert, W. L., Malloy, J. A., & Igo, B. (2009, November). *Academic and personal exchanges as a catalyst for authentic literacy learning.* Paper presented at the meeting of Association of Literacy Educators and Researchers, Charlotte, NC.

Gambrell, L. B., & Marinak, B. (1997). Incentives and intrinsic motivation to read. In J. T. Guthrie & A. Wigfield (Eds.), *Reading engagement: Motivating readers through integrated instruction* (pp. 205–217). Newark, DE: International Reading Association.

Gottfried, A. E. (1990). Academic intrinsic motivation in young elementary school children. *Journal of Educational Psychology, 82*(3), 525–538.

Guthrie, J. T. (2004). Teaching for literacy engagement. *Journal of Literacy Research, 36*(1), 1–29.

Guthrie, J. T., Hoa, A. L. W., Wigfield, A., Tonks, S. M., Humenick, N. M., & Littles, E. (2007). Reading motivation and reading comprehension growth in the later elementary years. *Contemporary Educational Psychology, 32*(3), 282–313.

Guthrie, J. T., & Humenick, N. M. (2004). Motivating students to read: Evidence for classroom practices that increase motivation and achievement. In P. McCardle & V. Chabra (Eds.), *The voice of evidence in reading research* (pp. 329–354). Baltimore: Brookes.

Guthrie, J. T., McRae, A., & Klauda, S. L. (2007). Contributions of concept-oriented reading instruction to knowledge about interventions for motivations in reading. *Educational Psychologist, 42*(4), 237–250.

Guthrie, J. T., & Wigfield, A. (2000). Engagement and motivation in reading. In M. L. Kamil, P. B. Mosenthal, P. D. Pearson, & R. Barr (Eds.), *Reading research handbook: Vol. 3* (pp. 403–424). Mahwah, NJ: Erlbaum.

Guthrie, J. T., Wigfield, A., Metsala, J. L., & Cox, K. E. (1999). Motivational and cognitive predictors of text comprehension and reading amount. *Scientific Studies of Reading, 3*(3), 231–256.

Guthrie, J. R., Wigfield, A., & Von Secker, C. (2000). Effects of integrated instruction on motivation and strategy use in reading. *Journal of Educational Psychology, 92*(2), 331–341.

Heathington, B. S. (1979). What to do about reading motivation in the middle school. *Journal of Reading, 22*(8), 709–713.

Hiebert, E. H. (2009). *Reading more, reading better.* New York: Guilford Press.

Kim, J. S. (2004). Summer reading and the ethnic achievement gap. *Journal of Education for Students Placed at Risk, 9*(2), 169–189.

Kim, J. S. (2006). The effects of a voluntary summer reading intervention on reading achievement: Results from a randomized field trial. *Educational Evaluation and Policy Analysis, 28*(4), 335–355.

Kim, J. S., & White, T. G. (2008). Scaffolding voluntary summer reading for children in grades 3 to 5. *Scientific Studies of Reading, 12*(1), 1–23.

Knapp, M. A. (1995). *Teaching for meaning in high-poverty classrooms.* New York: Teachers College Press.

Lepper, M. R., & Cordova, D. I. (1992). A desire to be taught: Instructional consequence of intrinsic motivation. *Motivation and Emotion, 16*(3), 187–208.

Lepper, M. R., & Green, D. (1978). Overjustification research and beyond: Toward a means-ends analysis of intrinsic and extrinsic motivation. In M. R. Lepper & D. Greene (Eds.), *The hidden costs of reward: New perspectives on the psychology of motivation* (pp. 109–148). Hillsdale, NJ: Erlbaum.

Malloy, J. A., Gambrell, L. B., & Williams, G. S. (2006). Supporting students' motivation to read. In C. Cummins (Ed.), *Understanding and implementing Reading First initiatives: The changing role of administrators* (pp. 116–126). Newark, DE: International Reading Association.

Malloy, J., Marinak, B., & Gambrell, L. B. (Eds.). (2010). *Essential readings in motivation.* Newark, DE: International Reading Association.

Marinak, B., & Gambrell, L. B. (2008). Intrinsic motivation and rewards: What sustains young children's engagement with text? *Literacy Research and Instruction, 47*(1), 9–26.

Marinak, B., & Gambrell, L. (2009, April 7). Rewarding reading? Perhaps authenticity is the answer [Editorial]. *Teachers College Record,* pp. 1–6.

Midgley, C. (1993). Motivation and middle level schools. In M. L. Maehr & P. R. Pintrich (Eds.), *Advances in motivation and achievement: Motivation in adolescent years: Vol. 8* (pp. 217–274). Greenwich, CT: JAI.

Mizelle, N. B. (1997). Enhancing young adolescents' motivation for literacy learning. *Middle School Journal, 24*(2), 5–14.

Moore, S. A., & Fawson, P. C. (1992, December). *Reading incentive programs: Beliefs and practices.* Paper presented at the forty-second annual meeting of the National Reading Conference, San Antonio, TX.

Morrow, L. M. (1992). The impact of a literature-based program on literacy achievement, use of literature, and attitudes of children from minority backgrounds. *Reading Research Quarterly, 27*(3), 250–275.

National Institute of Child Health and Human Development. (2000). *Report of the National Reading Panel. Teaching children to read: An evidence-based assessment of the scientific research literature on reading and its implications for reading instruction* (NIH Publication No. 00–4769). Washington, DC: U.S. Government Printing Office.

Neuman, S. B., & Celano, D. (2001). Access to print in low-income and middle-income communities: An ecological study in four neighborhoods. *Reading Research Quarterly, 36*(1), 8–26.

Ng, M. M., Guthrie, J. T., Van Meter, P., McCann, A., & Alao, S. (1998). How do classroom characteristics influence intrinsic motivations for literacy? *Reading Psychology, 19*(4), 319–398.

Paris, S. G., & Oka, E. R. (1986) Strategies for comprehending text and coping with reading difficulties. *Learning Disability Quarterly, 12*(1), 32–42.

Perie, M., Grigg, W., & Donahue, P. (2005). *The nation's report card: Reading 2005* (NCES 2006–451). Washington, DC: U.S. Department of Education.

Phillips, D. C., & Soltis, J. F. (1991). *Perspectives on learning.* New York: Teachers College Press.

Piaget, J., & Inhelder, B. (1969). *The psychology of the child* (H. Weaver, Trans.). New York: Basic Books.

Purcell-Gates, V., Duke, N., & Martineau, J. (2007). Learning to read and write genre-specific text: Roles of authentic experience and explicit teaching. *Reading Research Quarterly, 42*, 8–46.

Rettig, M. K., & Hendricks, C. G. (2000). Factors that influence the book selection process of students with special needs. *Journal of Adolescent and Adult Literacy, 43*(7), 608–618.

Reutzel, D. R., & Cooter, R. B. (2004). *Teaching children to read: Putting the pieces together* (4th ed.). Columbus, OH: Prentice Hall.

Ryan, R. M., & Deci, E. L. (2000). Intrinsic and extrinsic motivations: Classic definitions and new directions. *Contemporary Educational Psychology, 25*, 54–67.

Santa, C. M. (1997). School change and literacy engagement: Preparing teaching and learning environments. In J. T. Guthrie & A. Wigfield (Eds.), *Reading engagement: Motivating readers through integrated instruction* (pp. 218–233). Newark, DE: International Reading Association.

Schiefele, U. (1991). Interest, learning, and motivation. *Educational Psychologist, 26*(3), 299–323.

Schunk, D. H. (1989). Social cognitive theory and self-regulated learning. In B. J. Zimmerman & D. H. Schunk (Eds.), *Self-regulated learning and academic achievement: Theory, research, and practice* (pp. 83–110). New York: Springer-Verlag.

Schunk, D. H., & Zimmerman, B. J. (1997). Developing self-efficacious readers and writers: The role of social and self-regulatory processes. In J. T. Guthrie & A. Wigfield (Eds.), *Reading engagement: Motivating readers through integrated instruction* (pp. 34–50). Newark, DE: International Reading Association.

Skinner, E. A., & Belmont, M. J. (1993). Motivation in the classroom: Reciprocal effects of teacher behavior and students engagement across the school year. *Journal of Educational Psychology, 85*(4), 571–581.

Spaulding, C. L. (1992). The motivation to read and write. In J. W. Irwin & M. A. Doyle (Eds.), *Reading/writing connections: Learning from research* (pp. 177–201). Newark, DE: International Reading Association.

Sweet, A. P., Guthrie, J. T., & Ng, M. M. (1998). Teacher perceptions and student reading motivation. *Journal of Educational Psychology, 90*(2), 210–223.

Taylor, B. M., Frye, B. J., & Maruyama, G. M. (1990). Time spent reading and reading growth. *American Educational Research Journal, 27*(2), 351–362.

Thomas, R. M. (1985). *Comparing theories of child development* (2nd ed.). Belmont, CA: Wadsworth.

Tracey, D. H., & Morrow, L. M. (2006). *Lenses on reading.* New York: Guilford Press.

Turner, J. (1995). The influence of classroom contexts on young children's motivation for literacy. *Reading Research Quarterly, 30*(3), 410–441.

Turner, J., & Paris, S. G. (1995). How literacy tasks influence children's motivation for literacy. *The Reading Teacher, 48*(8), 662–673.

Vansteenkiste, M., Simons, J., Lens, W., Sheldon, K. M., & Deci, E. L. (2004). Motivating learning, performance, and persistence: The synergistic effects of intrinsic goal contents and autonomy-supportive contexts. *Journal of Personality and Social Psychology, 87*(2), 246–260.

Vellutino, F. R. (2003). Individual differences as sources of variability in reading comprehension in elementary school children. In A. P. Sweet & C. E. Snow (Eds.), *Rethinking reading comprehension* (pp. 51–81). New York: Guilford Press

Weiner, B. (1992). *Human motivation: Metaphors, theories, and research.* Newbury Park, CA: Sage.

Wigfield, A. (1997). Children's motivations for reading and reading engagement. In J. T. Guthrie & A. Wigfield (Eds.), *Reading engagement: Motivating readers through integrated instruction* (pp. 14–33). Newark, DE: International Reading Association.

Wigfield, A., & Eccles, J. (2000). Expectancy-value theory of achievement motivation. *Contemporary Educational Psychology, 25*(1), 68–81.

Wigfield, A., & Guthrie, J. T. (1997). Relations of children's motivation for reading to the amount and breadth of their reading. *Journal of Educational Psychology, 89*(3), 420–432.

Wigfield, A., Guthrie, J. T., Tonks, S., & Perencevich, K. C. (2004). Children's motivation for reading: Domain specificity and instructional influences. *Journal of Educational Research, 97*(6), 299–309.

Junko Yokota

Junko Yokota, PhD, is professor of reading and language at the National College of Education, National-Louis University, Chicago, and director of the Center for Teaching through Children's Books. A former elementary classroom teacher and school librarian, she has served as a consultant to numerous school districts, guiding curriculum development and providing professional development for teachers. She speaks on the topics of multicultural and international literature, literacy development of students of diversity, and improving literacy instruction through quality literature. Her publications include a coauthored college textbook, *Children's Books in Children's Hands*; columns that review children's books; journal articles; and book chapters. Yokota is past president of the U.S. national section of the International Board on Books for Young People, and is active in the International Reading Association and National Council of Teachers of English. She has served on the Caldecott, Newbery, Batchelder committees, and the IBBY Hans Christian Andersen Award jury. She is a recipient of the Virginia Hamilton Essay Award, and the Reading the World Award.

William H. Teale

William H. Teale, EdD, is professor of education in the Department of Curriculum and Instruction at the University of Illinois at Chicago. The author of more than one hundred publications, his work has focused on early literacy learning, the intersection of technology and literacy education, and children's literature. Teale has worked with organizations such as Children's Television Workshop, RIF, the Council of Chief State School Officers, and Reach Out and Read, and on productions like *Between the Lions*, *Sesame Street*, and the National Head Start Association's *HeadsUp! Reading* program. He is a former editor of *Language Arts* and a member of the Reading Hall of Fame. His current focal research projects are two U.S. Department of Education–funded Early Reading First projects that involve developing model preschool literacy curricula for three- and four-year-old children in urban Chicago schools (www.uic.edu/educ/erf/).

In this chapter, Yokota and Teale present general guidelines for choosing classroom reading materials, and then they outline age-specific ideas about key materials for elementary, middle, and high school classrooms.

Chapter 3

Materials in the School Reading Curriculum

Junko Yokota and William H. Teale

Walk into any good teacher's classroom and look around—carefully. The closer you look, the more materials you'll see that support student literacy learning. These materials are thematically rich, grounded in conceptual knowledge, support a wide variety of learning goals for a wide range of learners, and are present in both print and digital formats.

To do justice in discussing the wealth of materials related to reading in a literacy-rich classroom environment from kindergarten to high school would require a book-length manuscript; we have only a chapter. Therefore, we focus our remarks about this topic on the key materials that we believe teachers at different levels of schooling should have in their classrooms to provide the best support for reading growth. Since there are some general principles that apply to reading materials no matter what the grade, and there are also significant differences between grade levels, in this chapter we (1) examine what research says about overarching issues related to the role, nature, and importance of materials for reading instruction, no matter what the age or grade level of the student, and (2) present more age-specific ideas about key materials for reading in three sections: elementary (kindergarten through grade 5), middle school (grades 6 to 8), and high school (grades 9 to 12).

General Principles for Reading Materials

Materials matter—they impact how teachers teach and how readers read (Hoffman & Schallert, 2003). However, if teachers rely on materials to guide their decisions about how they teach reading, the needs of learners become secondary. Our position is that teachers first need to clearly define their own teaching philosophy and

> The materials a teacher uses in his or her classroom ultimately impact not only what students read about, but also how and how well they read and learn.

determine the learning standards that apply in their situation, then consider student assessment information (current achievement levels, needs, interests, and so on), and at that point select reading materials that align with results of the first two steps. Selecting materials is a very important part of planning and teaching, but the materials need to be understood in the context of the classroom. The materials a teacher uses in his or her classroom ultimately impact not only what students read about, but also how and how well they read and learn.

A Range of Materials Is Important

Given the relationship between materials and students' reading habits, processes, and skill levels, it is important that teachers at all grade levels ensure that students have ready access to a range of reading materials. It is helpful to keep in mind the following dimensions to provide such a range for your students.

Readability. How easy or hard a particular text is for a student to read is affected by a myriad of factors, some within the text (vocabulary load, syntactic complexity of sentences, and so on) and others within the reader (background knowledge, interest in the topic, how tired the reader is, and so on). Teachers are always trying to find materials that are at a "just right" reading level for a student (also known as the *instructional level*). Instructional-level materials are important because they allow students to have success in reading (in other words, the text is not at the frustration level), but they also stretch students a bit to develop new skills for processing texts.

Also important are materials that are at the student's *independent* reading level. These texts provide students with opportunities for a lot of practice reading. As with any activity (basketball, knitting, dancing, and so on), practice helps one develop fluency in orchestrating the actions that comprise the activity—in the case of reading, such factors as speed, accuracy, word recognition, phrasing, decoding, and so on.

Content. An aspect of level of difficulty that is frequently not considered but we believe is most important to consider is that students need to interact on a regular basis not only with materials at their reading level, but also with materials at their grade level. By grade-level materials we mean texts that contain the concepts and content in all subject areas that represent the achievement standards for that grade. This is, of course, especially critical for students who are reading below grade level. Consider that when we provide instruction for struggling readers at their reading (instructional) level (which, we have just said, is a good idea), they won't be encountering content at their grade level. Students progress in school (and in reading) by learning reading skills and strategies and by mastering content, or background knowledge. Without adequate background knowledge, all the reading skills in the world won't get students far enough. Thus, it is critical that even if a student is two or three years behind grade level in reading, that the student be exposed in some way—perhaps through read-alouds, perhaps through computer-assisted means—to texts at grade level.

Topics. There is a definite link between student interest and comprehension in reading (Anderson, Shirey, Wilson, & Fielding, 1987). A major factor contributing to student interest (or lack of it) is what the text is about. Certainly, when it comes to school, not every text that students read will be interesting to each individual reader. However, it is extremely important that there are many texts of interest to students in the overall collection of texts they read. Therefore, it is extremely important that texts on a variety of topics be part of the reading experience at each and every grade level and for each and every student.

Genres. Closely related to the need for variety in reading topics is the issue of variety in genre. Some students just love reading biographies, others go on science fiction or fantasy binges, and contemporary realistic fiction might capture the attention of others. Therefore, we highly recommend availability of a range of genres—realistic fiction, historical fiction, fantasy, science fiction, poetry, biography, informational texts, memoir, mystery, and so forth—at all grade levels. Keep in mind, however, that genres may be differentially appropriate and appealing across grade levels. For example, science fiction is not very central in the primary grades, and memoir generally works better with high school students, whereas fantasy is popular from kindergarten through twelfth grade.

Appeal. Even with our society's broadened conceptions of gender roles, there is still a degree of truth in the idea that some reading materials appeal more to males while others are significantly more appealing to females. "Chick lit," for example, is a well-documented phenomenon, and a number of programs and texts have cropped up recently on boys and reading. Examples include Guys Read (www .guysread.com), a web-based literacy program for boys; *Teaching Reading to Black Adolescent Males* (Tatum, 2005); and *For Boys Only: The Biggest, Baddest Book Ever* (Aronson & Newquist, 2007). Gender, culture, and individual interest all influence appeal. It is worth keeping this in mind as you think about the provision of reading materials, especially since the overwhelming majority of teachers at the elementary level is female. Likewise, readers may feel personal connection and motivation to read when the reading material aligns with their own cultural heritage or appeals to their personal interests.

Format. In addition to conventional texts (novels, informational books, and so on), we want to draw attention to three text formats that we recommend be included among a teacher's reading materials at any grade level: graphic novels, picture books, and multimedia texts. Graphic novels have grown significantly in use and stature during the past decade as reading materials for the classroom. A graphic novel is "a fictional or non-fictional book-length story told with images and verbal text using the conventions of a comic book" (Boerman-Cornell, Kim, & Teale, 2010, p. 1). Graphic novels have become quite popular with teens and are catching on more and more with younger readers. We recommend graphic novels as important materials because they offer readers opportunities for a unique, multimodal literary experience by immersing them in processing both text and images to create meaning. Such experiences can both extend children's responses to literature and enhance their dispositions toward reading. A few graphic novels are being taught with some regularity in the high school English curriculum (such as *American Born Chinese*, Yang, 2006, and *Persepolis*, Satrapi, 2003), and many school librarians and classroom teachers recommend them to students of all ages for independent reading. No collection of 21st century reading materials should be without graphic novels. (See Serchay, 2008, for recommended titles for middle and high school and Teale, Kim, & Boerman-Cornell, 2008, for recommended elementary titles.)

Learning to "read" and interpret the images in picture books is part of visual literacy. Of course, picture books are a staple in the primary grades, but they can also play a very important role in reading for grade 3 through 5 students because many picture books deal with sophisticated literary themes (such as *The Arrival* by Shaun Tan, 2007), complex scientific information (such as *The Tree of Life* by Peter Sís, 2003), and historical information (such as *Hiroshima No Pika* by Toshi Maruki, 1982). Realize also that certain picture books can be used to good effect with middle and high school students; there are various websites and professional books and articles focused on picture books as reading material for students of these ages (see Pearson, 2005). The California Young Reader Medal is even given in the category of Picture Books for Older Readers (see California Young Reader Medal, 2010, for a list of winners).

The final format for reading materials we suggest as critical for inclusion across all grades is multimedia texts. Multimedia texts combine the written word with still or moving images and/or audio to convey information or provide literary and artistic expression. Such texts are increasingly available on the Internet. We believe informational multimedia texts will soon completely replace the traditional print-based, content-area textbook (in history, biology, general science, geography, and so on) at all levels since complex concepts (such as DNA, westward expansion, or economic markets) can be conveyed to readers so much more effectively and with the most up-to-date interpretation with text, images, and sound rather than through a static image alone, as is the case with textbooks.

Reading Involves Knowledge, Not Just Skills and Strategies

Many educators, especially those at the elementary level and those working with struggling readers at the middle and high school levels, view learning to read as primarily a process of developing the skills and strategies involved in reading. Competence in skills, such as phonics and sight-word recognition, and in strategies, such as comprehension monitoring and questioning, are central to becoming a capable reader. However, it is important to regard reading as involving content (knowledge) as much as it involves skills and strategies. That is to say, all the reading skills in the world do little good without the accompanying world knowledge and content knowledge to go with them—especially for students beyond the primary grades. In fact, one of the strongest findings from the past half century of reading research is the close relationship between background knowledge and reading comprehension (Israel & Duffy, 2008).

> One of the strongest findings from the past half century of reading research is the close relationship between background knowledge and reading comprehension.

It is extremely important to include informational materials—from the various realms of the sciences and social studies, especially—as part of the reading/language arts curriculum as well as in our classroom libraries and in our recommendations for home and leisure reading. It is interesting to note the role of informational text reading in the National Assessment of Educational Progress (NAEP) and the Common Core State Standards. In the NAEP, materials on which students are tested shifts from 50 percent narrative/50 percent informational in grade 4 to 30 percent narrative/70 percent informational in grade 12 (National Center for Education Statistics, 2010). The recent Common Core State Standards include separate standards for literature and informational texts (Reading Standards for Literature K–5 and Reading Standards for Informational Text K–5) (Council of Chief State School Officers and the National Governors Association, 2010).

Cultural Content Is Critical

Likewise, it is important that reading materials are diverse in voice and content. Multicultural literature and international literature depict histories, stories, and experiences that are uniquely embedded within specific cultures or countries, yet they contain universal truths and themes for students to explore (Temple, Martinez, & Yokota, 2010). Multicultural literature is particularly important for students outside of mainstream culture who need to see their heritage reflected in the reading materials; however, all students need to be exposed to diversity through reading. Diverse literature expands readers' perspectives and aids in developing their critical understanding of the world around them.

Materials Should Meet Language Needs

Although most reading material in U.S. schools is in English, there is a need to include materials in other languages when warranted by the student population and the nature of the curriculum. Materials in languages other than English meet the needs of English language learners, and they offer additional support for those who are bilingual. Of course, for a school that has a bilingual education program or dual immersion program, materials in different languages (most typically English and Spanish) are essential. An added bonus of multiple language reading materials for all learners is that seeing text in different languages can impress upon students the importance of learning more than one language and of cross-cultural understanding.

Materials Matter

What students read impacts *how* they think; teachers need to be diligent in keeping the aforementioned criteria in mind as they select the highest quality and widest range of reading materials for their classrooms. It can be overwhelming, so it is helpful to partner with knowledgeable specialists, like the school librarian, whose job it is to know a wide range of good reading materials.

Implications for All Students

The thoughtful selection of reading materials manifests itself differently at the various grade levels. We find it useful to consider the implications of the previously elaborated criteria at three different levels: elementary school (kindergarten through grades 5 or 6), middle school (grades 5 or 6 through 8), and high school (grades 9 through 12).

Elementary School

Elementary school is traditionally thought of as the heart of reading instruction. The elementary years include what is for most students the most critical time in reading development in an alphabetic language like English or Spanish: beginning reading (typically grades K–2). The latter years of elementary school are very important as well. It is during grades 3–5 that readers consolidate their early skills to become fluent and comfortable engaging in higher levels of reading comprehension in both narrative and informational texts.

Basal reader programs. Basal reader programs continue to constitute the core reading materials in most elementary schools today. The appeal of such programs stems largely from the organized, complete package that they offer: carefully selected reading materials that are balanced for genre and provide lesson plans for teaching the skills that accompany each selection along with periodic assessments that document progress in reportable ways—all matched to learning standards for which teachers are responsible. The comprehensive preparation of such series appeals to administrators who often see them as fail-safe approaches and to many teachers because the lesson plans and materials are handed to them, ready to go. Recognizing the enormous impact of these series, the International Reading Association (IRA) has prepared guidelines for evaluating and selecting basals (IRA, 1994).

But are these series the best materials through which readers learn? Basal readers assume a grade-level audience, weighing the needs of the national range of students who represent each grade level. The programs are geared for a probable audience, with reference made to how to accommodate English learners, students with disabilities or exceptionalities, and others with special needs. These programs generalize grade-level interests and predict curricular teaching goals from the norm. But in reality, nobody knows the needs of an individual, specific reader like a student's own teacher. A well-prepared teacher with sensitive ability to adjust and accommodate can use his or her knowledge, imagination, and innovation to motivate and

> Nobody knows the needs of an individual, specific reader like a student's own teacher.

instruct learners by offering reading experiences closely matched to what each student needs.

Trade books. In well-stocked elementary classrooms, both variety and quantity are important in the materials the teacher uses for instruction and those available for student's independent use. Research suggests that making both narrative and informational texts readily available in a classroom library positively impacts students' reading habits and attitudes (Morrow & Weinstein, 1982). Intended to serve as an "at hand" library to augment the school library, the classroom collection should be relatively wide in scope, considering readers' needs and interests that span a range of readability and interests. As for quantity, a collection that includes four books for every child in the room is considered to be good, and one that has eight or more books per child is in the excellent category (Fractor, Woodruff, Martinez, & Teale, 1993). In no way should such a collection replace the even wider collection available in the school library; however, classroom library collections provide the immediacy and proximity necessary for promoting children's independent reading behaviors. The primary intent of these materials is motivation and engagement; therefore, they should include books, magazines, and audiobooks, as well as more traditional texts such as picture books, chapter books, informational books, and children's poetry —every possible reading material that could be of interest to students.

> Classroom library collections provide the immediacy and proximity necessary for promoting children's independent reading behaviors.

Guided reading and leveled readers. An outgrowth of the mid-1990s call for refocusing elementary reading instruction on the practice of guided reading (Fountas & Pinnell, 1996), "leveled readers" emerged as a way to provide students with reading material at their specific instructional reading level. These materials are written to or selected as conforming to a formula that limits the rate and number of words introduced. They are used in sets for small-group instruction. The aesthetic qualities of leveled readers are often lower than those of trade books created for literary and artistic intent. Guided reading is more widely defined than by merely using leveled readers, and offers lists and systems to level trade books. These systems of leveling books vary so widely, though, that the same trade books may be ranked anywhere on a range of difficulty depending on the system. Leveled readers are useful for offering students materials at their instructional reading level; however, care should be taken to allow and encourage students to read a wider range than just those texts that strictly adhere to a particular level.

The Accelerated Reader phenomenon. In many schools today, the use of Accelerated Reader, Reading Counts!, and other such programs has increased exponentially since the early 1990s. These programs use trade books, and in many cases the trade books are of high quality. That is the good news about the Accelerated Reader phenomenon—students are introduced to a range of high-quality books. These programs, based on the premise that readers become better by reading more, also offer tests for purchase to assess whether students have read and understood a particular book. Each book carries points for length and the publishing company's algorithm for measuring difficulty. The motivation for students to read and pass the tests comes from earning the points. That can be bad news for students: those who pass 70 percent of the quiz questions may not even bother to finish reading their books because they lack the motivation to do so (since the motivation is extrinsic and outside of the book itself). There are no consequences built in for repeatedly taking a quiz, so students may retake a quiz until they have read enough of the book (or guessed well enough) to pass and move on. Perhaps this extrinsic motivation increases a student's volume of reading in the short term, but how will it help readers develop intrinsic motivation to become lifelong readers? Another troubling aspect of Accelerated Reader is that it has become so deeply rooted in some schools that it is considered to be "the reading program," a highly problematic situation because even the Accelerated Reading program itself clearly recognizes that what it does is focus only on literal level of comprehension of details in a book, not on overall reading comprehension.

> Extrinsic motivation increases a student's volume of reading in the short term, but how will it help readers develop intrinsic motivation to become lifelong readers?

Materials for struggling readers. There is considerable debate about the kinds of materials that help struggling readers at the elementary level. One school of thought advocates that students be given highly decodable texts, books in which the vast majority of words are written in phonic patterns that have been taught in the reading program; another champions the use of leveled readers. In fact, the kinds of materials that prove to be successful with struggling readers are highly dependent upon the age of the student. Early reading intervention has proven more successful in helping struggling readers than attempts that begin in the later grades. Thus, materials for struggling students need to be especially helpful in promoting decoding and word recognition skills. Reading Recovery® has been shown to be an effective early reading intervention program (IES What Works Clearinghouse, 2008), so the kinds of materials it utilizes—texts that are (a) sequenced in terms of difficulty using a wide range of textual features (not merely what is measured by a readability formula) and (b) chosen for content that will appeal to the child reader—can be recommended. There are also a range of computer software programs and websites designed for struggling readers. These vary greatly in quality and effectiveness. We advise teachers to consult the IES What Works Clearinghouse for evaluations of these materials (see http://ies.ed.gov/ncee/wwc/reports).

Middle School

With respect to reading materials, middle schools truly are in the middle in many ways. Although it used to be that basal reading programs were developed for grades K–8, virtually all such programs these days extend through grade 5 only. Many high school English classes use literature anthologies that contain a variety of literary genres as well as a range of topics and authors, but such anthologies are not nearly as widely used in middle schools. Another factor contributing to the types of reading materials found in the middle school classroom is the design of the curriculum: is the curriculum integrated across traditional content areas, or does the school maintain a more high-school-like, subject-area approach with one period/teacher for English, another for social studies, and so on? Curricula that stress integrated studies tend to use more materials from magazine and Internet sources in addition to both informational and narrative trade books, whereas in the more traditional subject-area approach, one would tend to find novels in the English classroom and textbooks in science, social studies, and other content-area classrooms.

In middle schools, the fact that we are in the golden age of young adult literature means that the wealth of materials available for instructional as well as recreational reading is at a peak. This growth is not only in terms of the sheer amount of trade books being published with an older tween and teen audience in mind, but also in terms of the breadth of topics the literature addresses. Interestingly, the very topics that engender intense interest among middle school readers—sexuality, coming of age, identity, adult authority, death—are also the very ones that cause adults to engage in censorship of reading materials.

Censorship is a significant issue when considering reading materials for both middle school and high school students. The National Council of Teachers of English has a wealth of information on the topic of censorship and reading materials for this age group (see www.ncte.org/action/anti-censorship), as does the American Library Association (see www.ala.org/ala/aboutala/offices/oif/index.cfm).

Materials for struggling readers. The issue of struggling readers is a significant one for middle schools. This is often regarded as a critical time for overcoming reading problems. If a middle school student doesn't get up to grade-level proficiency, it is felt, the chances of his or her dropping out of school or continuing to experience extreme difficulty in school achievement are considerable (Biancarosa & Snow, 2006). A significant effort aimed at addressing this issue has been the Striving Readers initiative from the U.S. Department of Education. This program targets both middle and high schools with substantial numbers of struggling readers. The materials used through this program are quite varied, but one of the successful approaches is the use of short materials of high interest, such as articles from magazines, excerpted pieces from the Internet, relevant blogs, reviews, and shorter graphic novels (D. Ogle, personal communication, June 19, 2010). What these materials have in common is that (1) they are short enough to be used in targeted lessons—they don't need to be assigned for students to read at home, (2) they are selected to be at a readability level that is appropriate for these readers, and (3) they are of high enough interest that even if some of the vocabulary is challenging to struggling readers, there is enough personal interest to keep readers engaged and willing to work to comprehend the message of text.

High School

For many years, virtually all of the discussion about the critical time for reading focused on the primary grades and beginning reading. During the late 1990s and through the early 2000s, a host of reading educators sought to bring attention to the extreme importance of adolescent literacy (for example, Moore, Bean, Birdyshaw, & Rycik, 1999), the efforts of which culminated in the influential report *Reading Next: A Vision for Action and Research in Middle and High School Literacy* (Biancarosa & Snow, 2006). The research of this era had enormous implications for reading materials, many of which are being realized in high schools today.

Materials for English and the humanities. Without doubt, the major debate related to materials in the discipline of English centers on the canon. Since the beginning of English studies in the United States, scholars, teachers, and the public have weighed in on the merits of, and problems with, centering the high school curriculum on a core set of classic pieces of literature (Applebee, 1974, 1992). Most recently this debate has centered on refocusing the materials of high school English studies in two ways: making them more inclusive (having students read more multicultural literature, as well as works by women, more contemporary works, and so on) and including young adult literature as an integral part of the curriculum.

Restructuring English materials to include works by authors of color and by women started in the 1970s with texts used in college English courses and has affected the teaching of high school English in a significant way ever since. Both literature anthologies and departmental reading lists have expanded reading requirements for students beyond what was typical in high school freshman English, and American and British literature classes in the 1960s. For example, the literature of the Harlem Renaissance is widely studied in American high schools today. However, as Applebee's research has shown, the canon continues to dominate the materials assigned in English in most high schools today. We believe it is critically important for students to study the Anglo-American literary heritage as well as classics from around the world; however, we cannot overemphasize the importance of giving students opportunities to read and discuss the voices and stories traditionally underrepresented in English studies. High school students need a blend of both canonical literature and literature representing other perspectives, both in what they study in the classroom as well as what they choose for personal reading.

> High school students need a blend of both canonical literature and literature representing other perspectives, both in what they study in the classroom as well as what they choose for personal reading.

The issue of including young adult literature as part of the curriculum is in some respects even more contentious. The rise of young adult books can be traced to the 1970s, with such authors as S. E. Hinton and Paul Zindel. Young adult literature can be defined as "literature written for young people ages 11 to 18 and . . . marketed as 'young adult'" (Tomlinson & Lynch-Brown, 2010, p. 4). Currently, young adult publishing is one of the most robust sectors of the book industry, but such works typically have been given little role in the curriculum, probably for several reasons. One is the pure conservatism just discussed in relation to the canon—clearly, young adult literature is not part of those works. Also, there is the lingering belief that young adult literature is written "down" to a teen audience and therefore is not of high literary quality. It is true that many young adult books are written for popular appeal, but it is also the case—especially with works published in the past fifteen years—that a substantial number of young adult authors are creating works with considerable literary merit and thematic depth. Walter Dean Myers, Laurie Halse Anderson, Marc Aronson, and Jacqueline Woodson are several whose fiction and nonfiction books have been recognized by the National Book Award, Printz Award, and Margaret Edwards Award committees, not to mention teen readers themselves (with the International Reading Association's Young Adult Choices list, for example).

We believe it is extremely important that secondary teachers become familiar with the body of young adult literature so that they can selectively include high-quality young adult selections in their classroom teaching and be able to recommend such books to individual students for their personal reading.

> A substantial number of young adult authors are creating works with considerable literary merit and thematic depth.

The growth of the International Baccalaureate Programme has meant an increasing awareness and call for books that support student learning in three core areas that "broaden the educational experience and challenge students to apply their knowledge and understanding": the ability to write extended essays, show understanding of theory of knowledge, and actively learn through real tasks and service beyond the classroom (International Baccalaureate, 2005–2010).

Materials for struggling readers. In the 2000s, it has become increasingly common practice for programs for struggling high school readers to focus on first-year students so that students can succeed in reading across all subject areas in their high school curriculum. Teachers constantly voice their concern about a lack of suitable materials to accomplish such a goal. They are correct: there are relatively few high-interest/low-readability materials for these students. The American Library Association's Young Adult Library Services section produces a list of recommended titles called "Quick Picks for Reluctant Young Adult Readers" that teachers can access to help identify high-interest/low-readability materials. The Striving Readers initiative by the U.S. Department of Education (described previously in the section on middle schools), advocates using short materials of high interest, such as articles from magazines, excerpted pieces from the Internet, relevant blogs, reviews, and shorter graphic novels.

New Developments in Materials for Reading: Digital Literacy

Writing about the quickly changing world of digital materials for reading is tricky; it is impossible to stay current in a world in which text can change instantaneously, and even the delivery systems for providing digital texts undergo major changes periodically (think

Kindle™ or iPad). We have chosen to focus on two types of digital materials relevant to K–12 readers: audiobooks, and digitized books/digitally developed books.

Audiobooks

Audiobooks—recordings of texts being read aloud—have the potential to draw student readers into a story, and to support them as they follow along with the text. Audiobooks have become increasingly accessible; in many areas of the country, a public library card gives students access not only to boxed audio CDs that can be checked out of the library, but also to a huge range of textual MP3 files through an Internet connection. Many children's chapter books (both narrative and informational) and young adult novels are available as audiobooks.

Educators need to be aware of the literary merit as well as production quality of audiobooks because both impact engagement for readers. Journals such as *Booklist* and *School Library Journal* and specialized sources such as *Audiophile* regularly review audiobooks. Awards also help to identify quality: the American Library Association's Odyssey Award is given to the producer of the best audiobook for children and/or young adults with a focus on literary merit. The Audio Publishers Association's Audies has a longer history but focuses primarily on the merits of the technical aspects of the audio production.

> Educators need to be aware of the literary merit as well as production quality of audiobooks because both impact engagement for readers.

Although still costly, all-in-one audiobook players such as the Playaway® have been popular, especially with readers of young adult literature. The audiobook is preloaded onto a small MP3 player that hangs on a lanyard. Devices such as the Playaway are available at many public libraries, and some libraries also loan audiobooks that patrons can download onto their iPods or other devices for the duration of the loan.

Digital Books/Digitally Developed Books

Digital books are books in some sort of digitized format—readers can view them online on a computer, a smartphone, or an MP3 player. Digital books for adults are a strong presence in the market, and digital informational books and reference books are becoming increasingly sensible in retrieving the most current information, but digital children's books are not yet as plentiful. Digitized textbooks have particular potential for school markets as they would limit the physical weight of traditional textbooks that students take to and from school for homework. The interactive potential of digital books also makes them appealing for schools because students traditionally are not given permission to mark their books up for studying. With respect to digitizing trade books, companies are experimenting widely, but most are digitizing traditionally printed books. Perhaps when a new generation of creators of reading materials leads the way, there will be people who conceptualize, create, and teach through materials that are to be read from a different mindset than now, creating unique digitally developed books rather than merely adapting print books to a digital format.

Implications and Possibilities for the Future

Materials are changing greatly, both in system of delivery and in the nature of the materials themselves. Access to and types of reading materials are likely to be different in the future. Already, the emphasis on 21st century skills is leading teachers toward focusing on how students should access, consider, and process information in ways that are different than in the past. Kindles, nooks®, iPads, and other new technologies have already impacted our relationship to some reading materials.

How we consider materials that might be deemed traditional (such as print books) is also changing. In 1999 in her book *Radical Change*, Eliza Dresang asserted that readers need to be prepared for different literary experiences due to changes in materials. Dresang characterized changes in form and format as unusual graphics, nonlinear organization and format, multiple layers of meaning, and interactive format. She also noted the increase in unheard voices, multiple perspectives, unexplored settings, and unresolved endings. Such changes are profoundly evident today. For example, numerous picture books

> Readers need to be prepared for different literary experiences due to changes in materials.

characterized as "postmodern" in format have appeared increasingly in recent years. Such books present challenges to readers that differ from the visual understanding of traditionally created picture books (Sipe & Pantaleo, 2008).

In the past, literary reading materials have often been taught through a genre orientation. But increasingly, there are books that cross genre boundaries, leading to "genre blurring." This leads to the question of what organization is more valued or meaningful to student learning. Is understanding genre the most important element? Or is it more important to learn through the analysis of character development? Or perhaps theme wins as an organizer. For example, Brian Selznick's masterfully created book, *The Invention of Hugo Cabret* (2007), is a thick book, incorporating pages of black-and-white line drawings that weave through fast-paced pages, some with minimal text and others with a fair amount of text to read. If you go to the website for the book, you find the film that inspired Selznick as well as the music that could be used as a backdrop, and you quickly realize that this cinematic experience is somewhat akin to a silent film set to music. What, then, is this book? Is it historical fiction? Is it a picture book (after all, it won the Caldecott Medal)? Perhaps the implication for the future is that genre is not the primary organizer for teaching about literature; rather, educators should be seeking lasting ways to consider what's important in what these new works offer readers.

Books like these inspire greater possibilities for literary response in new ways that take advantage of web 2.0 technologies. These days, the impact of technology on student learning is such that educators must allow learners the opportunities to engage in and show their learning through interactive technology options. For example, literary response might have been through paper and pencil or dramatic or artistic expression in the past. While those formats continue, the possibilities have grown far beyond keyboarding and scanning, early steps in technology integration. These days, social media and web 2.0 technologies mean integrating visuals, video, and other formats and creating interactive spaces in virtual communities.

Teachers as Readers: Past, Present, and Future

Teachers need to be readers themselves (of a wide range of materials) if they are to make decisions about what to teach from and what to recommend to students; but more importantly, teachers need to experience for themselves the power of aesthetic and efferent reading. Only by being personally engaged in reading experiences that inspire and inform can teachers fully realize the intrinsic motivation to read for intellectual stimulation and emotional engagement. Although most teachers have studied literature for children and adolescents in teacher preparation programs, they must have a continued commitment to reading and knowing books as literature as the types of available reading materials change. Through their engagement as readers, teachers will be serving as models for their students, but also experiencing firsthand what it means to be a reader in a fast-changing world of new materials for readers.

References and Resources

Anderson, R. C., Shirey, L. L., Wilson, P. T., & Fielding, L. G. (1987). Interestingness of children's reading material. In R. E. Snow & M. J. Farr (Eds.), *Aptitude, learning, and instruction: Vol. 3. Cognitive and affective process analysis* (pp. 287–299). Hillsdale, NJ: Erlbaum.

Applebee, A. N. (1974). *Tradition and reform in the teaching of English: A history.* Urbana, IL: National Council of Teachers of English.

Applebee, A. N. (1992). Stability and change in the high-school canon. *The English Journal, 81*(5), 27–32.

Aronson, M., & Newquist, H. P. (2007). *For boys only: The biggest, baddest book ever.* New York: Feiwel & Friends.

Biancarosa, C., & Snow, C. E. (2006). *Reading next—A vision for action and research in middle and high school literacy: A report to Carnegie Corporation of New York* (2nd ed.). Washington, DC: Alliance for Excellent Education.

Boerman-Cornell, W., Kim, J., & Teale, W. H. (2010). *Secret identities: Graphic novels help students explore themes of self-discovery.* Manuscript submitted for publication.

California Young Reader Medal. (2010). *Booklist: Picture books for older readers.* Accessed at www.californiayoungreadermedal.org/booklist_picturebooks _older_readers.htm on June 19, 2010.

Council of Chief State School Officers and the National Governors Association. (2010). *Common Core State Standards.* Accessed at www.corestandards.org /assets/CCSSI_ELA%20Standards.pdf on August 17, 2010.

Dresang, E. (1999). *Radical change: Books for youth in a digital age*. New York: H. W. Wilson.

Fountas, I., & Pinnell, G. (1996). *Guided reading: Good first teaching for all children*. Portsmouth, NH: Heinemann.

Fractor, J., Woodruff, M., Martinez, M. G., & Teale, W. H. (1993). Let's not miss opportunities for promoting voluntary reading: Classroom libraries in the elementary school. *The Reading Teacher, 46*, 476–484.

Hoffman, J., & Schallert, D. (Eds.). (2003). *The texts in elementary classrooms*. Mahwah, NJ: Erlbaum.

International Reading Association. (1994). *Guidelines for the evaluation of commercial reading programs*. Newark, DE: Author.

IES What Works Clearinghouse. (2008). *Reading Recovery®*. Washington, DC: U.S. Department of Education Institute of Education Sciences. Accessed at http://ies.ed.gov/ncee/wwc/reports/beginning_reading/reading_recovery on July 4, 2010.

Israel, S. E., & Duffy, G. (2008). *Handbook of research on reading comprehension*. New York: Routledge.

Maruki, T. (1982). *Hiroshima no pika*. New York: HarperCollins.

Moore, D., Bean, T. W., Birdyshaw, D., & Rycik J. A. (1999). Adolescent literacy: A position statement. *Journal of Adolescent and Adult Literacy, 43*(1), 97–112.

Morrow, L. M., & Weinstein, C. S. (1982). Increasing children's use of literature through program and physical design changes. *The Elementary School Journal, 83*, 131–137.

National Center for Education Statistics. (2010). *National assessment of educational progress: The nation's report card*. Washington, DC: Author. Accessed at http://nces.ed.gov/nationsreportcard/reading/distributequest.asp on August 7, 2010.

Pearson, M. (2005). *Big ideas in small packages: Using picture books with older readers*. Santa Barbara, CA: Linworth.

Satrapi, M. (2003). *Persepolis: The story of a childhood*. New York: Pantheon.

Selznick, B. (2007). *The invention of Hugo Cabret*. New York: Scholastic.

Serchay, D. S. (2008). *The librarian's guide to graphic novels for children and 'tweens*. New York: Neal-Schuman.

Sipe, L., & Pantaleo, S. (Eds.). (2008). *Postmodern picturebooks: Play, parody, and self-referentiality*. New York/London: Routledge.

Sís, P. (2003). *The tree of life: A book depicting the life of Charles Darwin, naturalist, geologist and thinker*. New York: Farrar, Straus and Giroux.

Tan, S. (2007). *The arrival*. New York: Scholastic.

Tatum, A. (2005). *Teaching reading to black adolescent males*. Portland, ME: Stenhouse.

Teale, W. H., Kim, J., & Boerman-Cornell, W. (2008). It's elementary—Graphic novels for the K–6 classroom. *Book Links, 17*(5), 6–13.

Teale, W. H., Yokota, J., & Martinez, M. (2008). The book matters: Evaluating and selecting what to read aloud to young children. In A. DeBruin-Parecki (Ed.), *Effective early literacy practice: Here's how, here's why* (pp. 101–121). Baltimore: Brookes.

Temple, C., Martinez, M., & Yokota, J. (2010). *Children's books in children's hands: An introduction to their literature* (4th ed.). Needham Heights, MA: Allyn & Bacon.

Tomlinson, C., & Lynch-Brown, C. (2010). *Essentials of young adult literature* (2nd ed.). Needham Heights, MA: Allyn & Bacon.

Yang, G. L. (2006). *American born Chinese*. New York: First Second.

Yokota, J., Teale, W. H., & Quiroa, R. (2008). Literacy development for culturally diverse students. In S. B. Wepner, D. S. Strickland, & J. T. Feeley (Eds.), *The administration and supervision of reading programs* (4th ed., pp. 170–185). New York: Teachers College Press.

Lesley Mandel Morrow

Lesley Mandel Morrow, PhD, a former class-room teacher and reading specialist, is a professor at the Graduate School of Education at Rutgers University and chair of the Department of Learning and Teaching. She has received grants from the federal government for her research, which focuses in the field of early literacy with children from diverse backgrounds. Morrow is the author of more than 300 publications, including journal articles, book chapters, and books. She has received awards from Rutgers University for excellence in research, teaching, and service. She also received the International Reading Association's (IRA) Jerry Johns Outstanding Teacher Educator in Reading award and their William S. Gray Citation of Merit for Scholarship and Service to the field of Literacy. She is past president of the IRA and current president of the Reading Hall of Fame. She received her doctorate from Fordham University and was given their Outstanding Alumni Award several years later.

In this chapter, Morrow describes the characteristics of exemplary teachers and presents a comprehensive approach to early literacy instruction. She shows readers what literacy-rich classrooms look like and presents case studies of teachers using comprehensive exemplary instruction in the early grades for beginning readers.

Chapter 4

Developing Effective Reading Curricula for Beginning Readers and the Primary Grades

Lesley Mandel Morrow

In my observations of excellent teachers, I have discovered that these teachers encourage their students to function as a community of learners. The classroom atmosphere they create is one of acceptance of differences in cultures and achievement. They encourage their students to be academic risk takers who share ideas, which are valued by other students and the teacher. They give students responsibility for their learning. They view all students as capable learners who progress at their own developmental level. They provide uninterrupted periods of time for language arts instruction. Literacy instruction involves the integration of the language arts into content-area themes. They teach skills within a meaningful context and in an explicit manner. Their instruction is guided by assessment. Teachers meet with small groups and teach based on the specific needs of their students—according to their learning styles, interests, and achievement levels. They positively reinforce students to motivate them to want to learn. These excellent teachers provide their students with a comprehensive approach to literacy instruction.

In this chapter, I provide a description of the characteristics of exemplary teachers. I then present a comprehensive approach to early literacy instruction. Finally, I visit literacy-rich classrooms and explore case studies of teachers using comprehensive exemplary instruction in beginning and primary classrooms.

Characteristics of Exemplary Teachers

When seeking the most effective way to teach children, we often look for a silver bullet—the best program or the latest trend. However, research into strategies for reading success has found that the teacher—not the method—is the key element. In their position statement, the International Reading Association (1999) states that no method or combination of methods can teach all children to read; rather, it is the excellent teacher who knows his or her children from a social, emotional, physical, and intellectual perspective who creates reading success. Likewise, the National Institute of Child Health and Human Development (2000) found that the teacher is the most important element for student success—regardless of the method of instruction.

> When seeking the most effective way to teach children, we often look for a silver bullet—the best program or the latest trend. However, research into strategies for reading success has found that the teacher—not the method—is the key element.

Researchers who began exploring exemplary teaching wanted to know not only about good methods, but also about what teachers did in their classrooms. They wanted to know about the interactions between children and teachers, their routines, the design of environments, how the classroom as a community affected growth, and how and why teachers chose to do the things they did (Clark & Peterson, 1986; Coker, 1985; Duffy & Hoffman, 1999; Genishi, Ryan, Ochsner, & Yarnall, 2001; Haigh & Katterms, 1984; Roehler & Duffy, 1984; Shulman, 1986). In one large-scale study, teachers were nominated to participate in interviews and extensive classroom observations to determine characteristics of excellent teachers (Ruddell, 1995; Ruddell & Harris, 1989; Ruddell & Kern, 1986). The results of the study indicated that influential teachers do the following (Ruddell, 1995):

- Use highly motivating teaching strategies.

- Build strong affective relationships with their students.

- Create a feeling of excitement about what they are teaching.
- Adjust instruction to meet the individual needs of their students.
- Create literacy-rich physical environments to support their teaching.
- Have strong organization and management skills.

In other extensive studies (Morrow, Tracey, Woo, & Pressley, 1999; Taylor, Pearson, & Clark, 2000), researchers observed exemplary teachers from school districts ranging from at risk to middle class. Their findings revealed that these exemplary teachers created literacy-rich environments using a variety of learning settings, such as whole group, small group, and one on one, as well as teacher-directed instruction. Their students worked in centers and interacted with adults and peers. Classrooms included a rich variety of print materials for students to use daily. Teachers used varying instructional approaches, such as spontaneous, authentic, explicit, systematic, meaning-oriented, and problem-solving situations. They engaged children in shared, guided, oral, silent, independent, and collaborative reading and writing. They offered extensive writing experiences, word analysis, and comprehension instruction. They also made consistent efforts to connect reading and writing instruction to content areas. Student assessment guided instruction. These teachers carried out daily routines that were organized, well managed, and predictable. There was a great deal of communication with families.

A synthesis of investigations about exemplary literacy practice in the primary grades (Allington & Johnston, 2002; Block, 2001; Cantrell, 1999a, 1999b; Morrow & Casey, 2003; Morrow, Tracey, Woo, Pressley, 1999; Pressley, Rankin, & Yokoi, 1996; Taylor, Pearson, Clark, & Walpole, 1999; Taylor, Peterson, Pearson, & Rodriguez, 2002; Wharton, Pressley, Rankin, & Mistretta, 1997) found that effective teachers do the following:

- Provide explicit literacy instruction. They let students know what they are teaching and what students are to learn. They model explicitly the behavior they want students to acquire. They provide guidance as students practice the skill, and then students practice the skill independently.

- Engage students in constructive interactions. Excellent teachers are always building good relationships with students—especially during learning. Discussions expand student knowledge with high-level comprehension questions, and they allow students to do as much talking—if not more talking—than teachers do.

- Create a supportive, encouraging, respectful, and friendly atmosphere. Students in classrooms with excellent teachers learn that what they have to say is important and that there are no questions that can't be asked. There is time for fun, jokes, and being playful.

- Weave reading and writing throughout the curriculum by integrating content-area themes into the teaching of reading and writing. Learning to read without interesting material isn't very motivating, thus exemplary teachers know that they need to integrate literacy instruction into interesting content material.

- Create a literacy-rich environment in their classrooms with a variety of literacy materials to support instruction. Access to materials is crucial. Excellent teachers know how to supply their rooms with interesting materials that aren't expensive: they print materials from the Internet, collect free materials, buy low-cost materials (from flea markets, for example), and ask for donations.

- Teach to individual needs in small-group settings. By doing so, teachers are able to assess their students frequently and design differentiated instruction and strategies for learning by selecting appropriate materials for each child.

- Consistently monitor students' engagement and literacy progress through systematic accountability. Effective teachers collect daily performance samples; observe and record behavior; do informal assessments, such as running records; and administer standardized tests as well.

- Have excellent organization and management skills. Teachers establish rules for behavior and routines for work and play. Rules are consistent and enforced.

- Develop strong connections with students' homes. To be successful with students, effective teachers need to communicate their goals to parents so parents understand them and can help support the goals.

An Effective and Comprehensive Approach to Instruction

An effective and comprehensive approach to instruction is grounded in a rich model of literacy learning that encompasses both the elegance and complexity of reading and language arts processes. Such a model acknowledges the importance of both form (phonics, mechanics, and so on) and function (comprehension, purpose, and meaning) of the literacy processes and recognizes that learning occurs most effectively in a whole-part-whole context. This type of instruction is characterized by meaningful literacy activities that provide students with both the skill and desire to become proficient and lifelong literacy learners. A comprehensive program includes experiences in reading, writing, listening, speaking, spelling, and viewing. Literacy is taught both within a block of time set aside for uninterrupted instruction and throughout the school day in art, music, social studies, science, math, and so on.

To create interest in reading and writing, teachers and students select themes—such as sports, insects, plants, and current events—that provide a reason to read and write. The teacher meets with whole groups, small groups, and individual students. The classroom includes centers for independent and social learning. There are accessible literacy materials for reading and writing that include narrative, informational, and instructional texts as well as pencil-and-paper, technology, and manipulative materials. The teacher uses a systematic, explicit curriculum but allows for spontaneous learning that provides authentic experiences, construction of meaning, and problem solving. In the daily routine, the teacher makes sure to include shared reading and writing, guided reading and writing for skill development, oral and silent reading and writing, independent reading and writing, collaborative reading and writing, content-area reading and writing, and performance of reading and writing to an audience.

This comprehensive perspective is not a random combination of strategies or a broad and orderly sequence of strategies (such as doing whole-group instruction first, small-group instruction next, and then buddy reading, for example). A comprehensive perspec-tive includes careful selection from the best theories available and the use of different learning strategies to match the learning styles of individual children. In a comprehensive approach, a teacher might select strategies from different learning theories to provide the appropriate instruction for each child. One child, for example, may be a visual learner and will have a hard time mastering phonics. The teacher must find other routes for this student to become an independent reader. Alternately, a student whose strength is auditory learning will learn best with phonics instruction.

> This comprehensive perspective is not a random combination of strategies or a broad and orderly sequence of strategies. . . . A comprehensive perspective includes careful selection from the best theories available and the use of different learning strategies to match the learning styles of individual children.

The classroom characteristics of a comprehensive program are based on sociocultural theory. According to this theory, student learning is dependent upon what a teacher knows, how students come to understand that knowledge, and the context in which the learning takes place (Vygotksy, 1978). In a setting based on socio-cultural theory, schools are considered collaborative communities in which more capable adults or peers assist students. Teaching and the learning environment, or the culture of the classroom, are inextri-cably linked. A sociocultural concept of learning considers multiple contexts:

- The relationship between teacher and student
- The community of the classroom
- The larger community of the school
- How all of these are organized and managed together, and how they affect each other

Characteristics of Effective and Comprehensive Classrooms

The research provides a strong framework for what constitutes an effective and comprehensive approach to early literacy. But what does this framework look like in action? How are the classrooms of effective beginning and primary teachers organized? What materials do they include? How do teachers implement strategies to form an effective reading curriculum?

This section describes in detail what effective and comprehensive classrooms look like—what materials they contain, how they are organized, and so on. The case study section on pages 100–106 describes how teachers use the materials in a typical day to form an effective reading curriculum. The exemplary literacy-rich preK through third-grade classrooms described in the research looked very much alike. The major difference between grade levels was the difficulty of classroom materials and how teachers used them.

Kindergarten and First-Grade Classrooms

The classrooms of excellent kindergarten and first-grade teachers are inviting and organized into well-defined centers. Wall displays reflect the theme being studied and show evidence of students' growing literacy development. Displays include charts and samples of student writing. In the whole-group learning area is an easel with chart paper for the morning message, a calendar, a weather chart, a temperature graph, a helper chart, a daily schedule, classroom rules, a pocket chart, and a word wall. The teacher also has an interactive whiteboard, computers, and access to the Internet.

Literacy center. The largest center is the literacy center, which has a rug for independent reading and is also used for whole-class meetings. The area includes lots of space for storing books. One set of shelves holds books organized in two different ways: baskets of books leveled for difficulty that coordinate with the teachers' small-group reading instruction, and baskets organized by themes, such as dinosaurs, sports, and weather. The teacher rotates books in the baskets monthly. Colored stickers on the books and baskets assist students in returning them to the correct spot. Student-made class books and stories are in another basket. Books about the current theme are arranged on a display shelf.

The literacy center has a flannel board with flannel characters, puppets, and props for storytelling. There is a rocking chair for the teacher and other adults to use as they read to the class, and children use the rocking chair to read independently and to read to each other. The listening area has a compact disc player for listening to stories. There are manipulative materials for learning about print, including magnetic letters, puzzle rhyme cards, and letter chunks on small tiles for making words.

Writing center. The writing center is an extension of the literacy center. It has a table for small groups of children to meet with the teacher. Shelves hold many types of paper, a stapler, markers, crayons, colored pencils, dictionaries, alphabet stamps, and ink stamp pads. A word wall in the writing center has each of the letters of the alphabet taped on horizontally. When students learn a new word, the teacher writes it on a card and tapes it under the letter it begins with on the word wall. Students can refer to the word wall if they need help spelling a particular word. Students may be asked to think of words that begin with the same letter as a word on the wall or of words that rhyme with a word-wall word. Students' names are on the word wall along with high-frequency sight words they are expected to learn. Teachers also include theme-specific materials in the writing center. For example, for a dinosaur unit, students would find dinosaur-shaped blank books to write in, a dinosaur dictionary, and a dinosaur-shaped poster with words about dinosaurs.

Science center. The science center is the home of the class pets. Equipment in this center includes plants, magnets, and objects that sink and float; there are always new hands-on experiments to complete. Theme-specific materials, for a dinosaur unit, for example, would include books about dinosaurs and materials for writing stories or informational pieces about dinosaurs. It might include bones, a magnifying glass, and rubber gloves to examine the bones, dinosaur pictures to sort into "meat eater" and "plant eater" piles or "walked on two feet" and "walked on four feet" piles, and recording sheets for all activities.

Dramatic play center. This center includes a table, chairs, and a bookshelf. Part of the center is a restaurant where children read menus, take orders, and check their bills. The restaurant promotes learning about multicultural food and customs; it can be an Italian, Chinese, Mexican, Portuguese, or Japanese restaurant, or a Jewish deli, for example. Other options for dramatic play settings include a newspaper office, a post office, and a travel agency. During a dinosaur-themed unit, some of the dramatic play area could be transformed into a paleontologist's dig site with chicken bones embedded in plaster. Students then use carving tools and small hammers to remove the bones (while wearing safety goggles, of course). They label the bones and display them in trays. The center also includes dinosaur books and posters.

Block center. The block center includes wooden blocks of all sizes and shapes and other toys for construction, such as LEGOs®. There are toy trucks, cars, trains, busses, people, and animals in this area. Labels designate where the different toys go. There are 5 × 8 cards and tape so students can label their creations with "please save" signs for buildings under construction or signs naming finished structures along with the names of the builders. During special-theme units, such as a dinosaur unit, toy dinosaurs, trees, bushes, and some dinosaur books would be available in this center.

Art center. This center contains an easel, table, chairs, scissors, markers, crayons, and paper of many colors, types, and sizes. There are collage materials, such as cotton balls, doilies, foil, wallpaper, stickers, and paste. During a theme unit, teachers might add stencils and stamps related to the unit. A dinosaur unit might include clay models of dinosaurs and many pictures of dinosaurs for students to reference as they make their own sculptures. Students would discuss their sculptures and write about them.

Math center. The math center contains math manipulatives for counting, adding, measuring, weighing, graphing, and distinguishing shapes. There are felt numbers to use on the felt board; magnetic numbers for magnetic boards; numbers to sequence in a pocket chart; geometric shapes; and measuring tools with sheets of paper for recording objects' dimensions. Teachers add different objects for theme units. The dinosaur unit might include plaster bones of dinosaurs for measuring, dinosaur counters, small plastic dinosaurs in a jar for students to estimate the amount, and a basket containing small dinosaurs numbered from 1 to 50 to be put in sequential order. The new vocabulary introduced in the center enhances students' math knowledge.

Technology center. This center includes three computers with software specific to the unit the class is studying and quality interactive software for practicing skills. For example, during the dinosaur unit, the center contains *Eyewitness Virtual Reality: Dinosaur Hunter* (1996) by DK Multimedia for printing dinosaur stationary, postcards, posters, and masks, and for visiting a virtual museum exhibit about dinosaurs.

Second- and Third-Grade Classrooms

Upon entering these classrooms, it becomes immediately apparent how much value the teacher places on literacy. One area of the room is labeled "book nook" with a chair set on a carpet surrounded by numerous floor cushions and large bean bag chairs where students can settle in to read. Right next to the lounge chair is a book cart with a variety of books from which students can choose. The cart has many types of books, from light reading like *Squids Will Be Squids* (Scieszka, 1998), to the more serious *When I Was Young in the Mountains* (Rylant, 1982). A word wall made of felt containing different parts of speech takes up a large portion of the wall in the book nook. Posters of popular books cover the remainder of the wall. Next to them are book reviews written by students. There are posters that promote good reading hanging on the walls, filing cabinets, and bookcases. Chart paper with publishing guidelines (prewriting, drafting, revising, editing, and publishing) and definitions of literary terms, such as *onomatopoeia* and *alliteration,* hang from a rope strung diagonally across the room. Around the periphery of the chalkboard are various smaller posters of other literary terms and the class rules. On the back wall of the room is another word wall displaying the most commonly misspelled words.

The classroom has many bookcases filled with about 200 books of all levels and genres. They are labeled according to type—fiction, informational, biography, and so on. In the informational section there are books on the rainforest, planets, and reptiles, to name a few. Prominently displayed on a book rack are students' "personal choice" books. Popular books by well-known authors of children's literature are part of the collection, such as *Nighty Nightmare* (Howe, 1987) and *Runaway Ralph* (Cleary, 1970). They share space with trendy series books such as R. L. Stine's *Goosebumps* series (1990–1999). The remaining shelves contain books grouped by specific type: current science topics, biographies of important people from the current social studies unit, and so on. For the science topic of natural disasters, for example, the teacher would include on the shelf twenty books about volcanoes, tidal waves, hurricanes, and earthquakes. Most titles are single copies, but several would have multiple copies, such as *The Magic School Bus Inside a Hurricane* (Cole & Degen, 1995) and *Earthquakes* (Simon, 1995). On the wall near the shelf of science books is a corkboard with posters of the earth, weather patterns, earthquakes, hurricanes, and other similar topics.

Easels and bulletin boards featuring various topics are throughout the room. On one easel is a piece of paper with the headings "Said is Dead" on the top half and "Fun is Done" on the bottom half. Beneath the respective headings are lists of synonyms students have added for the overused words *said* and *fun*. Some of the suggested alternatives for *said* include *replied, uttered,* and *bellowed.* Synonyms for *fun* include *outstanding, excellent,* and *extraordinary.*

The students' desks are grouped in clusters of four or five. In addition, there are several tables where individuals or groups can work. The teacher's desk is towards the back of the room. Near the teacher's desk are four computers with access to the Internet and a printer. Students use the computer for researching, working on the class website, making PowerPoint presentations, sending emails to pen pals, and so on.

A learning environment such as the one described here can accommodate the differences in students' reading ability in second and third grade. In the third grade you might have students reading on a first-grade reading level and some reading on an eighth-grade level. Therefore, the materials and strategies they need must be available to them. Those who are not on level can only improve with materials and strategies appropriate for them and those above level deserve to be challenged with appropriate materials and strategies. This is true at all grade levels.

Effective and Comprehensive Instruction in Action: Case Studies

This section describes how teachers use the materials described in the previous section on a typical day to form an effective reading curriculum. These case studies come from our extensive research involving observation of exemplary classrooms in the primary grades in five different states.

Our team of researchers observed nine classrooms for each grade level for several days during a one-year period of time. Observers spent many full days in each classroom, often observing the same rooms to compare notes. Classroom teachers were selected for the study by their supervisors who had evaluated and observed them, and also by colleagues, parents, and students. They must have been teaching for at least five years. Their students must have scored well on standardized tests in the previous five years. When the study was complete, the data was coded for categories to determine how to define *exemplary*, noting similar and distinct characteristics among different grade levels.

We found in our observations that this effective and comprehensive instruction taught students to be independent; they knew what to do, where to go, and when. Purposeful learning occurred in all settings. The classrooms had routines and procedures, and students understood teachers' expectations and the consequences for their behavior. School proceeded in an orderly, calm, and productive fashion.

Kindergarten and first-grade classrooms. In exemplary kindergarten and first-grade classrooms where a comprehensive approach is used, children enter the room in the morning, take out their journals, and begin writing about something of interest. After all children are seated and the school's opening exercises end, students go to the rug for a morning meeting. The day begins by discussing the calendar and the weather. Students then count how many days have passed in the month and how many days are left. Then the teacher begins the morning message on chart paper by noting that they will have a guest who will help them with an exercise program as part of their "Healthy Bodies and Healthy Minds" unit.

Children dictate to the teacher sentences about healthy food they ate and healthy activities they participated in over the weekend, which becomes a part of the morning message. After the teacher writes and reads the message, she asks the class to look for print within the message related to word analysis elements the class is studying. For example, they notice that the word *healthy* uses the *th* chunk.

Following the morning message, several children share things they brought from home that relate to the current theme. Kyle has his mom's grocery list, and he reads the healthy foods on it. Keisha has a cookbook and reads a healthy recipe.

After the children's oral sharing, the teacher reads a piece of theme-related children's literature. The story, *Grandma's Helper* (Meyer, 1993), is about a Hispanic grandmother who speaks only Spanish. Because her granddaughter can speak English, the grandmother brings her grocery shopping. Prior to reading the story, the teacher discusses foods needed to keep our bodies healthy. Then the discussion turns to helping others as a way to make us feel good about ourselves. One student talks about helping her grandma walk because she has to use a cane.

Immediately before reading, the teacher sets a purpose for the children as they listen to the story. She asks them to listen to find out what ways the little girl helped her grandmother. After the story is finished, the class talks about how the little girl helped her grandma. The teacher asks the children how they have helped others. She asks students to write about a time when they helped someone, an activity to be done during center activities. To model the activity, the teacher writes on chart paper how she helped her mother prepare Thanksgiving dinner.

At the end of the morning meeting, the teacher reviews, and in some cases models, the center activities that students will be expected to complete later that day. In the math center, each student is instructed to find a partner. The students use a timer to count how many jumping jacks their partner can do in one minute. Then they write down the number, and the partners switch roles. In the science center, there is a figure of a child on a felt board and figures with felt backings of a brain, heart, lungs, and stomach. The students are to place these organs in the correct part of the body. There is also a sheet with a figure and body parts for each child to draw the organs in the correct position. In the art center, there are magazines and scissors for children to create healthy food collages. In the language arts center, children are instructed to write all the foods they can think of from A to Z. Working with a partner, using one sheet of paper per letter, children write the food name and draw the food. Students then "partner read" by selecting a book about nutrition, such as *Grandma's Helper* (Meyer, 1993), *Potatoes on Tuesday* (Lillegard, 1996), *Potluck* (Corbitt, 1962), *Cookies* (Pappas, 1980), *This Is the Plate* (Trussell-Cullen, 1995), and *Engelbert's Exercise* (Paxton, 1993). Partners read together, and when they finish, they talk about what they liked about the book.

While the children engage in their self-directed activities, the teacher meets with small groups for guided reading lessons. The first group is reviewing a book they have not read before. The teacher does a "picture walk" through the book to introduce it to the children by looking at the pictures and talking about each page. During the picture walk, the students are asked to find particular vocabulary words that are new to them and could cause some difficulty when first read. They also discuss the names of the animals in the book. As the group reads, the teacher notices that one student read the book quickly without any errors. She makes a note to think about moving him to a different reading group that would be more challenging.

After the children finish reading, the teacher asks everyone to turn to page 7. She says, "I noticed that James read, 'We saw the pot bear' and then changed it to 'polar bear,' since he looked back at the letters and took into account the meaning of the sentence. He remembered that the words have to match the letters, and what you read has to make sense." While the children are reading, the teacher does a running record on one child. She notes that this student reads "seals" instead of "otters" and "panda bears" instead of "bears." Although the student is not distorting the meaning of the text, the teacher notes that she has to help him pay more attention to the print.

The next reading group is more advanced and reading a more difficult book. The group has worked with this book before; therefore, the lesson will help students become more independent readers. The teacher continues to teach them how to figure out unknown words by using the meaning of a sentence. They begin with a game: Guess the Covered Word. The covered word in the sentence "I can run fast" is *run*. Students are encouraged to think of words that make sense in the sentence. Possibilities students generate for the missing word include *walk*, *eat*, *hop*, *sleep*, and *run*. The teacher writes these words on a sticky note placed over top of the covered word. The teacher then lifts the sticky note to reveal the right answer. The group repeats this activity using other sentences.

The last group the teacher meets with is made up of students who are still developing skills in sight words and beginning sounds. The teacher reads a poem about the theme "Healthy Bodies and Healthy Minds":

We like to eat toast in the morning.

We had tomato soup at lunch.

We got thirsty in the afternoon and had some iced tea.

We had turkey with trimmings and turnips for dinner.

Desert was very special with truffles and milk.

The students then echo read the poem with the teacher (the teacher reads one line then the children repeat it). They discuss the initial consonant and the *th* chunk since the poem has both. The teacher underlines the *t* and *th* words. Then the students chant the poem together emphasizing the *t* sound and the *th* sound when they come to a word that has them.

Writing workshop is in the afternoon. The teacher starts the workshop with a mini-lesson about capital letters at the beginning of sentences and periods at the end. Students write books about good nutrition. Those who are at the final editing stage of their stories have conferences with the teacher. Some students draw pictures for writing, some write a few letters, others write using invented spelling, and some use conventional writing.

At the end of the day comes a special activity that fits with the nutrition theme. It starts with a written recipe for fruit salad. The students discuss the types and amount of fruit they need. They make the fruit salad and then enjoy eating it. The day concludes with a review of the day's highlights, a reminder for students to complete their homework, and instructions about what they can think about for tomorrow.

Second and third-grade classrooms. When students enter the room in the morning, there is a "do now" message written on the chalkboard. This morning, the teacher has asked the students to use certain words in sentences in their journals. While students are responding, they are also carrying out morning housekeeping items described on several charts posted around the room. The teacher reviews the "do now" message and helps students who are struggling to complete the task.

Next on the agenda is a story to be read aloud. A child has brought a book from home to share with the class. The teacher announces the title: *The Saga of Stewy Stinker* (Burton, 1996). Before beginning to read, she leads a brief discussion. She asks, "What's a saga? Why do you think it could be called 'Stewy Stinker'?" They discuss the title and make predictions based on the cover illustration. They stop often during the reading to discuss issues prompted by the text. The teacher asks the children if they know what the Badlands are—the setting of the story. In this fashion, she ties the story to the content area of social studies and their current topic of the regions of the United States. When students are unable to provide the correct answer to the Badlands question, instead of giving the answer to them, the teacher replies, "I'll leave it as a challenge. See if you can figure it out."

During the course of the story, the teacher encourages active engagement with the text. The questions she asks during the read-aloud provide a model for the questions she hopes children will ask themselves as they read independently. She asks them to predict, seek clarification of story elements, and use context clues to understand vocabulary, and she guides them to make connections between the text and their own prior knowledge. She also reads with animated expression and portrays the characters in the story. She makes the reading an interactive experience during which she models effective comprehension strategies to enhance the enjoyment of reading literature.

The teacher selects a student volunteer to write and administer the weekly dictation. This is an assessment for spelling, capitalization, punctuation, and listening. Each sentence refers to subject matter from the social studies or science theme. The sentences on this day are "We're living in the United States, so we're Americans" and "Trenton is our state capitol." Upon completion of the writing, the class reviews the correct format of the sentences and choral reads them each three times.

The teacher uses literature circle groups, work centers, and guided reading groups for literacy instruction. The two literature circle groups consist of students who have selected the same book to read. One group is reading *Mrs. Frisby and the Rats of NIMH* (O'Brian, 1986), and the other is reading *I-Spy Treasure Hunt* (Marzollo & Wick, 1999).

Members have already read two chapters in their selected books. The groups know the routine well. After reading, the designated leader starts a discussion. One person is in charge of listing new vocabulary words to discuss, another member connects a part of the book to a real-life situation, and another member chooses an element of the book to draw.

Other students work in centers. The independent center activities are displayed in a pocket chart. Four children work at the computer center preparing a PowerPoint presentation about regions of the United States, another group fills in journals based on a science experiment they are conducting, and the last group participates in a literature circle activity related to a book they are all reading.

The teacher forms guided reading groups based on her knowledge of achievement levels and student needs and works with them. An easel is set up in front of them with a chart featuring the heading "Point of View." The students are currently reading the novel *Shiloh* (Foote, 1991). The teacher selected the book for this group because it is appropriate for their instructional level. The group discusses the nature of different characters from the book. They use a Venn diagram to list characters and their different and similar characteristics and how they would respond based on their points of view.

After reading groups, writing workshop begins. The teacher starts with a whole-class mini-lesson on the characteristics of an excellent informational news article. The students have been reviewing and publishing this type of writing in a class newsletter. The teacher reads two short newspaper articles and makes a T chart for each article. For each T chart, the students discuss what they think are the really good points and the not-so-good parts. They discuss such elements as: Is there a lot of description? Does the article follow a good sequence? Is there cause and effect or a problem solution? After the discussion, students write their own informational articles. The teacher holds conferences with individual students to help them with their ideas and skills.

In social studies, the class is nearing the end of a unit on the regions of the United States. The teacher gears her lesson toward literacy development and multiple intelligences. She uses a popular picture book, *Brown Bear, Brown Bear, What Do You See?* (Martin, 1996), as a sample for the format of a project. She asks students to construct their own books using a particular state as the topic. The teacher shows a finished product to the class and explains how she created it. She reads from her book, "Ohio, Ohio, what do you see? I see Columbus shining at me."

The next activity is independent, self-selected reading with the goal of writing down on a 3 × 5 card the part of the book that made the student laugh or feel sad. This activity is very quiet and calm as children make themselves comfortable. Some break off into pairs and trios, while others remain alone. Some choose to read in the hallway or outside the room's doorway. Reading materials include various genres. Two girls take turns reading from the picture book *Martha Calling* (Meddaugh, 1994). Another pair reads a tall tale from the anthology *From Sea to Shining Sea* (Thom, 1986). A pair of boys share the *Star Wars Trilogy* (Lucas, Kahn, Glut, 1993). All around the room, students read various other works of children's literature, including *The Encyclopedia of Dogs* (Coile, 2005) and *I-Spy Treasure Hunt* (Marzollo & Wick, 1999). After fifteen minutes, the teacher blinks the lights and asks the children to put their books away.

Building Literacy-Rich Environments

The effective teachers we observed filled their classrooms with the necessary reading and writing materials to support instruction. They purposefully placed these materials for student accessibility. They engaged students in whole-group, small-group, and one-on-one settings. They included both explicit instruction and time for periods of social interaction. They provided many strategies and opportunities for students to engage in reading and writing, including reading aloud, shared reading, independent reading, collaborative reading, guided reading, performance of reading activities, partner/buddy reading, literature circles, and content-area reading. Teachers provided many writing activities, including shared, journal, independent, reader-response, guided, and collaborative writing; writing fiction and informational text; writing activities for performance; and writing workshops.

All teachers advocated extended, uninterrupted periods of time devoted to language arts instruction. They noted the importance of designing programs around literacy themes, such as the study of poetry, authors, or elements of story structure. They also advocated the integration of content-area themes. They believed that instruction should integrate the use of all literacy skills concurrently (reading, writing, listening, speaking, and viewing). They believed that skills should be taught within a meaningful context and in an explicit manner when necessary.

Teachers had high, but attainable expectations for students. They treated students with respect, giving them positive and constructive feedback. All teachers felt a strong commitment to meeting the individual needs of their students. They recognized the importance of a supportive attitude toward students and positive atmosphere in their classrooms to motivate children to learn. Many also commented on the importance of home-school connections in supporting children's literacy development. Our observations of these teachers revealed that they truly put into practice ideas they expressed about student literacy learning.

How does a teacher become an excellent teacher? Excellent teachers are intelligent, they want to teach, they like children, and they are willing to constantly evaluate themselves, continue to learn more, take risks, and change. This will happen if teachers work with administrators who promote professional development that includes the entire school with long-term goals where administrators, supervisors, teachers, aides, and parents see themselves as a total community of learners along with students. We found that excellent teachers attended their school's professional development programs, and they also read about literacy instruction on their own. They went to professional development conferences. They worked to obtain graduate degrees.

Refining current practice is more important than constantly searching for a silver bullet. Early childhood education will thrive with excellent teachers who are always improving their craft.

References and Resources

Allington, R. L., & Johnston, P. H. (2002). *Reading to learn: Lessons from exemplary fourth-grade classrooms.* New York: Guilford Press.

Block, C. C. (2001, December). *Distinctions between the expertise of literacy teachers preschool through grade 5.* Paper presented at the Annual Meeting of the National Reading Conference, San Antonio, TX.

Burton, V. (1996). *Calico the wonder horse, or the saga of Stewy Stinker.* Boston: Houghton Mifflin.

Cantrell, S. C. (1999a). The effects of literacy instruction on primary students' reading and writing achievement. *Reading and Research Instruction, 39*(1), 3–26.

Cantrell, S. C. (1999b). Effective teaching and literacy learning: A look inside primary classrooms. *The Reading Teacher, 52*(4), 370–379.

Clark, C. M., & Peterson, P. L. (1986). Teachers' thought processes. In M. C. Wittrock (Ed.), *Handbook of reading research on reaching* (pp. 255–296). New York: MacMillan.

Cleary, B. (1970). *Runaway Ralph.* New York: Morrow Junior Books.

Coile, C. (2005). *Encyclopedia of dog breeds: Profiles of more than 150 breeds.* New York: Barron's Educational Series.

Coker, H. (1985). Consortium for the improvement of teacher evaluation. *Journal of Teacher Education, 36*(2), 12–17.

Cole, J., & Degen, B.(1995). *The magic school bus inside a hurricane.* New York: Scholastic.

Corbitt, H. (1962). *Potluck.* Boston: Houghton Mifflin.

DK Publishing. *Dinosaur hunter.* (1996). New York: Author.

Duffy, G. G., & Hoffman, J. (1999). In pursuit of an illusion: The flawed search for a perfect method. *The Reading Teacher, 53*(1), 10–16.

Foote, S. (1991). *Shiloh.* New York: Vintage Books.

Genishi, C., Ryan, S., Ochsner, M., & Yarnall, M. M. (2001). Teaching in early childhood education: Understanding practices through research and theory. In V. Richardson (Ed.), *Handbook of research on teaching* (pp. 1175–1210). Washington, DC: American Education Research Association.

Haigh, N., & Katterns, B. (1984). Teacher effectiveness: Problem or goal for teacher education. *Journal of Teacher Education, 35*(5), 23–27.

Howe, J. (1987). *Nighty-nightmare.* New York: Simon & Schuster.

International Reading Association. (1999). *Using multiple methods of beginning reading instruction: A position statement of the international reading association.* Newark, DE: International Reading Association.

Lucas, G., Kahn, J., & Glut, D. (1993). *Star Wars trilogy.* New York: Random House.

Martin, B. (1996). *Brown bear, brown bear, what do you see?* New York: Holt.

Marzollo, J., & Wick, W. (1999). *I-spy treasure hunt.* New York: Scholastic.

Meddaugh, S. (1994). *Martha calling.* New York: Houghton Mifflin.

Metsala, J. L., & Wharton-McDonald, R. (1997). Effective primary-grades literacy instruction = balanced literacy instruction. *The Reading Teacher, 50*(6), 518–521.

Meyer, L. (1993). *Grandma's helper.* Glenview, IL: Scott Foresman.

Morrow, L. M., & Casey, H. K. (2003). A comparison of exemplary characteristics in 1st and 4th grade teachers. *The California Reader, 36*(3), 5–17.

Morrow, L., Tracey, D., Woo, D., & Pressley, M. (1999). Characteristics of exemplary first-grade literacy instruction. *The Reading Teacher, 52*(5), 462–476.

National Institute of Child Health and Human Development. (2000). *Report of the National Reading Panel. Teaching children to read: An evidence-based assessment of the scientific research literature on reading and its implications for reading instruction* (NIH Publication No. 00–4769). Washington, DC: U.S. Government Printing Office.

O'Brian, R. (1986). *Mrs. Frisby and the rats of NIHM.* New York: Simon & Schuster.

Pappas, L. S. (1980). *Cookies.* San Francisco: Chronicle Books.

Paxton, T. (1993). *Engelbert's exercise (little celebration).* Upper Saddle River, NJ: Celebration.

Pressley, M., Rankin, J., & Yokoi, L. (1996). A survey of instructional practices of primary teachers nominated as effective in promoting literacy. *The Elementary School Journal, 96*(4), 363–383.

Roehler, L. R. & Duffy, G. G. (1984). Direct explanation of comprehension processes. In G. G. Duffy, L. R. Roehler, & J. Mason (Eds.), *Comprehension instruction: Perspectives and suggestions* (pp.265–280). New York: Longman.

Ruddell, R. B. (1995). Those influential literacy teachers: Meaning negotiators and motivation builders. *The Reading Teacher, 48*(6), 454–463.

Ruddell, R. B., & Harris, P. (1989). A study of the relationship between influential teachers' prior knowledge and beliefs about teaching effectiveness: Developing higher order thinking in content areas. In S. McCormick & J. Zutell (Eds.), *Cognitive and social perspectives for literacy research and instruction* (pp. 461–472). Chicago: National Reading Conference.

Ruddell, R. B., & Kern, R. B. (1986). The development of belief systems and teaching effectiveness of influential teachers. In M. P. Douglas (Ed.), *Reading: The quest for meaning* (pp. 133–150). Claremont, CA: Claremont Graduate School Yearbook.

Rylant, C. (1982). *When I was young in the mountains.* New York: Penguin Putnam.

Scieszka, J. (1998). *Squids will be squids: Fresh morals, beastly fables.* New York: Penguin Putnam.

Shulman, L. S. (1986). Paradigms and research programs in the study of teaching: A contemporary perspective. In M. C. Wittrock (Ed.), *Handbook of reading research on teaching* (pp. 3–36). New York: MacMillan.

Simon, S. (1995). *Earthquakes.* New York: Morrow.

Stine, R. L. (1990–1999). *Goosebumps* series. New York: Scholastic.

Taylor, B. M, Pearson, P. D., & Clark, K. (2000). Effective schools and accomplished teachers: Lessons about primary-grade reading instruction in low-income schools. *The Elementary School Journal, 101*(2), 121–165.

Taylor, B. M., Pearson, P. D., Clark, K. E., & Walpole, S. (1999). *Beating the odds in teaching all children to read.* (Ciera Report #2-006.) Ann Arbor, MI: Center for the Improvement of Early Reading Achievement.

Taylor, B. M., Peterson, D. S., Pearson, P. D., & Rodriguez, M. C. (2002). Looking inside classrooms: Reflecting on the "how" as well as the "what" in effective reading instruction. *The Reading Teacher, 56*(3), 270–279.

Thom, J. A. (1986). *From sea to shining sea.* New York: Random House.

Trussell-Cullen, A. (1995). *This is the plate.* Tuscon, AZ: GoodYear.

Vygotsky, L. S. (1978). *Mind in society.* Cambridge, MA: Harvard University Press.

Wharton-McDonald, R., Pressley, M., Rankin, J., & Mistretta, J. (1997). Effective primary-grades literacy instruction equals balanced literacy instruction. *The Reading Teacher, 50*(6), 518–521.

Timothy Shanahan

Timothy Shanahan, PhD, is professor of urban education at the University of Illinois at Chicago, where he is director of the UIC Center for Literacy. He has been director of reading for the Chicago Public Schools, and he has published more than 200 research articles, books, and other publications. His research emphasizes reading-writing relationships and improving reading achievement. Shanahan is past president of the International Reading Association (IRA), and in 2006, he received a presidential appointment to the advisory board of the National Institute for Literacy. He was a member of the National Reading Panel, convened by the National Institute of Child Health and Human Development at the request of Congress to evaluate research on successful methods for teaching reading, and he chaired the National Literacy Panel for Language-Minority Children and Youth, and the National Early Literacy Panel. He is a member of the English Language Arts Work Team for the Common Core State Standards. He received the Albert J. Harris Award for outstanding research on reading disability from the IRA, was 2009 Researcher of the Year at the University of Illinois at Chicago, and was inducted to the Reading Hall of Fame in 2007. He is a former first-grade teacher.

In this chapter, Shanahan examines the teaching of reading in fourth through twelfth grade, emphasizing what must be taught to improve the literacy of older students. He begins with some literacy basics before moving into discussions of reading comprehension, vocabulary instruction, and oral reading fluency.

Chapter 5

Developing Effective Reading Curricula Beyond the Primary Grades

Timothy Shanahan

Schools have long been enthralled by the appealing but foolish idea that students "learn to read" in the primary grades and from then on "read to learn." Because of this wrongheaded notion, reading instruction markedly diminishes, usually disappearing by the end of elementary or middle school. This "disappearing reading act" may once have been sufficient, but in the 21st century, it leaves far too many students without the literacy skills they need to participate fully in economic, social, and civic life.

According to the National Assessment of Educational Progress (Grigg, Donahue, & Dion, 2007), only about one in three high school seniors reads at a proficient level or higher, meaning that a significant proportion of students cannot read well enough to participate in higher education or meet the demands of the workplace. Ignoring literacy instruction in the upper grades—or depending on students to increase their literacy abilities incidentally on their own—is not working. This chapter examines the teaching of reading in fourth through twelfth grade, emphasizing what must be taught to improve the literacy of older students.

Some Literacy Basics

Before exploring the literacy curriculum for the upper grades, we will consider three basic ideas that underlie the successful implementation of such curricula. The first has to do with the dual nature of any literacy curriculum, the second deals with the role of text difficulty in reading, and the third considers the developmental aspects of literacy learning.

A Two-Part Curriculum

A curriculum usually divides a subject into component parts and then distributes those parts across the grades, thus ensuring that instruction addresses all necessary elements of a subject. However, what sounds straightforward can be a bit more complicated when the subject of reading is involved.

Reading is a twofold subject—it has both essential and aspirational aspects—and both aspects must be taught. Students must learn the essential aspects of a reading curriculum to ensure proficiency. For example, language growth requires an understanding of word meanings, so teaching vocabulary is not an arbitrary choice as much as an acknowledgment of what is necessary. We have substantial research support for these essential aspects of the curriculum; there are studies showing that teaching these components improves reading proficiency.

> Reading is a twofold subject—it has both essential and aspirational aspects—and both aspects must be taught.

A reading curriculum also contains aspirational aspects—decisions about what to teach that involve judgments. These judgments often depend on the values of a community, and they change from generation to generation. They reflect our shared values and hopes for our students. Look, for instance, at the coverage of minority groups in history books; our treatment of these groups has changed because we now want our students to know something different than before. An example from reading would be the kind of texts we emphasize in a curriculum. At times, we have emphasized either literary texts or functional texts, such as science materials. These days, we are choosing to teach technological reading since such texts have become so common and because the Internet differs in important ways from traditional book-based texts (Leu, 2006). This entails teaching search strategies, how to evaluate sources, how to use links, and so on. Perhaps the Common Core State Standards are now the best source for determining these aspirational elements of the curriculum since they serve as a summary of widely held values that are relevant to reading.[1]

Texts That Are Grade-Level Appropriate

Most curricula are no more than lists of reading skills, and these lists of skills do not provide an adequate description of what students must learn. For example, most curricula specify that students must learn to infer. Students from kindergarten to college English make inferences when they read, but the texts within which they do this are remarkably different. For example, making inferences in *The Three Bears* is not quite the same as doing so in *War and Peace*. There are many reasons *War and Peace* is harder: it is much longer (requiring greater perseverance), it includes a much more varied and abstract vocabulary, the sentences are longer and more complex, the subject matter is more complicated, the connections among ideas are more implicit, and the background knowledge a reader must rely upon is less common—and that barely scratches the surface. Whatever students need to know how to do in reading, they have to accomplish with grade-level appropriate materials. This chapter will discuss the kinds of comprehension abilities students must develop in the upper grades, but keep in mind that students must demonstrate these abilities within increasingly complex texts.

> Whatever students need to know how to do in reading, they have to accomplish with grade-level appropriate materials.

---

[1] In 2009–2010, the National Governors Association and the Council of Chief State School Officers, with the support of the Gates Foundation, began developing English language arts and math standards. Up to this time, all states had their own separate standards, and the idea here was to propose common educational standards that all states could aim for. At the time of publication of this chapter, thirty-eight states, and the District of Columbia had adopted these standards (see www.corestandards.org).

The Developmental Nature of Reading

Literacy learning becomes increasingly specialized as students advance. At the earliest levels, say through third grade, students learn the kinds of literacy skills that will be implicated in virtually all reading they will ever do. From fourth grade through eighth grade, they will continue to develop general all-purpose reading skills, though these intermediate skills will be more abstract and complicated than those on which they focused in the primary grade years. Finally, by high school, we hope students will be learning more specialized literacy skills that are closely linked to the disciplines and adult reading demands.

When students reach the upper grades, they should have the ability to recognize high-frequency words immediately without effort (words such as *is, of, the, what*). They also should have basic notions of reading comprehension. They need to learn that text has meaning, and they must develop the abilities to get the gist of simple texts—to make inferences that link closely related ideas or to interpret the motivations of central characters. Their meaning vocabularies must expand, too, if they are going to understand what they read. And, finally, students should be able to read fluently, which means they should be able to read grade-level texts with appropriate speed and automaticity (for example, about 110 words correct per minute for third grade), pausing in the right places and making the text sound like English (appropriate prosody).

With such accomplishments behind them, students are ready to confront higher levels of literacy. Of course, despite the best efforts of parents and teachers, some students will enter fourth grade with gaps or deficiencies. When this is the case, upper-grade teachers have little choice but to teach these more basic skills and provide opportunities to read less-demanding texts.

Reading Comprehension and Older Students

The most central component of the reading curriculum in the upper grades is reading comprehension. Reading comprehension can and should be taught directly and explicitly. Research shows that such instruction leads to better reading achievement (NICHD, 2000).

Establishing Coherent Mental Representations of Text

One theory of comprehension claims that to understand complex texts, readers must establish a rich and extensive set of coherent text memories, or mental representations of the content of earlier and easier texts; *coherence* means that the memories include all of the important information organized so that the parts are properly connected (Kintsch, 1998). These mental representations become templates that aid in future interpretation: readers read texts, identifying important information and mentally bookmarking it within existing memory templates. These templates include information from the texts, but also from the reader's other experiences and knowledge.

There are many things teachers can do to facilitate these coherent mental representations that have strong research bases attesting to their effectiveness (Best, Rowe, Ozuru, & McNamara, 2005). First and foremost, it is important that students read texts—stories, articles, books, chapters, critical essays, poetry, scripts—that are worth reading in terms of content and quality. Developing mental representations of worthless information or of poorly written texts forms a weak basis for supporting future reading interpretations. Assigning reading and turning kids loose is insufficient; teacher involvement increases the chance that students will build memories that will be comprehensive and coherent representations of the text.

Teachers can help enhance coherence by providing appropriate background information or guiding students to think about what they already know that is relevant to the text topic. Memories are not stored randomly, but in richly connected networks, so starting with what is known and then interpreting a new text within that context improves recall (Gagne & Memory, 1978; Neuman, 1988; Spires, Gallini, & Riggsbee, 1992). Also, research shows the potential benefits of guiding students to read with a minimum of interruption and distraction. Too often as teachers and students are reading a text together, there are detours to talk about word recognition or grammar. Research shows that minimizing such distractions, while

> Assigning reading and turning kids loose is insufficient; teacher involvement increases the chance that students will build memories that will be comprehensive and coherent representations of the text.

focusing all attention on trying to understand a text, improves student understanding (McKeown, Beck, & Blake, 2009).

Teachers can help students gain internally consistent and well-organized understandings of texts by engaging them in retelling activities in which students practice summarizing texts (Koskinen, Gambrell, & Kapinus, 1989; Law, 2008; Stevens, Madden, Slavin, & Farnish, 1987). Teachers can also focus discussions on the causal structures expressed in text, which helps to organize the information (Casteel, 1993; Varnhagen & Goldman, 1986; Shannon, Kameenui, & Baumann, 1988; Trabasso & Nickels, 1992; van den Broek, 1997), or they can use graphic organizers, such as story maps, to structure summaries (National Institute of Child Health and Human Development, 2000). Graphic organizers can make coherent even complex aspects of a story, such as the conflicting goals of multiple characters (Shanahan & Shanahan, 1997).

The development of coherent mental representations is complicated in the upper grades by the variety of texts to which students are exposed. The differences between stories and informational texts become more pronounced in the upper grades, and things get even more complicated as the disciplines diverge: high school science, history, math, and literature texts are distinct in purpose, organizational structure, vocabulary, author-reader relationship, expectation of precision or thoroughness, truth claims (the view within the discipline of whether discourse is a representation of fact or argument), and so on (Shanahan & Shanahan, 2008). Developing coherent mental representations for all kinds of texts and reading demands is a formidable challenge for advanced readers.

The development of coherent mental representations is even more complicated for English learners, who tend to struggle with reading comprehension. Their comprehension difficulty can be a reflection of the same problems native English speakers confront, such as poorly developed word recognition skills; however, English learners also often have the problem of not knowing English very well—they do not know the meanings of even basic words or do not understand grammatical relations within sentences. Such students have a tendency not to participate in the types of assignments described here, and because of the challenges of English, may compose understandings that are not accurate or coherent. Teachers have a special responsibility to try to steer these students to greater clarity. One way of accomplishing this is to encourage students to try to answer questions or formulate summaries in their home language first, before trying to do so in English.

Practicing With Question Types

Over the years, the teaching of question types—main ideas, supporting details, cause-and-effect relations, sequences, inferences, and so on—has often become the reading curriculum, rather than a means to assess student knowledge or understanding. In this type of teaching, teachers often ask students to practice answering certain question types, with the idea that they will improve with such practice. This is especially popular when teachers are pressured for higher test performance.

The problem with this thinking is that students don't perform differently on different question types. Teachers may claim that "Bob can answer main idea questions, but not supporting details questions" or that "Lisa can recall information that is explicitly stated, but she can't make inferences," but these are not accurate assessments. Studies show that variations in text difficulty overwhelm differences in question type. If a text is easy, students can answer all question types, and if a text is difficult, students struggle with all question types (American College Testing, 2006). Given this, the idea of mining a student's reading test to identify the kinds of questions that merit extra practice is a fool's errand; differences in such performance are not reliable, and no studies support the idea of such teaching.

That doesn't mean that we shouldn't ask students a varied set of questions about texts, questions that probe what an author has stated, what he or she has implied, the relationships among ideas in the text, and for critical responses; all can be appropriate, *depending on the text*. Rather than emphasizing particular question types and providing oodles of practice answering such questions, teachers should

> The idea of mining a student's reading test to identify the kinds of questions that merit extra practice is a fool's errand; differences in such performance are not reliable, and no studies support the idea of such teaching.

make sure the questions they ask actually help students think effectively about text ideas. That means some kinds of questions, depending on the text, are going to be asked more than others, and some will be irrelevant to particular texts.

Questions should change as the nature of the texts change. From fourth grade through eighth grade, it may be sufficient to give students practice in answering probing questions about the texts, and those questions might not differ much by subject matter as long as they require students to analyze, synthesize, and critique ideas. However, as the texts become more specialized, so should the questions teachers ask. For example, a science student might need to follow complex directions to execute an experiment and draw conclusions on the basis of the experiment, coordinating those conclusions with the information about a scientific principle explained in the text. A history student, however, could be expected to evaluate the information in a text from the perspective of a group or individual (like a slave perspective on a Lincoln speech). These kinds of questions or assignments are markedly different, but they are both aimed at developing the ways of thinking that are appropriate to the subject matter.

Teaching Strategies

Another important dimension of teaching reading comprehension in the upper grades is the need to develop effective comprehension strategies. Research shows that readers can enhance their understanding of text by engaging in particular mental routines or actions that guide them to process texts in particular ways (Brown, Pressley, Van Meter, & Schuder, 1996; Eilers & Pinkley, 2006; Kelly, Moore, & Tuck, 1994; NICHD, 2000; Rosenshine, Meister, & Chapman, 1996; Spörer, Brunstein, & Kieschke, 2009). These strategies include the following:

- Previewing a text to find out what it's about

- Predicting what might happen in a story or hypothesizing the outcome of a science experiment

- Setting a purpose to guide or focus the reading

- Self-monitoring comprehension and changing the approach if there is difficulty understanding the text

- Questioning oneself about a text as a way of thinking through the ideas

- Visualizing what is happening

- Story mapping or summarizing a story by structural parts (such as main character, problem, attempt to solve problem, and outcome)

- Identifying text structures that an author has used to organize the information (such as cause and effect and problem-solution)

- Summarizing or retelling what an author has stated

The use of multiple strategies is best, as different strategies focus attention on different aspects of the text or the reading process.

Students must master these intentional actions that support meaning making so they can use the strategies independently. Instruction usually employs an approach with gradual release of responsibility in which a teacher models the use of one or more strategies, then guides students to use those strategies with his or her support, and eventually provides students with opportunities to practice the strategies on their own (initially in groups and then individually).

Unfortunately, as effective as strategy teaching can be, it often does not work. There are several reasons for this. First, teachers—and commercial programs—tend to underestimate how difficult it is to learn strategies, so they do not present them thoroughly enough or over long enough duration. In most studies that found strategy teaching effective, this teaching continued daily for weeks; contrast this with the strategy-a-day approach of many schools, or the haphazard inclusion of strategies in many programs. Also, strategy teaching has been criticized for focusing students' attention too much upon their mental processes and not enough on the texts. Strategy experts have long emphasized the importance of teaching students how to use the strategies while maintaining sufficient emphasis on content learning, but often students are memorizing lists of strategies or carrying

> Unfortunately, as effective as strategy teaching can be, it often does not work.

them out in a rote fashion rather than using them as an avenue to better understanding. The students, in such circumstances, spend their time completing strategy assignments but not really learning how and when to use such strategies on their own. Remember, this is supposed to be mental practice—the point isn't to complete a chart or answer a question, but to develop the habit of doing these things mentally while reading. One useful tip is to initially try out strategies on texts that students are already familiar with or that should be easy for them; that way they can focus on the strategy without any loss of meaning. Then, as they gain proficiency with the strategy, introduce harder and less-familiar materials.

Generally, these strategies have been most effective with poor readers (Bereiter & Bird, 1985). I suspect this is because most general strategies, like predicting or summarizing, mainly help students to engage with the text. These strategies get students to pay attention mentally, not allowing their minds to wander. Most average or above-average readers don't have that problem; when they read a text, they can keep their head in the game without relying on strategies. Since they are already thinking about the text, such strategies don't help much. This distinction becomes even more apparent as students move from the intermediate stage of literacy to more disciplinary kinds of reading. As disciplinary texts become more distinctive, all-purpose strategies make less sense. We have found that more specialized strategies—those that may only be useful in particular kinds of materials—make more sense with disciplinary texts.

Instead of doing general summaries of chemistry chapters, for example, ask students to use structural summaries that cue them to identify the substances (samples of matter including elements and compounds), properties (such as reactivity, toxicity, and flammability), processes (how chemicals change or react), and interactions (what specifically happens when certain chemicals come together) (Shanahan & Shanahan, 2008). These four types of information are central to chemistry, so this kind of summarization familiarizes students with the structure of chemistry while ensuring that they learn the key text information. Similarly, while sourcing multiple texts (considering the authors' perspectives and purposes) can be a great a strategy for history, it is useless in a math book (Shanahan

& Shanahan, 2008; Wineburg, 1998). Thus, it makes great sense to teach general strategies during the intermediate stage of literacy, but to focus on more discipline-specific strategies related to particular texts and purposes at the disciplinary stage. These more sophisticated strategies may even facilitate reading for average and advanced readers, too, because they support discipline-specific thinking rather than merely ensuring that students are paying attention to what they are reading.

> It makes great sense to teach general strategies during the intermediate stage of literacy, but to focus on more discipline-specific strategies related to particular texts and purposes at the disciplinary stage.

Providing Opportunities for an Intellectually Rigorous Interpretive Experience

Reading comprehension is thinking. The best thinkers rigorously analyze, synthesize, and evaluate extensive amounts of diverse information. Students need opportunities to think deeply about information and to increase their knowledge of the world by mastering it. Teachers can facilitate reading comprehension by ensuring that students develop deep and specific knowledge about a wide range of information. This should be part of the province of reading teachers—making sure that students gain and retain information from what they read (Beck & McKeown, 1991).

Engagement in intellectually challenging discussions and interactions with text may provide students with habits of mind that allow them to better understand future texts. Similarly, expecting students to make sense of increasingly demanding and extensive texts as they move up the grades—not just stories or chapters, but books, too—makes sense, as does having students working on the synthesis of ideas across multiple sources (Hynd-Shanahan, Holschuh, & Hubbard, 2005); such experiences should increase students' intellectual stamina. Students demonstrate stronger reading comprehension in classrooms where teachers more frequently use higher-order questions (Andre, 1979; Taboada & Guthrie, 2006; Taylor, Pearson, Clark, & Walpole, 2000), and the use of writing to interpret text is also associated with stronger reading comprehension (Tierney & Shanahan, 1991), especially when the cognitive level and extensiveness of such writing is at a high level (Doctorow, Wittrock, & Marks, 1978).

Vocabulary Instruction and Older Students

A second area of focus in literacy instruction for the upper grades is vocabulary. It is impossible to interpret texts without a grasp of what words mean. It is obvious that students learn many word meanings incidentally, just from living and interacting in a social world. However, it is also true that the explicit teaching of vocabulary improves reading comprehension (Blachowicz & Fisher, 2007; Carlisle & Rice, 2002; NICHD, 2000), and the effects of vocabulary instruction seem to be even stronger with English learners (Shanahan & Beck, 2006). Given this, vocabulary is an essential part of any upper-grade reading curriculum.

Since students learn so many words just from watching television, surfing the web, talking with friends, reading, and from other daily activities, how could the direct teaching of a limited number of words make any real difference? One key to its success has to do with the actual words that are taught. Many words that appear frequently in text are not common in oral language, so students may have difficulty with these in reading. Another reason vocabulary teaching works is that English is a morphological language; many of its words are composites of meaningful parts, so when you learn a word, you end up knowing something about many words. Teaching a small number of words has multiplicative implications. Finally, explicit vocabulary instruction makes students aware of the importance of words to understanding, and this may lead them to pay greater attention to new and unknown words when they are on their own. Effective vocabulary instruction often supplements the teaching of words with direction in the use of dictionaries and thesauruses, including the electronic versions of these resources, which also, ultimately, can contribute to students' vocabulary growth.

Often, reading curricula indicate that vocabulary should be taught, but they are not specific about the words to teach. While it may not be a good idea for state or local curricula to be too detailed— selected words should reflect the texts being read—it is certainly too laissez-faire to provide teachers with no guidance in the selection of such words. Technical words that are specialized to a content area usually are a major focus of upper-grade teachers, and that is fine given their content teaching responsibilities. But it is also necessary to teach nontechnical words that are essential to understanding texts. For example, consider the words that are highlighted in a high school social studies chapter: *Mesoamerica, agricultural revolution, Maya,* and *pueblo.* But to understand this text and even these words, students will have to cope with an abundance of words that are uncommon in oral language and yet are not highlighted in the textbook. These include words like *nomadic, descendents, flourish, supplemented, motive,* and *abundant.* It is those kinds of words that should be the staples of an upper-grade reading vocabulary curriculum. It is easy enough to find such words in the literary, historical, scientific, mathematical, and technological texts that are available to students in the upper grades.

Whatever words are chosen, vocabulary teaching must be thorough and complete if it is to be effective. Teaching should emphasize the rich and detailed meanings of words—students' understandings of words should be more like encyclopedia entries than dictionary definitions. Copying definitions from dictionaries and glossaries is a bankrupt practice, the one vocabulary teaching approach proven to be ineffective (NICHD, 2000). Instead, students should be exploring definitions, synonyms, antonyms, categorizations, analogies, derivations, and comparisons. They should be interpreting and using these words in a variety of ways: in reading, writing, speaking, listening, acting, and drawing.

> Teaching should emphasize the rich and detailed meanings of words—students' understandings of words should be more like encyclopedia entries than dictionary definitions.

Instruction should emphasize how different forms of words are used grammatically (for example, *accommodate, accommodation, accommodated, accommodating*). This is especially helpful for English learners, as they need to know not just what words mean, but how to use them. Vocabulary teaching should guide students to connect words to other words in networks and comparisons, including learning words that are connected morphologically (for example, *doctrine, indoctrinate, document, dogma, dogmatic*), and words that are connected semantically (for example, *nutrient, provision, digestion, sustenance*). Finally, there is a need for a great deal of review in vocabulary instruction. Such repetition will not be evident in any curriculum guide, but without frequent review, students forget words they have supposedly learned. Vocabulary instruction of this kind, focused on essential words from texts that students are trying to understand, is a pillar of sound upper-grade reading instruction.

Oral Reading Fluency and Older Students

An effective upper-grade reading curriculum will include oral reading fluency. As with vocabulary, the point of teaching fluency is to increase students' understanding of texts. Studies show that significant numbers of older students are so lacking in fluency when they read that they have trouble understanding (Rasinski et al., 2005). Fluency instruction increases reading comprehension (NICHD, 2000), as fluency proficiency continues to develop during the upper grades (Hasbrouck & Tindal, 2006).

> Studies show that significant numbers of older students are so lacking in fluency when they read that they have trouble understanding.

Most approaches to teaching reading fluency involve oral reading, which older students will sometimes resist. From fourth grade on, students tend to be somewhat self-conscious, so the idea of making mistakes with everyone watching is not very appealing. Activities like paired reading, reading into a tape recorder, or reading while listening to a fluent rendering of the same text make much more sense with this age group than round-robin reading activities in which one student reads to the class while everyone else listens. Students should regularly practice reading texts aloud, trying to make the texts sound meaningful. Such activities should require rereading; students should read portions of a text multiple times, until it sounds like English (with appropriate and meaningful pausing), and with few errors. Teachers can draw the texts for such practice from the regular class materials. As students progress, it becomes increasingly important to have them try this with texts across the disciplines. Students who can read a literature book with sufficient speed, accuracy, and expression may still have difficulty with fluency in an algebra book, for instance, as they might be challenged by the combination of words and numbers, the use of mathematical symbols, and the alternation between English grammar and the order of operations of mathematical expressions.

The goal of fluency instruction is to get students to a point where they can read texts with sufficient word recognition automaticity when reading orally (approximately 150–160 words correct per minute), while making the text sound like English. Students should accomplish this speed not by hurrying through a text, but by becoming so skilled at reading texts that they can focus on interpretation. Average fourth graders can usually read grade-level appropriate texts at about 120 words correct per minute, and instruction should aim to get them to about 150 words sometime during the middle school years. To read text this quickly with understanding requires well-honed word reading skills and a reasonably strong knowledge of vocabulary meaning and punctuation. (Upper-grade students may have trouble interpreting some aspects of punctuation, such as split quotes: "Mary went to see the show," said John, "and we should go, too." Developing understanding of such conventions is a key part of the fluency curriculum during these years.) Students who read sentences so that they sound like sentences have an advantage when interpreting meaning. To interpret language, it is important to group the words in a way that facilitates interpretation; it is, for instance, easier to make sense of a sentence divided up like the first example than the second:

1. Mary went / to see the show / and / we should go too.

2. Mary went to / see the / show and we / should go too.

Successful Reading Instruction in the Upper Grades

The successful teaching of reading in the upper grades—no matter what the specifics of a particular curriculum—must include a substantial emphasis on reading comprehension, vocabulary instruction, and oral reading fluency. Students must master the meanings of hundreds of new words each year; not just the technical terminology of their subject matters, but all-purpose words that, though not common in oral language, are necessary to making sense of text. They must practice oral reading with sufficient repetition and guidance to allow them to read words with ease and translate written sentences into readily understandable spoken words.

Though skills work on fluency and vocabulary may require a great deal of repetition and review to get students to adequate levels of proficiency, the focus of this work should always be on facilitating meaning. This emphasis on meaning should be even more obvious with direct, explicit instruction in reading comprehension itself. Such teaching must ensure that students are reading both a variety and a multiplicity of texts at appropriate cognitive levels. It also must require that students be engaged in high-level thinking about the information in these texts in ways appropriate to the texts and the subject matter. Teachers must ensure that students are developing coherent understandings of the texts they read, both increasing their body of knowledge and also organizing that knowledge to facilitate future learning. They must help students develop intentional cognitive strategies—general strategies that initially may be helpful with any kind of text, and more disciplinary and specialized strategies that students need as text demands change. And this all must be accomplished in the context of intellectually rigorous work in which students are expected to make sense of challenging ideas from a variety of subjects.

References

American College Testing. (2006). *Reading between the lines: What the ACT reveals about college readiness in reading.* Iowa City, IA: Author.

Andre, T. (1979). Does answering higher-level questions while reading facilitate productive learning? *Review of Educational Research, 49*(2), 280–318.

Beck, I. L., & McKeown, M. G. (1991). Social studies texts are hard to understand: Mediating some of the difficulties. (Research Directions). *Language Arts, 68*(6), 482–490.

Bereiter, C., & Bird, M. (1985). Use of thinking aloud in identification and teaching of reading comprehension strategies. *Cognition and Instruction, 2*(2), 131–156.

Best, R. M., Rowe, M., Ozuru, Y., & McNamara, D. S. (2005). Deep-level comprehension of science texts: The role of the reader and the text. *Topics in Language Disorders, 25*(1), 65–83.

Blachowicz, C. L., & Fisher, P. J. (2007). Best practices in vocabulary instruction. In L. B. Gambrell, L. M. Morrow, & M. Pressley (Eds.), *Best practices in literacy instruction* (3rd ed.) (pp. 178–203). New York: Guilford Press.

Brown, R., Pressley, M., Van Meter P., & Schuder, T. (1996). A quasi-experimental validation of transactional strategies instruction with low-achieving second-grade readers. *Journal of Educational Psychology, 88*(1), 18–37.

Carlisle, J., & Rice, M. (2002). *Improving reading comprehension: Research-based principles and practices.* Timonium, MD: York Press.

Casteel, M. A. (1993). Effects of inference necessity and reading goal on children's inferential generation. *Developmental Psychology, 29*(2), 346–357.

Doctorow, M., Wittrock, M. C., & Marks, C. (1978). Generative processes in reading comprehension. *Journal of Educational Psychology, 70*(2), 109–118.

Eilers, L. H., & Pinkley, C. (2006). Metacognitive strategies help students to comprehend all text. *Reading Improvement, 43*(1), 13–29.

Gagne, E. D., & Memory, D. (1978). Instructional events and comprehension: Generalization across passages. *Journal of Reading Behavior, 10*(4), 321–335.

Grigg, W., Donahue, P., & Dion, G. (2007). *The nation's report card: 12th-grade reading and mathematics 2005* (NCES 2007–468). U.S. Department of Education, National Center for Education Statistics. Washington, DC: U.S. Government Printing Office.

Hasbrouck, J., & Tindal, G. A. (2006). Oral reading fluency norms: A valuable assessment tool for reading teachers. *The Reading Teacher, 59*(7), 636–644.

Hynd-Shanahan, C., Holschuh, J., & Hubbard, B. (2005). Thinking like a historian: College students' reading of multiple historical documents. *Journal of Literacy Research, 36*(2), 141–176.

Kelly, M., Moore, D. W., & Tuck, B. F. (1994). Reciprocal teaching in a regular primary school classroom. *Journal of Educational Research, 88*(1), 53–61.

Kintsch, W. (1998). *Comprehension: A paradigm for cognition.* Cambridge, UK: Cambridge University Press.

Koskinen, P., Gambrell, L. B., & Kapinus, B. A. (1989). The effects of rereading and retelling upon young children's reading comprehension. *National Reading Conference Yearbook, 38,* 233–239.

Law, Y-K. (2008). Effects of cooperative learning on second graders' learning from text. *Educational Psychology, 28*(5), 567–582.

Leu, D. J. (2006). New literacies, reading research, and the challenge of change: A deictic perspective. *National Reading Conference Yearbook, 55,* 1–20.

McKeown, M. G., Beck, I. L., & Blake, R. G. K. (2009). Rethinking reading comprehension instruction: A comparison of instruction for strategies and content approaches. *Reading Research Quarterly, 44*(3), 218–253.

National Institute of Child Health and Human Development. (2000). *Report of the National Reading Panel. Teaching children to read: An evidence-based assessment of the scientific research literature on reading and its implications for reading instruction* (NIH Publication No. 00–4769). Washington, DC: U.S. Government Printing Office.

Neuman, S. B. (1988). Enhancing children's comprehension through previewing. *National Reading Conference Yearbook, 37,* 219–224.

Rasinski, T. V., Padak, N. D., McKeon, C. A., Wilfong, L. G., Friedauer, J. A., & Heim, P. (2005). Is reading fluency a key for successful high school reading? *Journal of Adolescent & Adult Literacy, 49*(1), 22–27.

Rosenshine, B., Meister, C., & Chapman, S. (1996). Teaching students to generate questions: A review of the intervention studies. *Review of Educational Research, 66*(2), 181–221.

Shanahan, T., & Beck, I. (2006). Effective literacy teaching for English-language learners. In D. August & T. Shanahan (Eds.), *Developing literacy in second-language learners* (pp. 415–488). Mahwah, NJ: Lawrence Erlbaum Associates.

Shanahan, T., & Shanahan, C. (2008). Teaching disciplinary literacy to adolescents: Rethinking content-area literacy. *Harvard Educational Review, 78*(1), 40–59.

Shanahan, T., & Shanahan, S. (1997). Character perspective charting: Helping children to develop a more complete conception of story. *Reading Teacher, 50*(8), 668–677.

Shannon, P., Kameenui, E. J., & Baumann, J. F. (1988). An investigation of children's ability to comprehend character motives. *American Educational Research Journal, 25*(3), 441–462.

Spires, H. A., Gallini, J., & Riggsbee, J. (1992). Effects of schema-based and text structure-based cues on expository prose comprehension in fourth graders. *Journal of Experimental Education, 60*(4), 307–330.

Spörer, N., Brunstein, J. C., & Kieschke, U. (2009). Improving students' reading comprehension skills: Effects of strategy instruction and reciprocal teaching. *Learning and Instruction, 19*(3), 272–286.

Stevens, R. J., Madden, N. A., Slavin R. E., & Farnish, A. M. (1987). Cooperative integrated reading and composition: Two field experiments. *Reading Research Quarterly, 22*(4), 433–454.

Taboada, A., & Guthrie, J. T. (2006). Contributions of student questioning and prior knowledge to construction of knowledge from reading information text. *Journal of Literacy Research, 38*(1), 1–35.

Taylor, B. M., Pearson, P. D., Clark, K. & Walpole, S. (2000). Effective schools and accomplished teachers: Lessons about primary-grade reading instruction in low-income schools. *Elementary School Journal, 101*(2), 121–165.

Tierney, R. J., & Shanahan, T. (1991). Research on the reading-writing relationship: Interactions, transactions, and outcomes. In R. Barr, M. L. Kamil, P. Mosenthal, & P. D. Pearson (Eds.), *The handbook of reading research* (vol. 2) (pp. 246–280). New York: Longman.

Trabasso, T., & Nickels, M. (1992). The development of goal plans of action in the narration of a picture story. *Discourse Processes, 15*(3), 249–275.

Varnhage, C. K., & Goldman, S. R. (1986). Improving comprehension: Causal relations instruction for learning handicapped learners. *The Reading Teacher, 39*(9), 896–904.

van den Broek, P. (1997). Discovering the cements of the universe: The development of event comprehension from childhood to adulthood. In P. van den Broek, P. Bauer, & T. Bourg (Eds.), *Developmental spans in event comprehension: Bridging fictional and actual events* (pp. 321–342). Mahwah, NJ: Lawrence Erlbaum Associates.

Wineburg, S. S. (1998). Reading Abraham Lincoln: An expert/expert study in the interpretation of historical texts. *Cognitive Science, 22*(3), 319–346.

Richard L. Allington

Richard L. Allington, PhD, is professor of education at the University of Tennessee. He previously served as the Fien Distinguished Professor of Education at the University of Florida and as chair of the Department of Reading at the University at Albany, State University of New York. He is a past president of the International Reading Association (IRA), the National Reading Conference, and the Reading Hall of Fame. He was corecipient of the IRA's Albert J. Harris Award, the College Reading Association's A. B. Herr Award, the IRA's William S. Gray Citation of Merit, and the New York State Reading Association's Outstanding Reading Educator Award. He has been principal investigator on a number of research projects funded by the U.S. Office of Educational Research and Improvement, the Office of Special Education and Rehabilitation, and the National Institutes of Health. He is the author of over 150 articles and several books.

Patricia M. Cunningham

Patricia M. Cunningham, PhD, is a professor of education at Wake Forest University. Previously, she was an elementary teacher and a faculty member at Ohio University, and she served as Director of Reading for Alamance County, North Carolina. Her particular interest is in finding alternative ways to teach children for whom learning to read is difficult. She is the author of *Phonics They Use: Words for Reading and Writing*. Along with Richard Allington, she published *Classrooms That Work* and *Schools That Work*. Her most recent publications include *What Really Matters in Writing* and *What Really Matters in Vocabulary*. Along with Dorothy Hall, she developed the Four Blocks Literacy framework, which is currently used as the balanced literacy framework in classrooms throughout the country. She and Dorothy Hall are codirectors of the Four Blocks Literacy Center, which is housed at Wake Forest University.

In this chapter, Allington and Cunningham compare the characteristics of reading lessons we offer in our schools for struggling readers with those of their on-level counterparts. They provide a clear vision of what needs to done to reach the goal of all children reading on level.

Chapter 6

Developing Effective Reading Curricula for Struggling Readers

Richard L. Allington and Patricia M. Cunningham

One Tuesday morning, I (Patricia) was sipping coffee, packing a lunch, and making a mental list of what I needed to accomplish that day, which included working on this chapter. The local news show was on, but I didn't think I was paying attention to it until I heard the words, "Read and Ride." I glanced over at the TV, and there were a bunch of happy-looking nine-year olds pedaling away on stationary bikes and reading magazines. The reporter was at Ward Elementary school, fifteen minutes from my office. He was interviewing the students about how they liked their Read and Ride time. All the students were enthusiastic and shared their reasons for liking it.

A boy commented while still pedaling, "Well, you know, I love to ride my bike at home, and now I get to ride at school, too, and while I'm riding, I get to read any magazine I want. I usually read the *National Geographic for Kids* or the *Sports Illustrated for Kids*."

A girl explained, "I really like Read and Ride because you really get to read. In the classroom, you never really read. I mean, you read, but you don't really read—like read whatever you want. I brought a book with me today, but I like the magazines, too!"

Next they interviewed Scott Ertl, the guidance counselor at the school, who explained that the idea for Read and Ride came when he thought about the fact that children need to get more physical exercise and they need to read more. Why not combine the two? Currently the bike room has 30 stationary bikes—all donated—and subscriptions to popular magazines for kids. Each day, teachers bring their classes there for 15 to 20 minute Read and Ride breaks.

All day, I thought about this wonderful, clever, cost-free solution to get kids to read and exercise more. I was impressed by this school's ingenuity and the staff's ability to think outside the box and find a way to increase students' enthusiasm for reading without the help of additional funding. It shows that there are many things schools could be doing to help their struggling readers. Why, then, are we not providing better instruction for these students?[1]

All children reading on level—that has been our goal for at least three decades. As Alfred Tatum (2009) tells us, it isn't just about their literacies, it's about their lives. We know more than ever about how to accomplish this goal, but we still have not reached it. Little of what we know characterizes the reading lessons we offer in our schools, especially the lessons we offer our struggling readers. In this chapter, we provide a clear vision of what needs to be done to reach the goal of all children reading on level.

Struggling readers need what good readers need, except they need more of it and often a more expert version of what we provide our best readers. We'll begin by looking at the current situation in our schools.

Good Readers Read a Lot; Struggling Readers Don't Read Much

There are no studies indicating that struggling readers read very much, and none suggesting they read as much as our good readers do. Rather, many studies indicate that poor readers read much less than good readers, both in school and out of school (Allington, 1980, 1983, 1984, 2009; Anderson, Wilkinson, & Fielding, 1988;

---

[1] If you want to see the enthusiastic readers/riders and learn more about how to start your own Read and Ride program, you can take a virtual fieldtrip to Ward Elementary by going to www.kidsreadandride.com.

Cunningham & Stanovich, 1998; Martin-Chang & Gould, 2008; Samuels & Wu, 2003; Vellutino, 2003). The primary reason struggling readers do not read a lot is the way we design our reading lessons. The research shows that during instruction, poor readers are more likely to spend instructional time on skills work and completing low-level worksheets. In our efforts to teach struggling readers to read, we too often eliminate reading activity. Instead, we pile on work with reading skills. This seems like an appropriate instructional choice since poor readers often lack many reading skills, but it eliminates actual reading and thus the reasons that motivate students' desire to read: reading for meaning, reading to make them laugh or cry, reading that makes them think, reading that raises goose bumps on their arms. They are learning skills, but not reading to become readers.

> In our efforts to teach struggling readers to read, we too often eliminate reading activity.

In the following sections in this chapter, we will discuss in more detail the additional ways our poor design of reading lessons contributes to struggling readers' lack of time spent reading and the subsequent difficulty they face in the classroom. Struggling readers are:

- More likely to take turns reading aloud
- Less likely to talk about what they read
- Less likely to read independently
- More likely to read aloud word by word
- Less likely to be engaged in literate conversations
- Less likely to write about what they read

Good Readers Read Silently; Struggling Readers Read Aloud

It is unclear why poor readers are usually asked to read aloud during their lessons. It isn't just that they are behind. Even older struggling readers are more likely to be asked to read aloud than younger, achieving children (Allington, 1983). When struggling readers read aloud, they usually take turns reading. If there are eight pages of text and eight readers in a group, each student will probably read one page. Teachers tell us they ask struggling readers to read aloud so they can monitor their reading. But struggling readers need to learn to monitor their own reading, just as good readers do. If teachers constantly jump in to "help" struggling readers, these readers rarely develop self-monitoring skills (Allington, 1980) or an understanding of what they have read. In many cases, the books given to struggling readers are too hard for them. Thus, their self-monitoring abilities become overwhelmed by the difficulty of the text. But that is a reason to change the text, not interrupt the student.

So the first step in addressing this instructional difference is making sure the texts you select for struggling readers are of an appropriate difficulty level: texts that they can read with 99 percent accuracy, using appropriate phrasing, and with 90 percent comprehension. This level of text is what Betts (1946) labeled a student's "independent reading level." We call these high-success texts. It is high-success texts that our best readers read all the time. If we want struggling readers to maintain their silent reading activity, then we need to provide texts they can actually read successfully.

> If we want struggling readers to maintain their silent reading activity, then we need to provide texts they can actually read successfully.

This means we cannot provide adequate reading instruction from any single reading material or core reading program. Once you realize that the typical fourth-grade classroom has readers who can read ninth-grade level texts and others who can read only first-grade level texts (Hargis, 2006), it becomes clear that one-size-fits-all reading materials actually fit very few children in a typical classroom. Providing students with texts at an appropriate level of complexity is a critical feature of effective classroom and intervention reading instruction.

Here we mention intervention reading programs because there is much evidence that struggling readers rarely are offered texts at an appropriate level of difficulty in their Title I remediation classes or in their special education classes (Allington, Stuetzel, Shake, & LaMarche, 1986; Vaughn & Linan-Thompson, 2003). Most of the reading struggling readers do while in special classes is in texts that are too hard. More troubling even is that little actual reading—that is, reading of texts that are at least one paragraph long or longer—occurs during intervention lessons. On average, less than six hours of reading occurs during forty hours of intervention reading lessons! Struggling readers need regular access to texts they can read accurately and fluently, and they need to read these texts silently and for understanding.

Good Readers Talk About What They Read; Poor Readers Talk About Anything but Their Reading

If we were to give you a difficult text to read and then ask you to talk about it, we wouldn't be surprised if you sounded tongue-tied. For instance, read the following text. You might even want to time your reading to see if you meet adult reading rate standards.

> A further example of the potential comparative value of the dynamics for analysis, which especially draws out the dynamics of objectification and the dynamics of positioning, involves how Trinidadians use Internet practices for the performance of national identity. Trinidadians enter and practice the network "as a people who feel themselves encountering it from a place." Despite the broad dispersal of the Trinidadian diaspora, and despite the global commodification of culture, Trinidadians continually practice their national identities online and consume the Internet as a source of nationalism. (Leander, 2008, p. 41)

Could you accurately pronounce at least 99 percent of the words? Probably. Did you know the meanings of most of the key vocabulary? Probably not. Was your phrasing adequate? Probably not. Was your comprehension adequate? Probably not. If we asked you to tell us what you read, would you instead suggest the passage was too hard? Perhaps. Too unfamiliar a topic? Probably. Or would you attempt to change the topic, and talk, maybe, about how one of your students reads? Keep in mind that this exercise involves text made up of words you can read. Good word recognition is a beginning, but it is only a beginning when it comes to understanding.

On the other hand, you are reading this book chapter with far better than 99 percent accuracy, and if you read it aloud, your reading would likely be fluent and expressive. Your ability to discuss what you have read in this chapter is not only unimpaired, but you may be looking for a colleague with whom to discuss what you have read. In order to be willing and able to talk about what you read, you have to be able to read it accurately and fluently, connect meanings to most of the words, and be motivated to make sense of what you are reading.

There are other things you can do to improve the likelihood that struggling readers will not just be able to talk about what they have read, but that they will also look for someone with whom to talk about what they've read. For instance, you might have them read widely on a topic of high interest to them. Let's say your struggling reader is interested in snowboarding. How many books or articles on snowboarding can you find? How many of these books and articles could your struggling reader read with 99 percent accuracy and in phrases with 90 percent comprehension? How many books or articles on Miley Cyrus can you locate for the reader who expresses an interest in this pop-culture star? For both topics, you could find literally hundreds of texts. Not all of these will be written at a level of difficulty that your struggling reader can read, but some will be. You will notice that as the struggling reader reads more and more of the books and articles that you've found, he or she will begin to be able to read the more difficult books and articles as well. When struggling readers become "experts" on some topic they care about, they will talk about what they are reading and share their expertise with anyone who will listen.

> When struggling readers become "experts" on some topic they care about, they will talk about what they are reading and share their expertise with anyone who will listen.

Good Readers Read Independently; Struggling Readers Don't Read, Unless You Make Them

Good readers read widely and independently. Anderson et al. (1988) indicate that good readers read millions of words each year, while struggling readers read thousands (four million words a year for better readers, about a million words a year for typical readers, and less than 100,000 words for struggling readers). This is one reason why good readers are good readers—they engage in voluntary reading on a daily basis (Allington, 2009). It isn't just that reading lessons for struggling readers don't require much reading; struggling readers don't read much voluntarily, either.

We think this is often because they have had so few successful opportunities to actually read. Frequently there are few books in classroom libraries that struggling readers can read with a high level of accuracy, fluency, and comprehension. Look in the fourth- and fifth-grade classrooms in your schools. How many second-grade-level books are available in the classroom libraries? Look in the desks of struggling fourth- and fifth-grade readers and ask yourself, "How many of these books can this child read accurately with fluency and with understanding?" If the classrooms don't have many books these struggling readers can read, and if there are few such books in their desks, you have identified one source of the problem for struggling readers. If we want struggling readers to read independently—and we do—then classrooms with little or nothing struggling readers can read is a problem we must address.

So far we have only discussed books that struggling readers could read accurately, fluently, and with understanding. There is more to it, though. Some of those books have to be books that struggling readers want to read—books they cannot wait to read. But as Gallagher (2008) has noted, providing interesting books has never been a priority in schools. The International Reading Association conducts an annual competition called Children's Choices in which children vote for the best books. This is an attempt to locate books that kids find interesting. The American Library Association also conducts competitions in which librarians identify the "best books" for children. Interestingly, an analysis of these two sets of best books over a thirty-year period (Beach, 2006) found almost no overlap. Kids select different books than do librarians. But libraries stock the books from the American Library Association competition. It is unclear if most libraries order the books that children select. Classroom teachers select the books that the American Library Association lists, but they less often select the books that children pick as the best books.

Finally, we need to ask, "What percentage of the texts that readers read, especially struggling readers, are texts they can read and texts they selected to read?" Guthrie and Humenick (2004)

> If we want struggling readers to read independently—and we do—then classrooms with little or nothing struggling readers can read is a problem we must address.

conducted a meta-analysis on studies of improving classroom reading comprehension and reading motivation. Two factors stood out as contributing almost all of the variation in gains in both areas. These two factors were (1) easy access to interesting books and (2) student choice of reading materials. For our struggling readers to move forward, these two factors must be central to the design of classroom reading lessons and school intervention reading programs.

Good Readers Read Aloud Expressively; Struggling Readers Read Aloud Word by Word

When we do have good readers read aloud, they read expressively, while struggling readers are more likely to simply pronounce the words in a monotone voice. We suggest that there are two primary reasons for this difference. First, good readers have texts in their hands virtually all day long that they can read accurately and fluently and with good comprehension. This high-success reading practice is critical, and good readers get lots of it both in and out of school. Second, struggling readers often have had what we call "interruptive reading experiences" (Allington, 1983). That is, they are asked to read texts that are too difficult, and then teachers and other students interrupt them when they make mistakes when reading aloud or pause to decode a word. This steady stream of interruptions creates word-by-word readers, as does using text that is too difficult. Together, these two features literally ensure struggling readers rarely read aloud with fluency and expressiveness. While we ask good readers to read aloud less frequently than poor readers, we often have good readers reading aloud from texts they can read accurately and fluently. Poor readers are asked to read too-hard texts and are more likely to be interrupted during their reading-aloud experiences, which creates this opportunity for word-by-word reading.

We have found that small doses of repeated readings of appropriate-level texts can overcome this word-by-word reading—especially if a no-interruption rule for both students and the teacher is enforced in the classroom. As a teacher, it is hard to bite your tongue and let a reader continue reading when he or she makes a mistake, but it is the only way struggling readers will develop the monitoring system good readers already have. When a reader makes a mistake, wait until he or she reaches the end of the page, and then intervene. But intervene with questions such as, "Does that sentence make sense the way you read it?"

Combine the strategy of waiting until the end of the page with congratulating a reader who self-corrects: "Excellent monitoring. You realized the word you said didn't make sense, and you went back and figured out another word that did."

In our work with struggling readers, we find we can turn poor readers into expressive readers in three weeks or less with some repeated readings and much self-selected independent reading; other research has shown this to be effective as well (Kuhn, 2005). It is critical, however, to put texts of the right level of difficulty in students' hands and allow them to correct the errors they make if we expect them to become expressive readers.

Good Readers Engage in Literate Conversations; Struggling Readers Retell the Facts

Once struggling readers are reading expressively, we must then be concerned about their understanding of what they are reading. We have learned a lot about literate conversation and its power to foster comprehension. In fact, it seems that a few minutes of literate conversation about the texts children read works as well or better at improving comprehension, as measured on standardized tests, than similar amounts of comprehension-strategy instruction (Cunningham & Smith, 2008; Nystrand, 2006).

Literate conversation is different from literacy interrogation, yet interrogation is most commonly used in classrooms. Interrogation involves asking students questions you know the answer to. Figure 6.1 (page 142) shows examples of both questions that facilitate literate conversation and questions that represent literacy interrogation.

Notice that the questions that facilitate literate conversation have no single correct answer. Ask the first question to ten different readers, and you will get ten different—and all correct—answers. Each student response provides the opportunity for a follow-up question or comment, and the follow-up question won't typically have one correct answer either. Instead, follow-up questions provide the

---

Literate Conversation

What were you thinking about as you finished reading this piece?

Did this piece remind you of anything else you have read?

What did you learn from this piece that was new information for you?

Does Manny resemble anyone you know?

Literacy Interrogation

How does the author describe Manny in this piece?

What is the main idea the author is trying to convey?

Where did the children go first in this story?

Who was the general in charge of the Union troops at the Battle of Chattanooga?

Figure 6.1: Examples of literate conversation and literacy interrogation.

opportunity to engage with the reader's thinking. For instance, several students might respond to the second conversational question, each noting a different text that they were reminded of. The follow-up question might be, "Can you tell me what it was about the piece we just read that reminded you of that other text?" Alternatively, we could follow up with, "Many texts we have read have similar, but different, features. Why do you suppose so many authors choose to use this technique?

With interrogation questions, the follow-up is usually a confirmation that the student's response was correct, or the follow-up will indicate that the response is not acceptable and push the reader to expand, reread, or clarify. In other words, interrogation questions ask whether the reader remembers the bit of information that you asked about. They don't promote thinking.

Thinking, though, is what good readers do before, during, and after they read something. They weigh the information they have read, and they decide to, or try to, integrate that information into their world view. That is what reading is all about. We want readers who challenge authors, readers who are always a bit skeptical of what authors write. We want readers who work to make sense of what they have read rather than readers who simply recall what they read.

Readers who think critically about what they read are essential for any democratic society.

This doesn't mean that you should always avoid asking struggling readers questions that check for understanding; it means that if we want struggling readers to read more, like achieving readers, we will need to dramatically increase the opportunities we provide for struggling readers to engage in literate conversations that promote higher-level and critical thinking.

Good Readers Write About What They Read; Struggling Readers Rarely Write About Anything

> If we want struggling readers to read more, like achieving readers, we will need to dramatically increase the opportunities we provide for struggling readers to engage in literate conversations that promote higher-level and critical thinking.

A large meta-analysis looking at the effects of writing-to-learn activities (Bangert-Drowns, Hurley, & Wilkinson, 2004) concluded that asking students to write about what they are learning in science, social studies, and reading increases the amount of information they learn in those subjects. Students in classrooms where writing to learn is a regular activity demonstrated better performance on both teacher-made tests and standardized tests. Most teachers recognize that writing requires students to think about what they are learning and thus would result in increased learning; however, struggling readers often resist writing even more than they resist reading.

How can you get your struggling readers to write more? One painless way to get everyone—including your struggling readers—to write more is to use "think-writes" to help your students access and connect prior knowledge, make predictions about what they will learn, and summarize important information. Think-writes (Cunningham & Cunningham, 2010) are short bits of writing you can use to prompt your students to think more. They can help students access prior knowledge and make connections before they start to read.

Think-writes are a "painless" way to get struggling readers to write more. They are never corrected or graded, and they are finished before struggling writers even think about the fact that they don't like to write. Collect some recycled paper that has one side blank, cut it into quarters, and staple it into thinking pads. Put these thinking pads on your students' desks or tables. When you find yourself about to ask a prior knowledge/connection question ("What do you already know about . . . ?), a predicting/anticipating question ("What do you think will happen . . . ?"), or a summarizing question ("What important facts did we learn about . . . ?"), ask students to do a quick think-write before sharing their ideas. Following are some examples of when and how to conduct think-writes.

Begin by giving students the topic of the think-write:

Today you are going to read one of Gail Gibbon's wonderful animal informational books. Today's book is about bats. You probably already know some things about bats. Tear a piece of paper off your thinking pad. I am going to give you one minute to write down what you know about bats. Ready, set, go!

After exactly one minute, ask students to put their pencils down. Ask everyone to share their knowledge and ideas about bats (see fig. 6.2 for student samples of bat think-writes).

Imagine all the different places in your school day when you could use the think-write strategy to ask students the "What do you know about?" question. Following are some examples:

We are going to be learning about measurement this week in math. I know you know some thing about measurement. You have one minute to write down everything you already know about measurement.

Next week, we will be out of school on Monday to celebrate President's Day. We are going to be reading about some of our presidents this week. I know you already know a lot about presidents. Grab a piece of thinking paper, and see how much you can write about presidents in one minute.

You can also use think-writes to help your student anticipate or predict what they will learn, such as in the following example. Figure 6.3 (page 146) shows some sample student think-writes.

In science, today we are going to learn about two kinds of changes, physical changes and chemical changes. We are going

bats

come out at
night
live in caves
fly
eat inseks

bats
wings
brown
bite
scary

Bats

fly
wings
rabees

Figure 6.2: Sample student think-writes about bats.

to read about changes you see every day and why they are either physical or chemical changes. Take a piece of thinking paper, and label it Physical and Chemical Changes. I will write this on the board so that you will be able to spell these tricky words. Now, number your paper from one to five. I am going to write five things that change, and I want you to guess whether they are physical or chemical changes. Once you have your guesses, I will give you an article on physical and chemical changes, and you can read it with your partner to see if you guessed right.

You can also use prediction think-writes, such as the following, whenever you want students to predict or anticipate what they will learn:

Yesterday, we measured some objects using rulers and yardsticks. We determined how many feet and inches long some objects in

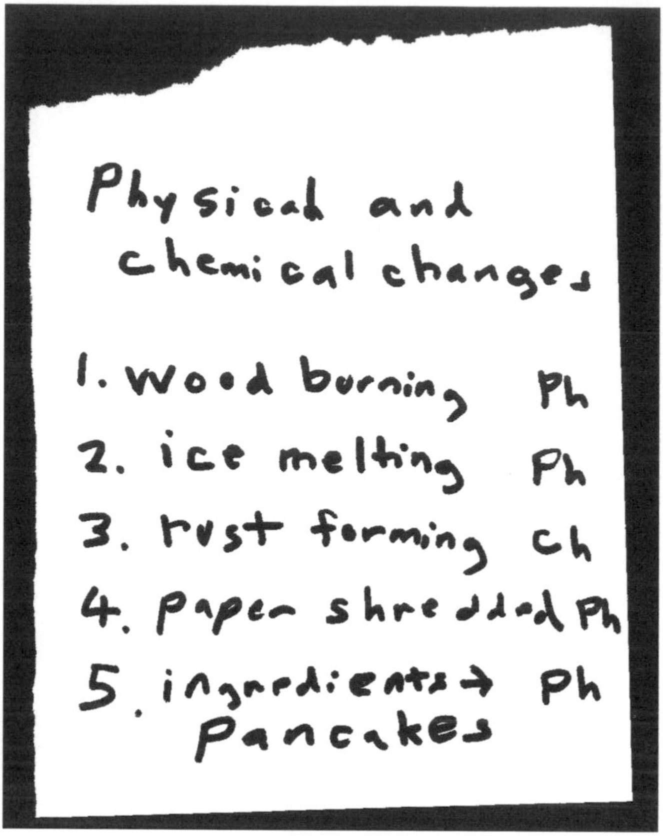

Figure 6.3: Sample student think-writes about physical and chemical changes.

our room were. Today we are going to use the meter sticks, and our measurements will be in centimeters and meters. Look at your thumb. The middle of your thumb is about one centimeter across. I am going to hold up some of the objects we are going to measure. On a piece of thinking paper, write the object name and how many centimeters long you think it will be.

Remember what was happening in our mystery when we finished reading yesterday. We are very near to solving the mystery of what happened to the bike. I know you all have some ideas about what happened to it. Take out a piece of thinking paper, and write how you think our mystery is going to end.

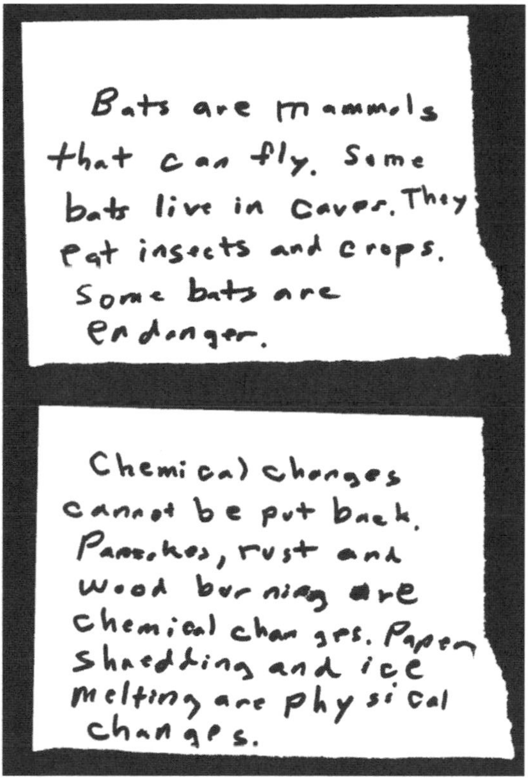

Figure 6.4: Sample student summary think-writes about bats and chemical and physical changes.

Teachers can also use think-write to ask students to write quick summaries of what they have learned. Figure 6.4 shows sample summary think-writes.

Good Readers Read Well Because of the Ways We Teach Them; Poor Readers Can Become Achieving Readers, Too

It is time to consider whether ineffective teaching is the primary reason struggling readers so often continue to struggle with reading. First we must look at the reading lessons we provide to good readers and struggling readers; they look so different from each other. Too often struggling readers have read very little during their reading lessons. In one observational research study (Allington, 1984), a struggling reader in first grade read a total of sixteen words during a whole week of reading lessons, and these words came from reading two pages aloud, one on Tuesday and one on Wednesday. By way of contrast, a good reader in that same classroom read 1,933 words that same week during his reading lessons. If reading ability is what we are attempting to develop, it is not difficult to understand why the good reader was making greater and faster progress with his reading skills.

Good readers read more when they are in school, and it is also true they read more outside of school (Anderson et al., 1988). Perhaps that is because they have more reading opportunities and more successful reading experiences in school. Maybe it's because they have more reading lessons in which silent reading is the objective and more opportunities to discuss, to engage in literate conversations about what they have read in school. It may also be because their classrooms are stocked with many books they can actually read, while struggling readers too often sit in classrooms where almost everything available is too hard for them to take on independently.

The self-teaching hypothesis (de Jong & Share, 2007; Share & Stanovich, 1995) suggests that much of what we call "learning to read" is accomplished during self-directed reading. We have known for a long time that wide independent reading is the major contributor to vocabulary size in students (Stahl, 1999), but what is becoming clearer is how every reading proficiency is fostered by wide independent reading.

Suggestions for Improving Instruction for Struggling Readers

We must change the current situation for struggling readers. Our first suggestion is to ensure that struggling readers have easy access—all day long—to interesting materials they can and want to read, that they have frequent opportunities to read these texts silently and to engage in literate conversations around these texts (Cunningham & Allington, 2011). By that we mean interesting science and social studies texts that struggling readers can read accurately and independently, as well as texts for reading lessons that fit the same criteria.

Our second suggestion is that struggling readers need to read independently in and out of school. We can accomplish this when we provide easy access to books students are interested in and that they can read. Finally, struggling readers need to write about what they are learning. Think-writes are one way to ensure everyone—including struggling readers—writes more and learns more.

None of this is to suggest that struggling readers don't need effective instruction in decoding (Cunningham & Cunningham, 2002), vocabulary (Graves, 2006), fluency (Allington, 2009), and comprehension (Cunningham & Smith, 2008). They do. However, we know a lot about how to teach all of these things, and as teachers, we spend more time instructing students in these pieces of proficient reading. We spend too little time on engaging struggling readers in the actual act of reading.

References

Allington, R. L. (1980). Teacher interruption behaviors during primary grade oral reading. *Journal of Educational Psychology, 72*(3), 371–377.

Allington, R. L. (1983). The reading instruction provided readers of differing abilities. *Elementary School Journal, 83*(5), 548–559.

Allington, R. L. (1984). Content coverage and contextual reading in reading groups. *Journal of Reading Behavior, 16*(1), 85–96.

Allington, R. L. (2009a). *What really matters in fluency: From research to practice.* New York: Allyn & Bacon.

Allington, R. L. (2009b). *What really matters in response to intervention: Research-based designs.* Boston: Allyn & Bacon.

Allington, R. L., Stuetzel, H., Shake, M., & Lamarche, S. (1986). What is remedial reading? A descriptive study. *Reading Research and Instruction, 26*(1), 15–30.

Anderson, R. C., Wilson, P., & Fielding, L. (1988). Growth in reading and how children spend their time outside of school. *Reading Research Quarterly, 23*(3), 285–303.

Bangert-Drowns, R. L., Hurley, M. M., & Wilkinson, B. (2004). The effects of school-based writing-to-learn interventions on academic achievement: A meta-analysis. *Review of Educational Research, 74*(1), 29–58.

Beach, J. D. (2006, November). *Why don't children read children's literature?* Paper presented at the National Council of Teachers of English, Nashville, TN.

Betts, E. A. (1949). Adjusting instruction to individual needs. In N. B. Henry (Ed.), *The forty-eighth yearbook of the National Society for the Study of Education, Part II: Reading in the elementary school* (pp. 266–283). Chicago: University of Chicago Press.

Cunningham, A. E., & Stanovich, K. E. (1998). The impact of print exposure on word recognition. In J. Metsala & L. Ehri (Eds.), *Word recognition in beginning literacy* (pp. 235–262). Mahwah, NJ: Lawrence Erlbaum Associates.

Cunningham, P. M., & Allington, R. L. (2011). *Classrooms that work: They can all read and write* (5th ed.). Boston: Allyn & Bacon.

Cunningham, P. M., & Cunningham, J. W. (2002). What we know about how to teach phonics. In A. Farstrup & S. J. Samuels (Eds.), *What research has to say about reading instruction* (3rd ed., pp. 87–109). Newark, DE: International Reading Association.

Cunningham, P. M., & Cunningham, J. W. (2010). *What really matters in writing: Research-based practices across the elementary curriculum.* Boston: Allyn & Bacon.

Cunningham, P. M., & Smith, D. R. (2008). *Beyond retelling: Toward higher level thinking and big ideas.* Boston: Allyn & Bacon.

de Jong, P. F., & Share, D. L. (2007). Orthographic learning during oral and silent reading. *Scientific Studies of Reading, 11*(1), 55–71.

Gallagher, K. (2009). *Readicide: How schools are killing reading and what you can do about it.* Portland, ME: Stenhouse.

Graves, M. F. (2006). *The vocabulary book: Learning and instruction.* New York: Teachers College Press.

Guthrie, J. T., & Humenick, N. M. (2004). Motivating students to read: Evidence for classroom practices that increase motivation and achievement. In P. McCardle & V. Chhabra (Eds.), *The voice of evidence in reading research* (pp. 329–354). Baltimore: Brookes.

Hargis, C. (2006). Setting standards: An exercise in futility? *Phi Delta Kappan, 87*(5), 393–395.

Kuhn, M. R. (2005). A comparative study of small group fluency instruction. *Reading Psychology, 26*(2), 127–146.

Leander, K. (2008). Toward a connective ethnography of online/offline literacy networks. In J. Coiro, M. Knobel, C. Lankshear, & D. Leu (Eds.), *The handbook of research on new literacies* (pp. 33–65). New York: Routledge.

Martin-Chang, S. L., & Gould, O. N. (2008). Revisiting print exposure: Exploring differential links to vocabulary and reading rate. *Journal of Research in Reading, 31*(3), 273–284.

Nystrand, M. (2006). Research on the role of classroom discourse as it effects reading comprehension. *Research in the Teaching of English, 40*(4), 392–412.

O'Connor, R. E., Bell, K. M., Harty, K. R., Larkin, L. K., Sackor, S. M., & Zigmond, N. (2002). Teaching reading to poor readers in the intermediate grades: A comparison of text difficulty. *Journal of Educational Psychology, 94*(3), 474–485.

Samuels, S. J., & Wu, Y. C. (2003). *How the amount of time spent on reading effects reading achievement: A response to the National Reading Panel.* Minneapolis: University of Minnesota Press.

Share, D. L., & Stanovich, K. E. (1995). Cognitive processes in early reading development: Accommodating individual differences in a model of acquisition. *Issues in Education, 1*(1), 1–57.

Stahl, S. A. (1999). *Vocabulary development: From reading research to practice.* Newton Upper Falls, MA: Brookline.

Tatum, A. W. (2009). *Reading for their life: Building textual lineages of African-American adolescent males.* Portsmouth, NH: Heinemann.

Vaughn, S., & Linan-Thompson, S. (2003). What is special about special education for students with learning disabilities? *Exceptional Children, 69*(4), 391–409.

Vellutino, F. R. (2003). Individual differences as sources of variability in reading comprehension in elementary school children. In A. P. Sweet & C. E. Snow (Eds.), *Rethinking reading comprehension* (pp. 51–81). New York: Guilford Press.

Shane Templeton

Shane Templeton, PhD, is Foundation Professor of Literacy Studies in the Department of Educational Specialties at the University of Nevada, Reno. A former elementary and secondary teacher, his research has focused on developmental word knowledge in elementary, middle, and high school students. He continues to explore students' developing understanding of morphology as reflected in the relationship between spelling and meaning. His books include *Teaching the Integrated Language Arts* and *Children's Literacy: Contexts for Meaningful Learning*; he is coauthor of *Words Their Way* and *Vocabulary Their Way: Word Study for Middle and Secondary Students*. He is a consultant with school districts across the country. He serves as university liaison with the Northern Nevada Writing Project. He is a member of the Usage Panel of the *American Heritage Dictionary* and educational consultant for *The American Heritage Children's Dictionary*.

Donald R. Bear

Donald R. Bear, PhD, is director of the E. L. Cord Foundation Center for Learning and Literacy and professor in the College of Education at the University of Nevada, Reno, where, together with preservice teachers, he assesses and teaches children who struggle to learn to read and write. He has been involved in innovative professional development grants; with colleagues, he has developed assessments used in school districts throughout the country. Bear is an author and coauthor of numerous articles, book chapters, and books, including *Words Their Way*, *Words Their Way With English Learners*, and *Words Their Way With Struggling Readers, 4–12*.

In this chapter, Templeton and Bear show why and how word study in the early school years can be an equally compelling and critical narrative in students' learning about phonemic awareness, spelling, and the roles they play in the development of word recognition.

Chapter 7

Teaching Phonemic Awareness, Spelling, and Word Recognition

Shane Templeton and Donald R. Bear

Shari Dunn, an exemplary educator with whom we work, taught first through third grade in a multigrade Title I classroom for three years. She then transitioned with the third graders and taught a fourth through sixth grade multigrade classroom for three years. This configuration allowed Shari to teach eleven of her students for six consecutive years, beginning in first grade. When these eleven students graduated from high school, Shari visited with them and asked them to reflect on and write about their experience. In their letters, the students mentioned the power of word study—phonics, spelling, and vocabulary. They wrote about how their conversations got them thinking about words in ways they never had before. No one else in their later school years ever talked about the interconnectedness among words like they did in Shari's classroom. They wrote about how they enjoyed working together in small groups to study words. For these eleven students, word study was a compelling narrative throughout their elementary years—so much so that its power was sustained through the middle and secondary grades in which they did not experience such engagement.

In this chapter, we attempt to show why and how word study in the early school years can be an equally compelling and critical narrative in students' learning about phonemic awareness, spelling, and the roles they play in the development of word recognition.

Efficient, fluent, and meaningful engagement with text depends upon students' understanding of the ways in which letters in printed words represent information about language—its sounds, structure, and meaning. For just about every child, this understanding takes quite a bit of time to develop. The focus in this chapter will be on the three areas that are critical for developing this understanding:

- Phonemic awareness—The ability to think explicitly about and manipulate the individual sounds or phonemes of spoken language

- Spelling—The ability to associate a letter or letter pattern with a particular sound

- Word recognition—The ability to accurately associate a printed word with a spoken word

Our focus will be situated within word study, the domain in which we have over the years invested much of our research and teaching. *Word study* is a collective noun that includes phonics, vocabulary, and spelling instruction. Instead of trying to focus on these three areas separately, we emphasize how they form an integrated approach to instruction (Bear & Barone, 1998; Bear, Invernizzi, Templeton, & Johnston, 2008; Templeton, 1997). Research consistently supports this interdependence (Ehri, 2005; Berninger, Abbott, Nagy & Carlisle, 2009). For instruction this means that when students study phonics, they are learning about spelling, and when they study spelling, they are also learning about phonics and vocabulary. For beginning readers and writers, phonics and spelling are really two sides of the same instructional coin: instruction in spelling—applying letters to sounds or *encoding*—supports instruction in phonics—applying sounds to letters or *decoding*. We take a developmental approach to this integrated instruction in word study. Knowing where students fall along a continuum of literacy development makes it easier to teach in small groups in a differentiated fashion. This is important, because we know that developmental instruction is productive and allows students to make generalizations about words. In contrast, attempting to teach students at their frustration level can effectively destroy their motivation and learning.

Where We Must Begin: The Nature of the Spelling System

Phonemic awareness, spelling, and word recognition all reflect and rely upon *orthographic* knowledge, a learner's underlying knowledge of how printed words are structured. Orthographic knowledge guides learners' efforts to write and read the language they have learned to speak and understand. The orthography of English—its spelling system—represents information about printed words on three levels: alphabet, pattern, and meaning. At the alphabetic level, sounds and letters are matched in a straightforward left-to-right fashion as in the words *mad, plop,* and *me.* When we examine the spelling of most long vowel sounds in single-syllable words, however, we note that the system is no longer strictly left to right: long vowel sounds are usually signaled by the presence of accompanying "silent" letters as in *tame, bike, coat, rain,* and *play.* Such spellings illustrate patterns in which a group of letters, rather than a single letter, corresponds to sound. Different spellings for the same sound often reveal homophones, words that sound the same but have different meanings, such as *brake/break* and *sail/sale.* Homophones illustrate the role that meaning can play in determining spelling, a role that should become predominant in the later school years. This pattern principle also applies to a majority of two-syllable words. Doubling a final consonant when adding –*ed* or –*ing* to *mop* and *mope* depends on whether there is a short or long vowel sound in the first syllable of the base word: *mopping* versus *moping.* In the case of *mope,* nothing is doubled, but a letter is dropped. This same principle, learned first in the context of exploring the addition of –*ed* and –*ing,* later extends to other words such as *happen* (short vowel in the first syllable, so the *p* is doubled) and *robot* (long vowel in first syllable, so the *b* is not doubled).

A number of polysyllabic words, however, do not as reliably follow these sound-based patterns. This is because *meaning* takes precedence. For example, why isn't the *n* doubled in *punish* as we would expect because of the "double the consonant after a short vowel" principle? Because the spelling preserves the word's visual relationship to the words *punitive* and *impunity*; the common spelling

-*puni*- represents the fact that these words share a core meaning, despite the varying pronunciations of the letter sequence -*puni*-. This tendency to spell similarly words that share a common meaning illustrates the *spelling-meaning connection* (Templeton, 1992): "Words that are related in meaning are often related in spelling as well, despite changes in sound" (p. 194). This connection reflects the morphologically based nature of English spelling. Consider the word pairs *colum<u>n</u>/colum<u>n</u>ist*, *resi<u>g</u>n/resi<u>g</u>nation*, and *autum<u>n</u>/autum<u>n</u>al*, in which the silent consonant in the first word becomes sounded in the other. Note the changes in pronunciation but visual consistency in the underlined letters of the pairs *d<u>e</u>fine/d<u>e</u>finition*, *m<u>e</u>ntal/m<u>e</u>ntality*, *d<u>i</u>vine/d<u>i</u>vinity*, and *all<u>e</u>ge/all<u>e</u>gation*. Though the pronunciation of the italicized letters in each word pair changes, the spelling does not—it visually preserves the meaning relationships the words share.

Over the course of the school years, learners may develop an understanding of the three layers as they learn and exercise their developing word knowledge. This occurs more productively, however, if teachers understand these layers and how to assess and provide appropriate word study accordingly (Henderson & Templeton, 1986; Invernizzi & Hayes, 2004; Wong-Fillmore & Snow, 2005).

The Foundations of a Developmental Approach to Phonemic Awareness, Spelling, and Word Recognition

There are innumerable studies going back a good many years that have informed our understanding of what young children must learn as they develop knowledge about printed words. The challenge has always been, however, *how* to help children develop this knowledge. As we address the issues of phonemic awareness, spelling, and word recognition, we will emphasize how our instructional focus must reflect the *interrelatedness* among these abilities. Simply put, developing the ability to recognize and remember words in print efficiently and reliably depends on the developing awareness and understanding of the relationship between sounds and the letters that represent those sounds.

Why are explicit awareness and manipulation of consonants and vowels within syllables so challenging for many children, and how might we better support the development of this awareness when children appear to struggle? Before looking at how some research has addressed this question, let's step back and consider some deeper issues regarding the nature of the task and why many children may struggle. Olson (1994) observed that a writing system is a model for thinking about language, not a direct representation of language itself. Some writing systems are based on the representation of syllables, and that is how readers of those systems think about language: the smallest unit of analysis is the syllable. Other writing systems, such as English, are based on the representation of units *within* syllables, consonants and vowels. Letters, therefore, are a model for thinking about how the stream of speech might be segmented. The sounds to which we believe letters (or graphemes) correspond, however, do not themselves clearly exist in speech. Phonemes are primarily concepts in the mind and not distinct perceptual realities.

Building the foundation of this phoneme/grapheme model takes time. It may be instructive to note that humans had been representing their world symbolically, first in drawing and later in writing, for approximately 50,000 years *before* an alphabetic system was developed that represented both consonant and vowel sounds. The classical Greeks attained this insight; they borrowed a system of letters already developed by the Phoenicians but which represented syllables and adapted it to their own language. At a conceptual level, this was quite an accomplishment (Havelock, 1983). Given how long it took historically to develop this understanding—that consonants have their own letters or graphemes and vowels have theirs—it is important to pause and reflect on our expectation that young children develop this understanding in kindergarten (Templeton, 1986). Children don't have to reinvent the alphabet, of course, but they do have to reinvent the alphabetic principle, discovering what some very clever and insightful Greeks discovered after a number of other advanced civilizations had been tinkering with the problem for thousands of years. Young children learning to read in English must perceive a need to split consonant sounds from vowel sounds and assign a letter or grapheme to each—just like the Greeks. Analyzing the stream of speech down to the level of the phoneme, in other words, is a very challenging task. This is especially true because phonemes, as we noted, do not really exist in speech as isolated, discrete units. This is why it took thousands of years for the concept of a phoneme to develop historically; this is why it may take some time for children to develop this concept.

Learning about words—what they are and how their printed form corresponds to their spoken form—is a developmental process. Children's brains are not like cameras, taking pictures of printed words as wholes while preserving both their meaning and their pronunciation. Rather, once children are phonemically aware, they recognize words first through their parts—their beginning, ending, and then middle letters and the sounds those letters represent. What does the research addressing the teaching of phonemic awareness suggest we do to help children construct concepts in their minds for individual consonants and vowels?

Of course, children must learn the alphabet, because letters help make speech stand still and provide a foundation for beginning to think about sounds (Ehri & McCormick, 2004; National Early Literacy Panel, 2008; Treiman, 1993, 1998). Along with our teaching of the alphabet and our modeling of how print works as we read to and with young kindergarten children and write for and with them, we can explicitly teach about beginning consonant sounds. Children also must make the match between the words they are reading and the words they are saying—a concept of word in text (Flanigan, 2007; Morris, Bloodgood, Lomax, & Perney, 2003; Invernizzi, Justice, Landrum, & Booker, 2004/2005). This is the "voice to print match" that Clay described (Clay, 1972). Without a concept of word in text, children's understanding of the nature and purpose of sounds and the letters that represent them is disorganized and potentially confusing (Henderson, 1981). The concept of word in text—the ability to accurately finger point as they read lines of memorized text—leads most directly to full phonemic awareness. Once children can "read the spaces," they know and can attend to where words begin and end, and to what's in the middle. They can "finger-point read" (Uhry, 1999) because they now have a conceptual frame that defines the location and sequence of sounds and into which their understanding of sounds and letters can fit. As Morris et al. explained, "The word begins 'to stand still' for analysis, [and children] can attend to other letter-sound properties within the word unit (e.g., the ending consonant)" (2003, p. 321).

Encouraging children's writing is also critical, because their attempts to spell will enhance their attention to phonemes and reinforce letter-sound relationships (Morris et al., 2003; Martins & Silva, 2006; Uhry, 1999). These experiences establish the alphabetic principle, the understanding that letters or graphemes represent sounds in a left-to-right fashion. Alphabet knowledge, beginning-consonant awareness, the concept of word in text, writing, the alphabetic principle, and full phonemic awareness all work towards a major developmental milestone: the child's ability to develop a sight-word vocabulary, words the child can identify immediately out of context.

Learners' sight-word vocabulary and their advancing knowledge of grapheme-phoneme relationships support the development of word recognition in text. Teachers can gain the best understanding of their students' developing knowledge of words by examining their students' spelling. The role that spelling knowledge plays in children's learning to read words is not widely understood among many educators, although its importance has been acknowledged for decades (Ehri, 1989; Read, 1975; Henderson, 1981; Henderson & Templeton, 1986; Perfetti, 1997; Templeton & Bear, 1992). In table 7.1 (page 160), the types of spellings characteristic of each level of reading development reveal the types of information that learners use to read words (Ehri, 1997; Henderson, 1990; Templeton, 2011; Templeton & Bear, 1992); these spellings are the most precise and accurate measure of these learners' developing word knowledge and inform teachers what to teach in phonics and spelling. Spellings such as JREP (the word *drip*), for example, reveal that a child is phonemically aware, attending to consonant and vowel sounds within syllables. When reading, the child perceives words as a series of linear, left-to-right letter-sound match-ups.

It is quite fascinating that Letter Name/Alphabetic learners are often more phonetically sensitive than literate adults (Read, 1975), noting features such as the "voiced" and "unvoiced" affricates at the beginning of *drip* and *try*. In contrast, older readers whose perception is influenced by their orthographic knowledge think these words begin with a /d/ and a /t/ sound, respectively. Beginning readers finger point when they read, and their reading is out loud, choppy, and dysfluent. Transitional readers learn to discern the vowel plus

Table 7.1: Common Types of Spelling Errors as a Function of Level of Reading Development and Spelling Phase

Level of Reading Development				
Early Beginning (preK/K and Grade 1)	Beginning (Grades 1 and 2)	Transitional (Grades 2 and 3)	Intermediate (Grades 4 and 5)	Skilled/ Proficient (Grade 6 and above)
Spelling Phase				
Early Letter Name	Letter Name/ Alphabetic	Within-Word Pattern	Syllables and Affixes	Derivational Relations
YT–*went*	JREP–*drip*	TRANE–*train*	ROPPING– *roping*	CONTRABUTION– *contribution*
CUS–*see you soon*	WATEN– *waiting*	BOTE–*boat*	CATTEL– *cattle*	CONFRENCE– *conference*
BTM–*bottom*	CHRIY–*try*	BATOL–*battle*	PLESURE– *pleasure*	FEASABLE–*feasible*

Grade levels are approximate. As grade level advances, there is usually greater variability among reading levels. The grade designation here represents where the majority of students may fall within those levels.

the letter or letters that follow it as a unit or pattern rather than as individual letters (Bear, 1992; Invernizzi, 1992). This is a significant advance beyond the grapheme-phoneme, alphabetic level processing of the beginning reading phase, and it allows these readers to recognize words more efficiently and accurately when reading. There is some expression when reading as these readers move toward fluency, and they will become silent readers during this phase (Bear, 1991). For students in the primary grades, our objective is to support their learning of the ways in which letters represent the several different syllable types in English. This takes more time than in languages such as Spanish and German, in which there are fewer syllable types and a more consistent relationship between letters and sounds within those types. There is more to be learned with English, and it will take longer than in many other languages. This exploration calls upon both letter-sound, part-to-whole learning ($b + a + t$ = /bat/) and analogical, whole-to-part reasoning (if you know *light*, that will help you decode *fright*) (Bear et al., 2008; National Reading Panel, 2000; Zeigler & Goswami, 2005).

The next two phases of literacy development, Intermediate and Advanced/Proficient, are beyond the scope of this chapter, but two important aspects must be noted about instruction in spelling at these levels: the role of *morphology*, the spelling-meaning connection, will become primary, and it will impact spelling knowledge, vocabulary knowledge, and recognition of polysyllabic words (Taft, 2003; Templeton, 2004, 2011). In summary, analyzing learners' spellings provides (1) the best indicator of what to teach with respect to phonemic awareness and phonics as well as spelling, and (2) the best window into the information learners use to read words (Henderson, 1981; Perfetti, 1997; Ouellette & Sénéchal, 2008), in turn providing the best indicator of where learners fall along the continuum of literacy development.

Breadth and Depth in Word Study

In order to provide breadth and depth in phonics and spelling instruction, we need to ensure that students are experiencing, examining, and talking about words from a variety of perspectives. We begin by assessing students' word knowledge through a developmental spelling inventory (Bear et al., 2008; Ganske, 1999) and by examining students' writing. This information reveals the letter-sound correspondences or spelling patterns that students are ready to explore, and helps teachers differentiate instruction accordingly.

> In order to provide breadth and depth in phonics and spelling instruction, we need to ensure that students are experiencing, examining, and talking about words from a variety of perspectives.

Activities that afford this type of instructional breadth and depth involve sorting or classification; such comparison and contrast of spoken and written words and word features are the essence of word study. Students will organize what they are learning about words and form generalizations about letters, patterns, and words (Bear et al., 2008). Three types of sorting and classifying activities are as follows:

- Picture sorts—Sorting pictures helps young children develop awareness of sounds within words and categorize words according to different types of sounds. Teachers model how to sort or categorize pictures of different objects and actions according to beginning sounds or onsets, and a bit later, the vowel and what follows, or rhymes. For example, working with a group, the teacher pronounces the name of each picture as she places it under the letter associated with its beginning sound. After this guided activity, the children will work independently to sort the pictures and sounds. Picture sorts are used throughout the primary grades as children explore phonics or grapheme-phoneme relationships—listening for and sorting according to different beginning, ending, and medial sounds within single-syllable words.

- Word sorts—Word sorts are similar to picture sorts in that children are attending to different beginning, ending, and medial sounds. As they look at and pronounce each word, however, they are now thinking about how the letters within each word correspond to the sounds they hear. Throughout the grades, children will sort words according to increasingly advanced spelling features and patterns. There are a number of variations on the basic word sort format: teacher-directed "closed" sorts versus student-centered "open" sorts, writing sorts, blind sorts, pattern sorts, buddy sorts, speed sorts, and "guess my category" sorts (Bear et al., 2008).

- Word study notebooks—These notebooks are an ongoing record of children's investigations of words. Children often write or record a word sort they have just completed and write an explanation of why they sorted the words as they did. As they encounter other words in their reading that they believe have the same feature or spelling pattern, they add those words to their categories. These notebooks may include content vocabulary word study notes and sorts. Teachers make specific word study assignments for the differentiated word study groups. The word study notebooks are a physical record of what the students have studied and can be included as a part of the grading in reading or spelling. We like to see students sharing their notebooks with partners and adding to their notebooks when they meet with their English learner or intervention instructors.

Notebooks with brads or three rings make it possible to insert pages as needed.

Sorting or classification activities reflect the fundamentals of effective learning and instruction:

1. Learning is active as students manipulate and say the words and names of the pictures they sort.

2. Students make choices and have control of how they sort and manipulate the words.

3. Students examine the words through repeated practice. Teachers demonstrate and guide the word study and word sorts, and then students have independent and partner time to practice sorting and in playing word games.

4. The final step in most word study is for students to explain *why* they sorted the way they did. This verbal reflection and social interaction deepen learning.

To reiterate, the depth of processing of orthographic structure afforded by this type of approach to examining words supports both the encoding and the decoding of words. The number and types of engagements with words support more accurate and rapid recognition of words during reading.

Because the developmental approach to word study requires time for students to sort, think, discuss, and write, teachers often ask how they might go about organizing word study within their literacy block. For example, because they wish to differentiate their word study instruction, must they plan for an additional layer of instructional groups? Importantly, teachers will find that their spelling assessments reliably and validly predict their reading groups. In other words, differentiated guided reading groups and differentiated word study groups will usually contain the same students. Because of this, they may introduce a new set of words to be explored on Monday for ten minutes during their guided reading time. Part of students' partner and independent work throughout the week focuses on word study; for example, after the initial sorting and discussion on Monday, students may do "open sorts" with their words on Tuesday in which they determine their own categories for sorting the words; on Wednesday they may go on a word hunt, looking in selections they've already read for other words that have the features or patterns they have been studying, and adding these words to the recorded sorts in their word study notebooks; on Thursday they may play word games that reinforce the features and patterns; on Friday the teacher may assess the studied words, or students may work in pairs to assess each other.

Where do the words for sorting activities come from? Increasingly, published reading curricula provide words arranged according to a scope and sequence that reflect what we know about the nature of orthographic development. Resources devoted to word study in particular are available in hard copy, software, and online (such as Bear et al., 2008; Fresch & Wheaton, 2004; Ganske, 2000; Flanigan, Hayes, Templeton, Bear, Invernizzi, & Johnston, 2011; Invernizzi, Johnston, Bear, Templeton, 2009; Johnston, Bear, Invernizzi, Templeton, 2009).

Applying the Developmental Model to Instruction

To illustrate how understanding the development of phonemic awareness, spelling, and word recognition can support instruction, we present the assessments and instructional activities for two students: Stan, a second grader, and Hakim, a fourth grader. Their cases are also of interest because they illustrate how the recent response to intervention (RTI) paradigm (Lipson & Wixson, 2010) supports developmental instruction as soon as possible, with appropriate intensity and duration. In contrast to the traditional discrepancy and difference model, RTI is grounded in research supporting a delay and development model.

Stan

Stan became a student in our program when he was repeating kindergarten, and he illustrates how students progress developmentally even when they experience learning difficulties. Stan is a twin who experienced developmental delays in his speech and in his literacy development. During more than thirty years of teaching in reading centers, we have observed that approximately half of the students with reading difficulties who attend such centers have some history of being involved in speech and language testing and remediation. This was the case with Stan. His speech was delayed in both articulation and structure. He was difficult to understand, and he spoke in a rather shrill voice. Like most students who experience a developmental or language delay, Stan still followed a typical developmental sequence, though at a slower pace. During two years of tutoring, Stan progressed from an emergent reader and speller to being a transitional reader and within-word-pattern speller.

Here we show the types of word study and reading activities that Stan pursued and describe how he grew in a developmental fashion over the two years he attended the literacy center.

Year 1. As seen in the first spelling sample (fig. 7.1, page 166), Stan represented just the first sound of words, indicating that he was an emergent reader and speller. He knew eighteen letters of the alphabet and was learning how to form the letters. He was unable to point to the words of a rhyme or dictation that he had memorized, indicating that his concept of word in text was still developing.

Stan's tutoring focused on learning the letters of the alphabet through singing the alphabet song while pointing to the letters, forming the letters, and developing phonemic awareness for beginning sounds, focusing on some of the most frequent and distinctive beginning sounds (for example/b/ and /m/). Stan pasted the pictures of his beginning sound sorts into his word study notebook and spelled as much of each word as he could (fig. 7.2, page 166).

To develop a rudimentary concept of words, during each session, Stan practiced pointing to the words of a familiar rhyme or dictation. When his tutor had a birthday, "Happy Birthday" became a favorite text for him to practice tracking. The two-syllable words were most difficult for him to follow, and his teacher was there to support accurate pointing. Stan especially liked using a fancy pointer with a plastic hand attached. Another favorite rhyme was "Five Little Monkeys." Stan concentrated on finger pointing accurately to just the first line, which we turned into two: *Five little monkeys / swinging through the trees.* We enjoyed singing the poem, and then, with his classmates, we rambled down the hall swinging our arms like monkeys. The young children enjoyed the movement and characterization.

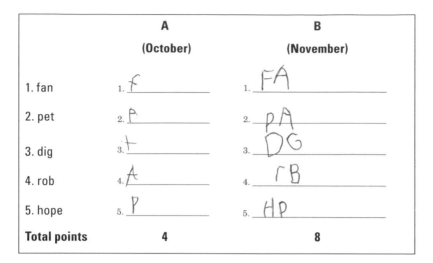

	A **(October)**	**B** **(November)**
1. fan	1. f	1. FA
2. pet	2. P	2. PA
3. dig	3. t	3. DG
4. rob	4. A	4. rB
5. hope	5. P	5. HP
Total points	4	8

Figure 7.1: Stan's spelling in year 1 in October and November. From the Primary Spelling Inventory (Bear et al., 2008).

Figure 7.2: A page from Stan's word study notebook.

Likewise, Stan's word study often involved movement, hopping from letter to letter on the floor as he named the letters.

By the end of tutoring in late November, Stan was assessed as a late-emergent reader and speller. He had begun to point accurately to the words of familiar two-line poems and dictations. He was now spelling both the beginning and final sounds of words (fig. 7.1, column B). Notice that he omitted the vowels. Emergent students whose primary language is English tend to spell only the consonants. Acoustically, the consonants are the noisy sounds, the vowels are the musical sounds, and the students attend to the noise first. In addition, consonants are more salient and concrete when articulated. (Interestingly, Spanish speakers include more vowels at this stage; in Spanish, the vowels are more prominent, with many words ending in a vowel.)

In his reading, Stan read simple poems and personal dictations repeatedly over several weeks. The poems and dictations were stored in his personal reader (Bear, Casserta-Henry, & Venner, 2004), and he reread four or five selections each tutoring session with a sticker or a tic mark noting each time he reread a selection (fig. 7.3, page 168). Stan also collected sight words from these dictations; these sight words were written on 1 × 2 card stock and deposited in his word bank. Stan looked through his word-bank cards for appropriate words to use in his beginning-consonant word study.

Year 2. For a year, Stan was a solid letter name–alphabetic speller. He consistently included a vowel in each syllable and used a letter-name strategy to spell short vowels based on articulation (Read, 1975; Ouellette & Sénéchal, 2008). For example, in the sample from mid-April, note how Stan substituted the long vowel A for the short *e* sound (fig. 7.4, page 169). This is because A is the closest letter name to the short *e* sound (PAT for *pet,* SLAD for *sled*). It is important to note that while Stan progressed in a developmental fashion, some of his speech delays were evident in his spelling, for example, FLT for *fright,* JOD for *chewed,* FON for *thorn,* FRD for *third*. We worked to coordinate his instruction with what he was learning in speech and conducted sound sorts with pictures and

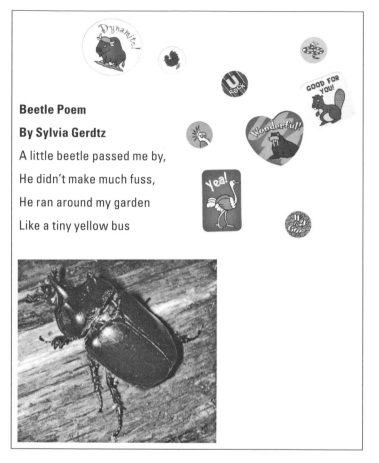

Beetle Poem

By Sylvia Gerdtz

A little beetle passed me by,

He didn't make much fuss,

He ran around my garden

Like a tiny yellow bus

**Figure 7.3: A sample from Stan's personal reader
with stickers for rereadings.**

words that drew his attention to some of the sounds he had difficulty articulating (Figure 7.5, page 170).

In reading, Stan was reading easy first-grade texts, and he added to the number of poems and personal dictations that he reread regularly in his personal reader. In word study, Stan studied short-vowel patterns. At first, he studied word families of short vowels, and then he began to compare short-vowel sounds across vowels (short *e* and short *a*, short *i*, and short *o*). Sorts often began with picture sorts so that he had to focus on the sounds themselves, and then he compared short-vowel words so that he could see the consistency of the spelling of short vowels. Stan wrote these sorts into his word study

1. fan	1. FaN
2. pet	2. Pat
3. dig	3. diG
4. rob	4. raB
5. hope	5. HoP
6. wait	6. Wit
7. gum	7. GuM
8. sled	8. SLad
9. stick	9. Sit
10. shine	10. SaN
11. dream	11. Dre
12. blade	12. BLad
13. coach	13. Coo
14. fright	14. FLt
15. chewed	15. UoL
16. crawl	16. roU
17. wishes	17. WIS
18. thorn	18. Fary
19. shouted	19. SoU
20. spoil	20. SoL
21. growl	21. GaN
22. third	22. Frd
23. camped	23. CuP
24. tries	24. trS
25. clapping	25. draP
26. riding	26. rNN

Figure 7.4: Stan's spelling in April of Year 1. From the Primary Spelling Inventory (Bear et al., 2008).

Figure 7.5: Stan sorts pictures of words that begin with consonant digraphs *wh, sh, ch,* and *th.*

notebook, and later looked through his repeated reading selections for words that fit the patterns and add those words to his word study notebook. At the same time, Stan studied beginning-consonant digraphs and blends. He sorted pictures by sounds, then attached letters to the sounds, and then he wrote these words on pages dedicated to particular blends and digraphs. This study of vowels and digraphs took some time, and we found Stan correcting himself when he came across spelling errors for consonant digraphs in his writing; for example, changing FAK to *thank.*

The final spelling sample in figure 7.6 reveals that by the end of the spring of his second year, Stan was moving from beginning reading/late letter name–alphabetic spelling to transitional reading/within-word-pattern spelling. He spelled most short vowels correctly, and he was beginning to "use but confuse" (Invernizzi &

1. fan	1. fahe
2. pet	2. pet
3. dig	3. dig
4. rob	4. rob
5. hope	5. hope
6. wait	6. wate
7. gum	7. gum
8. sled	8. sled
9. stick	9. stik
10. shine	10. shine
11. dream	11. drem
12. blade	12. blade
13. coach	13. coch
14. fright	14. fitl
15. chewed	15. chud
16. crawl	16. dol
17. wishes	17. wichis
18. thorn	18. fone
19. shouted	19. spolt
20. spoil	20. gnowd
21. growl	21. thrd
22. third	22. cah4At
23. camped	23. tise
24. tries	24. capen
25. clapping	25. riden
26. riding	26. swoaid

Total Points 43

Figure 7.6: Stan's spelling in April of year 2. From the Primary Spelling Inventory (Bear et al., 2008).

Hayes, 2004) long vowel patterns (WATE for *wait*, FITE for *fright*). He overgeneralized the silent *e*, spelling *fan* as FANE. There were still a number of sounds he struggled to spell, such as final consonant blends and digraphs. Often these reflected his continued speech delay (CLOL for <u>crawl</u>, FONE for <u>thorn</u>). His word study at this time focused on these final sounds in the context of comparing short vowel patterns (CVC) with long vowel patterns (CVCe, CVVC). He was more expressive and fluent in his reading, and he enjoyed reading longer books at a second-grade level. It was this spring that his tutor was rewarded with the question, "Time to go already?" at the end of a lesson when Stan realized that the session was already over. Stan will benefit from continued tutoring, and we hope that, should he need our support, he will continue with us for a few more years.

Hakim

Our second student, Hakim, is a fourth-grade English learner who was born in Ethiopia. His spelling reveals that he is at a within-word-pattern developmental stage; he is a transitional reader, reading second- and third-grade level materials at an instructional level.

One thing that we have learned about teaching English learners is that we need to bend developmental instruction to match instruction to their specific language needs (Bear, Helman, & Woessner, 2009). Clearly, Hakim has learned to spell many short- and long-vowel words (fig. 7.7). What at first appeared unusual is his misspelling of some short vowels (RAB for *rob*, SLID for *sled*, STANK for *stick*) that we would think he could spell given his ability to spell more challenging words (*blade, coach, spoil*). Hakim's misspellings illustrated the sounds in English he was learning: short *o, e,* and *i*. In his word study, Hakim continued to study short vowels with picture and word sorts for short vowels. In addition, in a small group, Hakim studied *r*-influenced words; and because the words sound so much alike to the students, they made the meaning and spelling connections among homophones *war* and *wore*. While backfilling some of the sounds in English of single-syllable words, Hakim continued to learn the meaning and spelling of many more complex words than these (such as *clapping*/CLAPING and *riding*/RIDDING). More fluent reading will come with a deeper knowledge of the sounds and

Word	Student Spelling
1. fan	✓
2. pet	✓
3. dig	✓
4. rob	rab
5. hope	✓
6. wait	✓
7. gum	✓
8. sled	slid
9. stick	stank
10. shine	✓
11. dream	✓
12. blade	✓
13. coach	✓
14. fright	freight
15. chewed	chawing
16. crawl	crall
17. wishes	✓
18. thorn	throawn
19. shouted	shated
20. spoil	✓
21. growl	✓
22. third	✓
23. camped	camn't
24. tries	✓
25. clapping	✓
26. riding	Ridding

Figure 7.7: Hakim's spelling in fourth grade. From the Primary Spelling Inventory (Bear et al., 2008).

spelling of single-syllable words. Hakim recorded his word sorts in his word study notebook, and he continued to add words to these sorts as he discovered them in his word hunts. For example, he had three pages of different *r*-influenced words that followed different patterns. In addition, there were separate sections in his notebook for content-area vocabulary (social studies and science).

Hakim's reading was constrained both by his orthographic knowledge and vocabulary knowledge. As a fourth grader reading at a second-grade level, it was difficult for Hakim to keep pace with his classmates reading on grade level. Like other English language learners in his class, Hakim would "read around" in difficult grade-level content-area texts, skipping over some words and focusing on the key vocabulary. His teacher audio-recorded several sections of his textbooks, and she found books on related topics that were written at easier levels. She paid particular attention to texts appropriate for transitional readers who were just approaching fluency in their reading and who would achieve greater fluency, orthographic, and vocabulary knowledge by reading these slightly easier texts.

These two case studies illustrate the synchronous relationship between reading and spelling behaviors across developmental phases. The developmental model is a roadmap for expectations and suggests the types of word study and reading instruction to plan. A qualitative spelling assessment makes it possible to understand how to bend instruction for Stan and Hakim's individual needs. While they are delayed in their development, they follow in general the same developmental sequence as other students. In order to keep from falling so far behind that they never achieve grade-level reading, students such as Stan and Hakim will need intense developmental instruction over a long period of time. Such instruction should be provided in the contexts of both the regular classroom and intervention plan.

The emergent, beginning, and transitional phases of literacy are delicate periods requiring a teacher's knowledgeable response to developmental benchmarks. Like the students we discussed at the beginning of this chapter, in word study, students such as Stan and Hakim have opportunities to understand words in brand new ways. The development of orthographic knowledge—the knowledge of how printed words work—underlies learners' attempts both to spell and to read words. Children need support as they invent the alphabetic principle for themselves, and they need careful guidance as they apply their developing understanding to the conventional spellings of words they encounter and learn to read. In such fashion will phonemic awareness, spelling, and word recognition develop.

References

Bear, D. (1991). "Learning to fasten the seat of my union suit without looking around": The synchrony of literacy development. *Theory Into Practice, 30*(3), 149–157.

Bear, D. (1992). The prosody of oral reading and stage of word knowledge. In S. Templeton & D. Bear (Eds.), *Development of orthographic knowledge and the foundations of literacy: A memorial Festschrift for Edmund H. Henderson* (pp. 137–189). Hillsdale, NJ: Lawrence Erlbaum Associates.

Bear, D. R., & Barone, D. (1998). *Developing literacy: An integrated approach to assessment and instruction.* Boston: Houghton Mifflin.

Bear, D. R., Caserta-Henry, C., & Venner, D. (2004). *Personal readers and literacy instruction with emergent and beginning readers.* Berkeley, CA: Teaching Resource Center.

Bear, D. R., Helman, L., & Woessner, L. (2009). Word study assessment and instruction with English learners in a second grade classroom: Bending with students' growth. In J. Coppola & E. V. Primas (Eds.), *One classroom, many learners: Best literacy practices for today's multilingual classrooms* (pp. 11–40). Newark, DE: International Reading Association.

Bear, D. R., Invernizzi, M., Templeton, S., & Johnston, F. (2008). *Words their way: Word study for phonics, spelling, and vocabulary* (4th ed.). Boston: Allyn & Bacon.

Berninger, V. W., Abbott, R. D., Nagy, W., & Carlisle, J. (2009). Growth in phonological, orthographic, and morphological awareness in grades 1 to 6. *Journal of Psycholinguistic Research—Online First.* Accessed at http://0-www. springerlink.com.innopac.library.unr.edu/content/gpu4572318l52242/ on October 16, 2009.

Clay, M. (1972). *Reading: The patterning of complex behaviour.* London: Heinemann.

Ehri, L. C. (1989). Development of spelling knowledge and its role in reading acquisition and reading disabilities. *Journal of Learning Disabilities, 22*(6), 356–365.

Ehri, L. C. (1997). Learning to read and learning to spell are one and the same, almost. In C. A. Perfetti, L. Rieben, & M. Fayol (Eds.), *Learning to spell: Research, theory, and practice across languages* (pp. 237–269). Mawah, NJ: Lawrence Erlbaum Associates.

Ehri, L. C. (2005). Learning to read words: Theory, findings, and issues. *Scientific Studies of Reading, 9*(2), 167–188.

Ehri, L. C., & McCormick, S. (2004). Phases of word learning: Implications for instruction with delayed and disabled readers. In R. B. Ruddell, M. R. Ruddell, & H. Singer (Eds.), *Theoretical models and processes of reading* (5th ed.). Newark, DE: International Reading Association.

Flanigan, K. (2007). A concept of word in text: A pivotal event in early reading acquisition. *Journal of Literacy Research, 39*(1), 37–70.

Flanigan, K., Hayes, L., Templeton, S., Bear, D. R., Invernizzi, M., & Johnston, F. (2011). *Words their way with struggling readers: Word study for reading, vocabulary, and spelling instruction.* Boston: Allyn & Bacon.

Fresch, M., & Wheaton, A. (2004). *The spelling list and word resource book.* New York: Scholastic.

Ganske, K. (1999). The Developmental Spelling Analysis: A measure of orthographic knowledge. *Educational Assessment, 6*(1), 41–70.

Ganske, K. (2000). *Word journeys.* New York: Guilford Press.

Havelock, E. (1983). *The literate revolution in Greece and its cultural consequences.* Cambridge, MA: Harvard University Press.

Henderson, E. H. (1981). *Learning to read and spell: A child's knowledge of words.* DeKalb, IL: Northern Illinois University Press.

Henderson, E. H. (1990). *Teaching spelling* (2nd ed.). Boston: Houghton Mifflin.

Henderson, E. H., & Templeton, S. (1986). A developmental perspective of formal spelling instruction through alphabet, pattern, and meaning. *Elementary School Journal, 86*(3), 305–316.

Invernizzi, M. (1992). The vowel and what follows: A phonological frame of orthographic analysis. In S. Templeton & D. R. Bear (Eds.), *Development of orthographic knowledge and the foundations of literacy: A Memorial Festschrift for Edmund H. Henderson* (pp. 105–136). Hillsdale, NJ: Lawrence Erlbaum Associates.

Invernizzi, M., & Hayes, L. (2004). Developmental-spelling research: A systematic imperative. *Reading Research Quarterly, 39*(2), 216–228.

Invernizzi, M., Johnston, F., Bear, D. R., & Templeton, S. (2009). *Words their way: Word sorts for within word pattern spellers* (2nd ed.). Boston: Allyn & Bacon.

Invernizzi, M., Justice, L., Landrum, T. J., & Booker, K. (2004/2005). Early literacy screening in kindergarten: Widespread implementation in Virginia. *Journal of Literacy Research, 36*(4), 479–500.

Johnston, F., Bear, D. R., Invernizzi, M., & Templeton, S. (2009). *Words their way: Word sorts for letter name-alphabetic spellers* (2nd ed.). Columbus, OH: Allyn & Bacon.

Lipson, M. Y, & Wixson, K. K. (Eds.). (2010). *Successful approaches to RTI: Collaborative practices for improving K-12 literacy.* Newark, DE: International Reading Association.

Martins, M. A., & Silva, C. (2006). The impact of invented spelling on phonemic awareness. *Learning and Instruction, 16*(1), 41–56.

Morris, D., Bloodgood, J. W., Lomax, R. G., & Perney, J. (2003). Developmental steps in learning to read: A longitudinal study in kindergarten and first grade. *Reading Research Quarterly, 38*(3), 302–328.

National Early Literacy Panel (NELP). (2008). *Developing early literacy.* Jessup, MD: National Institute for Literacy.

National Reading Panel (NRP). (2000). *Teaching children to read: An evidence-based assessment of the scientific research literature on reading and its implications for reading instruction.* Washington, DC: National Institute of Child Health and Human Development.

Olson, D. (1994). *The world on paper: The conceptual and cognitive implications of writing and reading.* Cambridge, England: Cambridge University Press.

Ouellette, G. P., & Sénéchal, M. (2008). A window into early literacy: Exploring the cognitive and linguistic underpinnings of invented spelling. *Scientific Studies of Reading, 12*(2), 195–219.

Perfetti, C. A. (1997). The psycholinguistics of spelling and reading. In C. A. Perfetti, L. Rieben, & M. Fayol (Eds.), *Learning to spell: Research, theory, and practice across languages* (pp. 21–38). Mawah, NJ: Lawrence Erlbaum Associates.

Read, C. (1975). *Children's categorizations of speech sounds in English* (Research Report No. 17). Urbana, IL: National Council of Teachers of English.

Taft, M. (2003). Morphological representation as a correlation between form and meaning. In E. G. H. Assink & D. Sandra (Eds.), *Reading complex words: Cross language studies* (pp. 113–137). New York: Kluwer Academic.

Templeton, S. (1986). Metalinguistic awareness: A synthesis and beyond. In D. B. Yaden, Jr., & S. Templeton (Eds.), *Metalinguistic awareness and beginning literacy: Conceptualizing what it means to learn to read and write.* Portsmouth, NH: Heinemann.

Templeton, S. (1992). Theory, nature, and pedagogy of higher-order orthographic development in older students. In S. Templeton & D. R. Bear (Eds.), *Development of orthographic knowledge and the foundations of literacy: A memorial Festschrift for Edmund H. Henderson* (pp. 253–277). Hillsdale, NJ: Lawrence Erlbaum Associates.

Templeton, S. (1997). *Teaching the integrated language arts* (2nd ed.). Boston: Houghton Mifflin.

Templeton, S. (2004). The vocabulary-spelling connection: Orthographic development and morphological knowledge at the intermediate grades and beyond. In J. F. Baumann E. J. & Kame'enui, (Eds.), *Vocabulary instruction: Research to practice* (pp. 118–138). New York: Guilford Press.

Templeton, S. (2011). Teaching spelling in the English/language arts classroom. In D. Lapp & D. Fisher (Eds.), *The handbook of research on teaching the English language arts* (3rd ed.). IRA/NCTE: Lawrence Erlbaum Associates.

Templeton, S., & Bear, D. R. (Eds.). (1992). *Development of orthographic knowledge and the foundations of literacy: A memorial Festschrift for Edmund H. Henderson.* Hillsdale, NJ: Lawrence Erlbaum Associates.

Treiman, R. (1993). *Beginning to spell.* New York: Oxford University Press.

Treiman, R. (1998). Why spelling? The benefits of incorporating spelling into beginning reading instruction. In J. L. Metsala & L. C. Ehri (Eds.), *Word recognition in beginning literacy* (pp. 289–313). Mahwah, NJ: Lawrence Erlbaum Associates.

Uhry, J. K. (1999). Invented spelling in kindergarten: The relationship with finger-point reading. *Reading and Writing: An Interdisciplinary Journal, 11*(5–6), 441–464.

Wong-Fillmore, L., & Snow, C. (2005). What teachers need to know about language. In C. T. Adger, C. E. Snow, & D. Christian (Eds.), *What teachers need to know about language* (pp. 7–54). Washington, DC: Center for Applied Linguistics.

Ziegler, J. C., & Goswami, U. (2005). Reading acquisition, developmental dyslexia, and skilled reading across languages: A psycholinguistic grain size theory. *Psychological Bulletin, 13*(1), 3–29.

Timothy V. Rasinski

Timothy V. Rasinski, PhD, is a professor of literacy education at Kent State University. He has written numerous articles and chapters and has authored, coauthored, or edited more than forty books and curriculum programs on reading education. He is author of the best-selling book *The Fluent Reader*, now in its second edition. His scholarly interests include reading fluency and word study, and readers who struggle. His research on reading has been cited by the National Reading Panel and has been published in journals such as *Reading Research Quarterly*, *The Reading Teacher, Reading Psychology,* and the *Journal of Educational Research*. Rasinski is the coauthor of the fluency chapter for Volume IV of the *Handbook of Reading Research.*

Rasinski recently served a three-year term on the International Reading Association Board of Directors and has served as coeditor of *The Reading Teacher*, the world's most widely read journal of literacy education, and the *Journal of Literacy Research*. Rasinski is past president of the College Reading Association and winner of the A. B. Herr Award and the Laureate Award from the College Reading Association for his scholarly contributions to literacy education. In 2010, he was elected to the Reading Hall of Fame.

Rasinski received his doctorate from The Ohio State University. He taught at the University of Georgia and as an elementary and middle school classroom and intervention teacher in Nebraska.

In this chapter, Rasinski explores the journey of reading fluency in the public and academic consciousness from its status of important to ignored. He defines reading fluency and presents a brief summary of research; he addresses how reading fluency has become a pariah in the eyes of the reading community, despite research that demonstrates its importance; and he explores how to address reading fluency instructionally to take advantage of its great potential.

Chapter 8

Teaching Reading Fluency

Timothy V. Rasinski

After decades of benign neglect (Allington, 1983), reading fluency was finally reidentified as a critical element in proficient reading and effective reading instruction (National Reading Panel, 2000). After reviewing the empirical research on reading fluency, the National Reading Panel concluded that fluency was associated with success in becoming a proficient reader, and it recommended that instructional reading programs include reading fluency as an integral component.

Fast-forward ten years, and we find that reading fluency may no longer be considered as critical as the National Reading Panel thought. In their annual survey of reading education experts, Cassidy and Cassidy (2010) reported that reading fluency is no longer a hot topic in reading education and that it does not deserve to be a hot topic. What happened from 2000 to 2010 that resulted in reading fluency going from critical to criticized in the minds of reading experts and practitioners? Indeed, a recent study (Gamse, Bloom, Kemple, & Jacob, 2008) found that in primary grade classrooms where daily fluency instruction was mandated, less than five minutes per day, on average, was allotted for such instruction. Fluency apparently is no longer hot, and it is barely being taught.

In this chapter, I explore this journey of reading fluency from important to ignored. I begin by defining reading fluency and presenting a brief summary of research. Next, I address how reading fluency has become a pariah in the eyes of the reading community, despite research that demonstrates its importance. Finally, I explore how teachers can take advantage of reading fluency's great instructional potential, while at the same time addressing the concerns.

Defining Fluency

Fluency has been called a bridge between phonics or word decoding and comprehension (Pikulski & Chard, 2005). The bridge metaphor is a good one. First, fluency links to phonics through automaticity—readers decode or sound out words not just accurately but automatically, with minimal cognitive effort. Fluency then completes the bridge by linking to comprehension through the construct of prosody—readers read texts with expression that reflects and amplifies the author's intended meaning.

Automaticity refers to the ability to do a task with minimal attention or cognitive energy or resources, thus allowing a person to simultaneously devote attention to other tasks. LaBerge and Samuels (1974) described how automaticity plays a role in reading. In the act of reading, a reader has at least two major tasks to accomplish: decode the words in the text, and comprehend the meaning that the author is sharing through the texts. Proficient readers decode most words they encounter in the text accurately and automatically. By decoding words automatically, proficient readers free up their limited amount of cognitive energy for the more important task in reading—comprehension.

Less proficient readers, on the other hand, may be able to decode words accurately, but not automatically. They have to invest more of their cognitive energy into the decoding task than more proficient readers. These are readers whose reading is characterized by slow, effortful reading of the text. By having to employ an excessive amount of attention to word decoding, they have less attention available for comprehension.

One goal of fluency instruction, then, is to develop word decoding to the point of automaticity so that readers can maximize their attention on meaning, not word decoding. This is best accomplished through plenty of supportive practice in reading. A simple way to assess automaticity is by measuring a reader's rate of reading and comparing it to grade-level norms. Readers who are more automatic in their word recognition are generally faster in their reading; readers who are automatic in their word recognition also tend to have better comprehension of what they read.

Automaticity frees the reader's cognitive resources from phonics and allows him or her to focus on making meaning. Prosody is the fluency component that is actually involved in making meaning. *Prosody* is a linguistic term that refers to the use of one's voice to construct meaning while reading—expression in oral reading. When reading orally (or speaking), proficient readers will raise and lower the pitch and volume of their voices, use their voices to phrase text into syntactically and semantically appropriate units, emphasize words, and embed pauses of various duration into their oral presentations. All this is done to complement and supplement the meaning embedded in the text itself. In other words, readers use their voices to comprehend what they read.

Research has found that readers at a variety of grade levels who read with good prosody tend to have good comprehension when reading silently; and readers whose oral reading is marked by poor prosody tend to be less proficient in silent reading comprehension. Thus, we can infer that one way to improve reading comprehension is through improving oral reading prosody. Additionally, I would argue that elements of oral reading prosody are also operational during silent reading (Rasinski, 2004, 2010; Wright, Sherman, & Jones, 2004). That is, helping students develop that internal voice when reading silently will also lead to improved comprehension.

Teaching Reading Fluency

I will begin this section with a discussion of how *not* to teach fluency. It may seem odd that I would begin this important section on teaching fluency by exploring negative approaches to teaching fluency. I do so, however, because some approaches to reading fluency instruction, while well intentioned, are counterproductive in developing fluent or proficient readers.

Earlier in this chapter, I mentioned that reading speed is a valid and reliable measure of automaticity. And because automaticity correlates with comprehension, it has also been used as a proxy for comprehension and overall reading achievement.

Correlation, however, does not imply causation. Nevertheless, such a causal connection between speed in reading and comprehension has apparently been inferred. Thus, fluency programs and methods have been developed where the primary focus of the instruction is having students improve their rate of reading. Students are subtly and sometimes directly instructed to read faster and faster. The result of such instruction are readers who may be able to read fast, but find little meaning or satisfaction in their reading. We see this in our university reading clinic quite often, when students who are asked to read a passage in an informal reading inventory query the examiner as to whether they should read the passage as fast as they can. We see this also in students who, when asked to identify the characteristics of a proficient reader, respond with "fast reading." I know of no compelling research that shows that teaching students to read faster results in better readers. Indeed, I have seen cases where students in such routines regress in their reading development, and more importantly, learn to dislike reading.

Although speed in reading may be an indicator of one aspect of fluency, it is not the way to teach fluency. We want students to develop speed in the same way that most proficient readers develop their reading speed—through plenty of wide and deep reading practice. This overt focus on reading speed development has led reading experts to call fluency a topic that is not hot and should not be hot (Cassidy & Cassidy, 2010).

> Although speed in reading may be an indicator of one aspect of fluency, it is not the way to teach fluency. We want students to develop speed in the same way that most proficient readers develop their reading speed—through plenty of wide and deep reading practice.

Teaching Fluency the Right and Real Way

Instruction is most effective when it adheres to a gradual release of responsibility (GRR) model (Pearson & Gallagher, 1983). This model suggests that the initial stages of instruction in a new area of learning should be characterized with the teacher taking on the greatest portion of responsibility for doing the task to be learned. Then, over time, responsibility is gradually shifted from the teacher to the student until the student is able to complete the learning task independently without support.

Research has identified several promising approaches to developing reading fluency in students. I will present these methods within the framework of a GRR model.

Model Fluent Reading

For students to learn to be fluent readers, they need to have an understanding of what fluency is. This can be best done by the teacher, or some other fluent reader, reading to students in a fluent, expressive, and meaning-filled manner. When the reading is complete, the teacher can chat with students about how she was able to use her voice to complement the meaning of the text. The teacher might note prosodic features that added to the meaning of the passage, such as phrasing, emphasis of words, dramatic pauses, and so on, as well as how she was able to automatically recognize the words to read. Done regularly, this strategy will help students develop an authentic understanding of what reading fluency means and its relationship to comprehension.

Use Assisted Reading

When teachers read to students, they take full responsibility for reading the text. The next step in the GRR framework is for students and teacher to share the learning task—*both* taking responsibility for the reading. This is done in fluency instruction through assisted reading. In assisted reading, the student reads a text while simultaneously listening to a fluent oral rendition of the same passage. The oral support acts as a scaffold that allows the student to be successful in the reading.

Assisted reading can take a variety of forms. Paired reading (Topping, 1987a, 1987b, 1989) and its variations (Eldredge & Quinn, 1988; Heckelman, 1969) are probably most useful with students working to acquire fluency in their reading. In paired reading, a less fluent reader reads a text he or has chosen orally with a more fluent partner (tutor) who sits at his or her side for ten to fifteen minutes. The more fluent reader adjusts the pace and volume of his or her voice to make the reading accessible to the student. If the student is feeling confident in a particular portion of the text, he or she can signal (touch of the hand) the partner to read quietly while he or she continues to read orally. If the student runs into difficulty, the partner immediately returns to reading orally to provide the needed support.

Normally we think of the more fluent partner as the teacher. However, the partner can be a parent, classroom aide, older student, or even a classmate. Paired reading is a simple procedure that tutors can learn in less than an hour. Research into this form of assisted reading has shown it to be remarkably robust in promoting fluency and general reading achievement (Topping, 1987a, 1987b, 1989).

Another form of assisted reading commonly found in primary grade classrooms is choral reading (Rasinski, 2010). Choral reading generally involves reading one text with a group of other readers simultaneously. In choral reading, more fluent readers support their less fluent classmates with their voices. If a group were to read a text chorally several times, less fluent students would eventually be able to read the text without the assistance of the group.

Choral reading can take a variety of forms: whole-group choral reading (or singing), antiphonal reading (breaking the class into smaller groups, each group having a different part) and echo choral reading are among the most common forms I have seen. Not only does choral reading develop fluency in students, it helps to develop and reinforce a sense of group cohesion and teamwork, which is an important characteristic we should try to nurture in our classrooms.

> Not only does choral reading develop fluency in students, it helps to develop and reinforce a sense of group cohesion and teamwork, which is an important characteristic we should try to nurture in our classrooms.

Teachers can also use technology for assisted reading. Prerecorded audio texts are a good example. When students read a text while simultaneously listening to a fluent recorded version of the same text, they will have the same assisted reading experience as the student who reads with a partner. Although cassette tapes and compact discs have been the mainstay of recorded texts, the advent of podcasting (using your computer as the recording device) has the potential to revolutionize this form of assisted reading. Teachers and students can create podcasts on the computer, they are easily orga-nized much in the same way as word processing files, and they can easily be transported from one computer to another as email attach-ments or put onto websites where students can access the recordings at their leisure.

Research into the use of audio-recorded texts as a tool for assisted reading has been long standing and very promising (Carbo, 1978; Chomsky, 1976; Pluck, 1995). In her early classic piece on assisted reading, Carol Chomsky (1976) found, for example, that teaching students to be proficient in phonics was not sufficient. They had to move their knowledge of word recognition beyond accu-racy to automatic and prosodic in order for them to access meaning as they read. Assisted reading in the form of audio-recorded texts and repeated reading allows this to happen.

> Research into the use of audio-recorded texts as a tool for assisted reading has been long standing and very promising.

Practice Wide and Deep Reading

Generally when we think of practice in reading, we think of wide reading, the kind of reading most readers do. As a reader fin-ishes one text, he or she moves on to the next, and then the next. Clearly, wide reading is an essential type of practice that is necessary for developing all aspects of reading. However, for our less-than-fluent readers, reading a text once in a mediocre manner (which they often do), and then moving on to read a new text in a mediocre manner, seems to be good way to practice mediocre reading. These students never get the opportunity to become fully proficient at reading any text.

Reading fluency practice needs to be not only wide, but also deep. By deep, I mean students need to read a text (or a portion of a longer text) more than once until they become proficient with that text. The more common terms for deep reading practice are *repeated reading* (Samuels, 1979) and *rehearsal*. Beginning with the seminal research of Samuels (1979), a body of research into repeated readings (Rasinski, Reutzel, Chard, & Linan-Thompson, in press) found that when students practice a text repeatedly to the point of proficient reading, they not only improve on the text practiced, but also on new never-before-read texts. In other words, real learning and real improvement in reading occur through deep, repeated reading.

> Real learning and real improvement in reading occur through deep, repeated reading.

Most fluency instruction approaches embed repeated reading into their programs. However, the primary goal of repeated reading is often to increase reading speed. This is not a terribly authentic approach to repeated reading. It is not often in real life that readers are asked to read a text repeatedly for the purpose of increasing reading speed. A more authentic approach for repeated reading comes when we substitute the word *rehearsal* for *repeated* reading. Rehearsal is done in anticipation of a performance for an audience, with the aim of communicating meaning to the audience.

A more authentic and engaging approach to repeated reading, then, employs the repeated reading of story segments, scripts, poetry, song lyrics, monologues, dialogues, jokes, and other texts meant to be performed for an audience. Students rehearse a text over the course of several days and eventually perform it for an audience of classmates, parents, and others. The research into this approach to repeated reading has shown very promising results (for example, Biggs, Homan, Dedrick, & Rasinski, 2008; Martinez, Roser, & Strecker, 1999; Griffith & Rasinski, 2004; Rasinski & Stevenson, 2005; Young & Rasinski, 2009).

The Importance of Phrasing in Fluency

I think that most teachers would agree that staccato, word-by-word reading with minimal attention to phrasing is a chief characteristic of nonfluent reading. Fluent readers (and speakers) attend to phrasing. For example, I recently had the opportunity to visit the William J. Clinton Presidential Library & Museum in Little Rock and discovered that the actual written texts of several of his speeches had slash marks embedded in the text to aid in phrasing his speech. President Clinton realized that his ability to communicate meaningfully depended on his ability to parse his message into phrasal units.

The phrase (for example, noun phrases, verb phrases, and prepositional phrases) is, as much as the word, a natural unit of meaning in reading. Function words such as *the, as, if,* and *which* carry little meaning unless they are embedded in a syntactically appropriate phrase. Moreover, researchers have found that one of the major functions of prosody in oral speech and oral reading is to aid the speaker, listener, and reader in phrasing the text into meaningful units (Schreiber, 1980, 1987, 1991; Schreiber & Read, 1980).

Parsing text into phrasal units occurs not only in oral reading, but in silent reading as well. Studies have found that readers who read orally with good expression and appropriate phrasing tend to be good comprehenders when reading silently (Daane, Campbell, Grigg, Goodman, & Oranje, 2005; Pinnell, Pikulski, Wixson, Campbell, Gough, & Beatty, 1995; Rasinski, Rikli, & Johnston, 2009), and every declination of expression and phrasing is also marked by a decline in silent reading comprehension.

> Parsing text into phrasal units occurs not only in oral reading, but in silent reading as well.

Reading scholars have used this research to recommend that fluency instruction include emphasis on prosody and phrasing (Rasinski, 1994). Indeed, I reviewed a number of studies (most conducted several decades ago) that provided instruction in phrasing as part of the reading curriculum. Nearly every study found some facilitative effect in reading for students who were provided such instruction (Rasinski, 1990).

Because prosody is so closely correlated with phrasing, working with students on reading orally with appropriate expression has an embedded focus on phrasing. Readers need to attend to phrase and sentence boundaries in order to know when to pause and when to lengthen the last sound in a phrase. Beyond simply teaching students to read with good expression, there are several more direct ways to focus on phrasing.

Teach Phrases

Perhaps the easiest way to include an element of phrasing in fluency and word study instruction is to teach students common phrases (see fig. 8.1, page 190) or phrases that include common, high-frequency words. Most elementary and many middle grade teachers have a word wall in their classroom that students practice reading regularly and use in their oral and written language.

Teachers can take a similar approach with phrases. Authors use many common phrases in their writing. Phrase walls can include these common phrases that students can practice regularly. This will help students when they encounter these same phrases in their reading.

Once upon a time	In the nick of time
By the time	My best friends
Pros and cons	By the way
By and by	Birds of a feather
Happily ever after	Out of the blue
The next day	Long, long ago
Easy as pie	In other words
By and large	All's well that ends well

Figure 8.1: Common reading phrases and expressions.

Clearly, there are a limited number of such expressions worth teaching. Another approach might be to teach high-frequency words embedded in phrases and short sentences (see fig. 8.2). By practicing regularly and chorally several times a day, students will receive the double facilitative effect of learning high-frequency words and learning to read these words in the context of meaningful and syntactically appropriate sentences (Fry & Rasinski, 2007).

The people	Up in the air
Write it down	What are these?
By the water	If we were older
Who will make it?	There was an old man
You and I	It's no use.
What will they do?	It may fall down.
He called me.	With his mom
We had their dog.	At your house
What did they say?	From my room
When would you go?	It's been a long time.
No way	Will you be good?

A number of people	Give them to me.
One or two	Then we will go.
How long are they?	Now is the time.
More than the other	An angry cat
Come and get it.	May I go first?
How many words?	Write your name.
Part of the time	This is my cat.
This is a good day.	That dog is big.
Can you see?	Get on the bus.
Sit down.	Two of us
Now and then	Did you see it?
But not me	The first word
Go find her.	See the water.
Not now	As big as the first
Look for some people.	But not for me
I like him.	When will we go?
So there you are.	How did they get it?
Out of the water	From here to there
A long time	Number two
We were here.	More people
Have you seen it?	Look up.
Could you go?	Go down.
One more time	All or some
We like to write.	Did you like it?
All day long	A long way to go
Into the water	When did they go?
It's about time.	For some of your people
The other people	

All the words in these phrases come from the first 100 words of Edward Fry's Instant Word List (Fry, 1980).

Figure 8.2: High-frequency word phrases.

Use Phrased Text

Teaching is the process of making visible that which is often invisible to students. Phrase boundaries in texts are often invisible to students, as punctuation marks are not reliable indicators of syntactic boundaries in written text. One way of making phrase boundaries more visible for students is to physically mark the boundaries in texts that you will have students read (much in the same way that President Clinton used them in his own speeches). I use slash marks in my own work with students to help them develop an awareness of where they should pause in oral reading—one slash mark for a slight pause within sentences and two slashes for longer pauses, normally between sentences. Consider the following excerpt from President Kennedy's inaugural address:

> In the long history of the world /, only a few generations / have been granted the role of defending freedom / in its hour of maximum danger //. I do not shrink from this responsibility /—I welcome it //. I do not believe / that any of us would exchange places / with any other people / or any other generation //. The energy /, the faith /, the devotion which we bring to this endeavor / will light our country / and all who serve it //. And the glow from that fire / can truly light the world //. And so /, my fellow Americans /, ask not / what your country can do for you //; ask / what you can do / for your country //. My fellow citizens of the world /, ask not / what America will do for you /, but what together / we can do / for the freedom of man //.

Although this is a fairly complex and challenging text, my insertion of the phrase boundaries makes it easier for developing readers to break it into readable chunks. As students become more proficient in their reading, some of the slash marks can be removed in order to make the reading flow a bit smoother. Eventually, as students develop skill in reading text with appropriate phrasing, they can phrase texts on their own in advance of their oral reading.

Putting It All Together—Synergy in Fluency Instruction

Modeling fluent reading, assisted reading, repeated reading, and phrased reading are components of effective fluency instruction. To get the greatest impact out of these individual elements, effective teachers of fluency will combine them in synergistic ways so that the combination and interaction of one component with another results in an instructional effect that is greater than the sum of the individual components by themselves.

The Text-Phrased Fluency Lesson

The text-phrased fluency lesson (TPFL) combines the use of phrased texts with modeled, repeated, and assisted reading. The lesson usually spans two days and requires approximately ten minutes per day.

To prepare for the TPFL, the teacher finds a suitable text of approximately 100–200 words. The text segment can come from material that students have read recently or will read in the future. The teacher prepares the text in two forms for students: the Day 1 form has the text parsed so that the phrase boundaries are visibly apparent for students—sentential breaks are marked with two slashes, and intersentential breaks are marked with single slashes. The teacher then makes a copy for every student. The Day 2 text is simply the original text without the marked phrased boundaries.

The teacher then presents the TPFL in the following manner:

Day 1

1. The teacher presents the Day 1 text to students and reads it to them as they follow along.

2. The teacher and students discuss the content of the text as well as how the teacher conformed her reading to the marked phrased boundaries in the text and how the phrasing added to the meaning of the passage.

3. The teacher and students read the text chorally once or twice.

4. Students practice reading the text one to three more times on their own or with a partner.

5. The teacher concludes the lesson with a brief discussion that focuses again on content and the expression of meaning through phrasing and expression.

Day 2

1. The teacher reads the Day 2 text to students while they follow along.

2. The teacher and students discuss the content and nature of the teacher's reading, especially in regard to her use of phrasing and expression.

3. Students practice the text on their own once or twice more.

4. Individuals or small groups of students read or perform the passage. These final readings can be done in front of the class, or they can be recorded.

5. Students engage in comprehension activities from the passage and/or word work based on selected words from the passage.

The Fluency Development Lesson

The fluency development lesson (FDL) is another approach to synergistic instruction. The FDL is a proven approach to teaching reading fluency that involves modeling fluency reading, assisted reading, repeated reading, performance reading, word study, and home and school involvement. It was recognized by the National Reading Panel (2000) as an effective approach to fluency instruction. The FDL (Rasinski, Padak, Linek, & Sturtevant, 1994) employs relatively short reading passages (poems, rhymes, songs, story segments, or other texts) that students read and reread over a brief period of time. The format for a lesson follows a routine of the teacher taking responsibility for reading the daily passage and gradually shifting responsibility for the reading to the students:

1. The teacher introduces a new short text and reads it to the students two or three times while they follow along silently. The text can be a poem, segment from a basal passage or trade book selection, and so on.

2. The teacher and students discuss the nature and content of the passage as well as the quality of the teacher's reading of the passage.

3. The teacher and students read the passage chorally several times. They use antiphonal reading and other variations to create variety and maintain engagement.

4. The teacher organizes students into pairs or trios. Each student practices the passage three times while his or her partner listens and provides support and encouragement.

5. Individuals and groups of students perform their reading for the class or other audience, such as another class, a parent visitor, the school principal, or another teacher.

6. The students and their teacher then choose four to five interesting words from the text to add to the individual students' word banks and/or the classroom word wall.

7. Students engage in five to ten minutes of word study activities (such as word sorts with word-bank words, word walls, flash card practice, defining words, word games, and so on).

8. The students take a copy of the passage home to practice with parents and other family members.

9. The following day, students read the passage from the previous day to the teacher or a fellow student for accuracy and fluency. Students and groups of students also read, reread, group, and sort words from the previous day. Students may also read the passage to the teacher or a partner who checks for fluency and accuracy.

10. The instructional routine then begins again with step 1 using a new passage.

Done on a regular (daily) basis, the FDL is very likely to improve students' fluency, word recognition, comprehension, and overall reading achievement (Rasinski, Padak, Linek, & Sturtevant, 1994).

Fluency Instruction That Works

Fluency is important. Difficulties in acquiring fluency in reading are a major cause of reading difficulty for many struggling readers (Duke, Pressley, & Hilden, 2004). Fluency needs to be taught on a regular, consistent basis. Rather than the five minutes per day found in recent research, I would love to see teachers devote fifteen to thirty minutes per day to fluency instruction.

Fluency needs not only to be taught daily and consistently, it also needs to be taught in authentic, engaging, and supportive ways to students. Adults, adolescents, and children should participate outside of the classroom in instructional methods that resemble authentic reading activities. The instructional components of modeling fluent reading, assisted reading, wide and repeated reading, and phrased-focused reading are the building blocks that teachers, clinicians, school leaders, and parents can use to create fluency instruction that will work for all students.

References

Allington, R. L. (1983). Fluency: The neglected reading goal. *The Reading Teacher, 36*(6), 556–561.

Biggs, M., Homan, S., Dedrick, R., & Rasinski, T. (2008). Using an interactive singing software program: A comparative study of middle school struggling readers. *Reading Psychology, 29*(3), 195–213.

Carbo, M. (1978). Teaching reading with talking books. *The Reading Teacher, 32*(3), 267–273.

Cassidy, J., & Cassidy, D. (2010). What's hot for 2010. *Reading Today, 27*(3), 1, 8.

Chomsky, C. (1976). After decoding: What? *Language Arts, 53*(3), 288–296.

Daane, M. C., Campbell, J. R., Grigg, W. S., Goodman, M. J., & Oranje, A. (2005). *Fourth-grade students reading aloud: NAEP 2002 special study of oral reading.* Washington, DC: U.S. Department of Education, Institute of Education Sciences.

Duke, N. K., Pressley, M., & Hilden, K. (2004). Difficulties in reading comprehension. In C. A. Stone, E. R. Silliman, B. J. Ehren, & K. Apel (Eds.), *Handbook of language and literacy; Development and disorders* (pp. 501–520). New York: Guilford Press.

Eldredge, J. L., & Quinn, W. (1988). Increasing reading performance of low-achieving second graders by using dyad reading groups. *Journal of Educational Research, 82*(1), 40–46.

Fry, E. (1980). The new instant word list. *The Reading Teacher, 34*(3), 284–289.

Fry, E., & Rasinski, T. (2007). *Increasing fluency with high frequency word phrases.* Huntington Beach, CA: Shell Education.

Gamse, B. C., Bloom, H. S., Kemple, J. J., & Jacob, R. T. (2008). *Reading first impact study: Interim report.* Washington, DC: National Center for Education Evaluation and Regional Assistance, U.S. Department of Education.

Griffith, L. W., & Rasinski, T. V. (2004). A focus on fluency: How one teacher incorporated fluency with her reading curriculum. *The Reading Teacher, 58*(2), 126–137.

Heckelman, R. G. (1969). A neurological impress method of reading instruction. *Academic Therapy, 4*(4), 277–282.

LaBerge, D., & Samuels, S. A. (1974). Toward a theory of automatic information processing in reading. *Cognitive Psychology, 6*(2), 293–323.

Martinez, M., Roser, N., & Strecker, S. (1999). "I never thought I could be a star". A readers theatre ticket to reading fluency. *The Reading Teacher, 52*(4), 326–334.

National Reading Panel. (2000). *Report of the National Reading Panel: Teaching children to read. Report of the subgroups.* Washington, DC: U.S. Department of Health and Human Services, National Institutes of Health.

Pearson, P. D., & Gallagher, M. C. (1983). The instruction of reading comprehension. *Contemporary Educational Psychology, 8,* 317–344.

Pikulski, J. J., & Chard, D. J. (2005). Fluency: Bridge between decoding and reading comprehension. *The Reading Teacher, 58*(6), 510–519.

Pinnell, G. S., Pikulski, J. J., Wixson, K. K., Campbell, J. R., Gough, P. B., & Beatty, A. S. (1995). *Listening to children read aloud.* Washington, DC: U. S. Department of Education, Office of Educational Research and Improvement.

Pluck, M. (1995). Rainbow Reading Programme: Using taped stories. *Reading Forum, 1,* 25–29.

Rasinski, T. V. (1990). *The effects of cued phrase boundaries in texts.* Bloomington, IN: ERIC Clearinghouse on Reading and Communication Skills (ED 313 689).

Rasinski, T. V. (1994). Developing syntactic sensitivity in reading through phrase-cued texts. *Intervention in School and Clinic, 29*(3), 165–168.

Rasinski, T. V. (2004). *Assessing reading fluency.* Honolulu: Pacific Resources for Education and Learning. Accessed at http://www.prel.org/products/re _/assessing-fluency.htm on September 30, 2010.

Rasinski, T. V. (2010). *The fluent reader: Oral and silent reading strategies for building word recognition, fluency, and comprehension* (2nd ed.). New York: Scholastic.

Rasinski, T. V., Padak, N. D., Linek, W. L., & Sturtevant, E. (1994). Effects of fluency development on urban second-grade readers. *Journal of Educational Research, 87*(3), 158–165.

Rasinski, T. V., Reutzel, C. R., Chard, D., & Linan-Thompson, S. (in press). Reading fluency. In M. L. Kamil, P. D. Pearson, P. Afflerbach, & E. B. Moje (Eds.), *Handbook of Reading Research* (Vol. 4). New York: Routledge.

Rasinski, T., Rikli, A., & Johnston, S. (2009). Reading fluency: More than automaticity? More than a concern for the primary grades? *Literacy Research and Instruction, 48*(4), 350–361.

Rasinski, T., & Stevenson, B. (2005). The effects of Fast Start Reading, a fluency based home involvement reading program, on the reading achievement of beginning readers. *Reading Psychology: An International Quarterly, 26*(2), 109–125.

Samuels, S. J. (1979). The method of repeated readings. *The Reading Teacher, 32,* 403–408.

Schreiber, P. A. (1980). On the acquisition of reading fluency. *Journal of Reading Behavior, 12*(3), 177–186.

Schreiber, P. A. (1987). Prosody and structure in children's syntactic processing. In R. Horowitz & S. J. Samuels (Eds.), *Comprehending oral and written language* (pp. 243–270). New York: Academic Press.

Schreiber, P. A. (1991). Understanding prosody's role in reading acquisition. *Theory into Practice, 30*(3), 158–164.

Schreiber, P.A., & Read, C. (1980). Children's use of phonetic cues in spelling, parsing, and—maybe—reading. *Bulletin of the Orton Society, 30,* 209–224.

Topping, K. (1987a). Paired reading: A powerful technique for parent use. *The Reading Teacher, 40*(7), 604–614.

Topping, K. (1987b). Peer tutored paired reading: Outcome data from ten projects. *Educational Psychology, 7*(2), 133–145.

Topping, K. (1989). Peer tutoring and paired reading. Combining two powerful techniques. *The Reading Teacher, 42*(7), 488–494.

Wright, G., Sherman, R., & Jones, T. B. (2004). Are silent reading behaviors of first graders really silent? *The Reading Teacher, 57*(6), 546–553.

Young, C., & Rasinski, T. (2009). Implementing readers theatre as an approach to classroom fluency instruction. *The Reading Teacher, 63*(1), 4–13.

Camille L. Z. Blachowicz

Camille L. Z. Blachowicz, PhD, is professor of education and director of the Reading Program and The Reading Center at National College of Education of National-Louis University, Chicago, Illinois. She is the author of numerous chapters, articles, and books, primarily in her research area of vocabulary instruction, and speaks widely nationally and internationally.

She was named to the roster of Outstanding Teacher Educators in Reading by the International Reading Association and has been the recipient of grants and fellowships from the Institute of Educational Sciences and the Spencer and Fulbright Foundations. She serves on the RtI Commission of the International Reading Association and has been a board member of the National Reading Conference. She has been co-principal investigator of the Multifaceted Vocabulary Instruction Project, funded by the Institute of Educational Science, which looks at how upper-elementary teachers can achieve a balanced approach to vocabulary in their classrooms.

Peter J. Fisher

Peter J. Fisher, PhD, is a professor of education in the National College of Education at
National-Louis University where he teaches
graduate classes in literacy education. His
research interests include vocabulary development and the teaching of storytelling. In
1997 he was inducted into the Illinois Reading Council Hall of Fame. Peter is coauthor
of *Teaching Vocabulary in All Classrooms* and
numerous chapters and articles. He has been
involved in many long-term professional development projects in Chicago
and Chicago-area schools. He has been a featured speaker at state and
local conferences.

Susan Watts-Taffe

Susan Watts-Taffe, PhD, is an associate professor in the Literacy and Second Language
Studies Program at the University of Cincin-
nati. She holds a BS in Exceptional and Elementary Education from the State University
College of New York at Buffalo and an EdM
and PhD in Reading Education from the State
University of New York at Buffalo. She has
experience as a special education teacher
and a reading diagnostician. She has written
numerous articles for journals such as *The
Reading Teacher, Language Arts, Journal of Literacy Research,* and *Reading Research Quarterly* and is the coauthor of two books. Her research is
characterized by long-term collaborations with teachers and administrators to aid struggling readers in urban schools. She serves on the RtI Commission of the International Reading Association and has recently served
on the IRA's Committee on Technology, Communication, and Literacy. She
is a frequent speaker at regional and national conferences.

In this chapter, the authors examine current knowledge about vocabulary instruction. They follow with an analysis of recent research about vocabulary instruction for all students, including English learners and other learners, and discuss the potential role of technology in that learning. They then take a look into the future of research and practice.

Chapter 9

Teaching Vocabulary: Leading Edge Research and Practice

Camille L. Z. Blachowicz, Peter J. Fisher,
and Susan Watts-Taffe

Over decades of research, interest in vocabulary development and vocabulary instruction has ebbed and flowed. In their periodic reviews of "What's Hot . . . and What's Not," Cassidy and Cassidy (2005, 2009) have chronicled this fluctuation by looking at the number of articles on vocabulary appearing in literacy journals. In our work, we have seen the "temperature" continue to rise from the 1960s, when a comprehensive review concluded that "the teaching profession seems to know little of substance about the teaching of vocabulary" (Petty, Herold, & Stoll, 1967, p. 85); to the first decade of the new century, when the National Reading Panel noted, "The Panel knows a great deal about the ways in which vocabulary increases under highly controlled conditions" (National Reading Panel, 2000, p. 4); to the present, when vocabulary issues are again "hot" (Cassidy & Cassidy, 2009).

Attention to vocabulary often can be traced to larger issues in education. When instructional foci were skills-based, an instrumental view of vocabulary—which focuses on the importance of learning discrete words—stimulated individual word-learning studies (Beck & McKeown, 1991). When the focus in reading shifted to prior knowledge, learning vocabulary through wide reading and context received more emphasis (Anderson, Wilson, & Fielding, 1988). Currently, concern about the "vocabulary gap" that emerges in early childhood (Hart & Risley, 1995) and persists over the school years (Becker, 1977) has focused on vocabulary development for readers who are at risk (National Reading Panel, 2000).

In this chapter, with apologies to Donna Ogle, we will present not a K-W-L (Ogle, 1986) but rather a K-L-W. We will begin by looking at what we think we *know*—the state of the art of knowledge about vocabulary instruction. We will follow this with what we think we have *learned* from recent research about vocabulary instruction for all students, including English learners (ELs) and other learners, and we will discuss the potential role of technology in that learning. Lastly, we will share some ideas about what we *want* to know by looking at future research and practice.

What We Think We Know From Vocabulary Research

Across the shifting landscape of research, two things have remained constant: the emphasis on the importance of vocabulary to school performance and the variety of ways that teachers have attempted to interpret and apply this research in their classrooms.

In addition to numerous articles and books, three edited volumes since 2004 have summarized various aspects of the research on vocabulary instruction and drawn implications for teaching:

- *What Research Has to Say About Vocabulary Instruction* (Farstrup & Samuels, 2008)

- *Teaching and Learning Vocabulary: Bringing Research to Practice* (Hiebert & Kamil, 2005)

- *Vocabulary Instruction: Research to Practice* (Baumann & Kame'enui, 2004)

Each of these volumes is over two hundred pages long, and it is a little daunting to summarize them in less than five thousand words. Nevertheless, from this wealth of knowledge, we have teased out some issues regarding vocabulary instruction on which there is consensus and that we feel can be useful to classroom teachers

(Blachowicz et al., 2006). The research shows that effective vocabulary instruction does the following:

- Takes place in classrooms where lots of reading, writing, and meaningful talking are going on. We know that students learn many words incidentally through reading (Anderson, Wilson, & Fielding, 1988; Kim & White, 2008; Swanborn & de Glopper, 1999) and through exploring word meanings and nuances in writing and discussion. Discussion and use are also critical for deep learning. Students also learn from listening to texts read aloud, especially when teachers scaffold this learning through elaboration, example, and definition (Blachowicz & Obrochta, 2005; Elley, 1988; van Kleek, Stahl & Bauer, 2003).

- Includes the teaching of individual words. Teachers know that specific vocabulary can be taught using a number of different strategies (Beck & McKeown, 1991; Blachowicz & Fisher, 2010; Jitendra, Edwards, Sacks, & Jacobson, 2004) including definitional, contextual, and usage instruction and feedback (Stahl & Fairbanks, 1986).

- Includes teaching word-learning strategies and the generative elements of words, such as roots and affixes, in ways that give students the ability to learn new words independently. Work by Baumann and his associates (2003) and others has demonstrated that when students are taught the meanings of prefixes and suffixes and a strategy for how to use affix-meaning knowledge, they can use these strategies when encountering unknown words. The same is true of context clues, which students can be taught to recognize and use (Baumann, Edwards, Font, Tereshinski, & Kame'enui, 2002; Baumann et al., 2003; Baumann, Ware, & Edwards, 2007; Blachowicz & Zabroske, 1990; Buikema & Graves, 1993; Fukkink & de Glopper, 1998).

- Fosters word consciousness. Graves (2006) defined *word consciousness* as "an awareness of and interest in words and their meanings" (p. 7). Nagy (2005) elaborated, stating that word consciousness includes "various aspects of words—their meanings, their histories, relationships with other words, word parts, and most importantly, the way writers use words effectively to communicate" (p. 30). For example, when students learn that words can be related to words with similar meanings (synonyms) or opposite meaning (antonyms) they are becoming conscious not only of the word and its related terms, but also of categories of relatedness. Students develop word consciousness by engaging in playful language activities; by making visual representations of categories, webs, and maps; and by exploring words authors use in writing and accomplished speakers use in speaking (Beck, McKeown, & Omanson, 1987; Graves & Watts-Taffe, 2002; Nagy, 2007; Scott, Jamieson-Noel, & Asselin, 2003).

However, even with benefit of these extensive reviews of research, examinations of instruction in upper-elementary classrooms over the years have revealed little rich or deep vocabulary instruction (Beck, McCaslin, & McKeown, 1980; Blanton & Moorman, 1990; Durkin, 1978–1979; Ryder & Graves, 1994; Scott, Jamieson-Noel, & Asselin, 2003; Walsh, 2003; Watts, 1995). This has left many questions for practice unaddressed (Blachowicz, Watts-Taffe, & Fisher, 2006).

In the next section, we address two areas of work that we believe may contribute to this dialogue: first, what we have learned from current work that can inform teachers' attempts to diversify vocabulary instruction for all students, including ELs; and second, what we have learned about the potential of technology for vocabulary learning. We conclude this chapter with consideration of an important goal for ongoing vocabulary research—helping teachers orchestrate both what is new and what is well established within the context of their own classrooms.

What We Have Learned From Recent Research About Teaching Vocabulary to All Students

In some ways, word learning can be really simple, but in other ways, it is extremely complex. For example, we can teach the meaning of an adjective or an adverb (such as *horrible*, for example) with a synonym (*dreadful*), and we can write essays to explore the connotations and denotations of the meanings of a single word. In order to organize some of the more recent research about instruction, we find it helpful to use the following characteristics of words and word learning described by Nagy and Scott (2000): interrelatedness, polysemy and heterogeneity, and multidimensionality.

Interrelatedness

Interrelatedness refers to the ways that one word in a semantic domain is linked to another—for example, if you know the meanings of *warm* and *tepid,* you are better able to learn the meaning of *lukewarm.* Recent research in this area has focused on the teaching of morphemes and the teaching of cognates.

Morphemes. A morpheme is the smallest meaningful unit in the grammar of a language—for example, a word or a suffix. Various published programs exist to teach morphemes and word analysis to elementary and middle school students (Padak, Newton, Rasinski, & Newton, 2008). In general, such programs have been successful. For example, Kieffer and Lesaux (2007) implemented a program of morphology instruction with fourth- and fifth-grade students, some of whom were ELs (Spanish speaking) and some native English speakers. They found that both the ELs and native English speakers with greater understanding of morphology had higher reading comprehension scores.

Nagy and his colleagues (Nagy, Berninger, & Abbott, 2006; Nagy, Berninger, Abbott, Vaughan, & Vermeulen, 2003) explored the relationships between morphological awareness, orthographic knowledge, vocabulary, reading comprehension, and other variables related to literacy. They found that from fourth grade on, morphological awareness—in addition to the contribution of vocabulary knowledge—had an impact on reading comprehension. McCutchen, Logan, and Biangardi-Orpe (2009) found a similar sensitivity with fifth- and eighth-grade students, and Kieffer and Lesaux (2008) with fourth- and fifth-grade ELs. Programs that link teaching morphemic awareness and using context to determine word meaning have been particularly successful with fifth-grade students (Baumann et al., 2002: Baumann et al., 2003), middle-grade students (Baumann, Font,

Edwards, & Boland, 2005), and fourth-grade students with language-learning disabilities (Carlisle, 2007).

Cognates. Cognates are a particular form of morphemes. A cognate is a word in a native language that is similar to the English form of the word, for example *calendario/calendar* or *comprender/comprehend*. English learners often rely on phonological similarity to identify cognates (Dressler & Kamil, 2006). The importance of cognates has been recognized by the recent development of a test for cognate recognition (Malabonga et al., 2008). Studies have also explored teaching cognates as part of broader vocabulary instructional programs. Work by Carlo and her associates (Carlo et al., 2004; Carlo, August, & Snow, 2005) using a multiple-strategy, long-term approach has been successful in developing vocabulary learning. Their approach incorporates multiple modalities to analyze word structure and meaning in cognate as well as noncognate words that were encountered multiple times. The researchers focused on creating relational sets of words by looking at synonyms, antonyms, and multiple meanings using Spanish-language texts to support the English-language texts. Although the use of cognates was only one part of this comprehensive program, the results, when related to previous research, demonstrate the effectiveness of cognate instruction for English language students when linked with other instruction.

Polysemy and Heterogeneity

Polysemy is the idea that words may have different meanings in different contexts. For example, the word *mild* has a different meaning when applied to weather than when applied to food, although the meanings are linked. In recent years, the idea of polysemy has been important in relation to content-area vocabulary. Many common words take on different meanings depending on the content area in which they are used (for example, the word *force* means something different in physics than it does in military strategy).

Heterogeneity refers to the idea that (1) different words require different kinds of knowing and (2) different word users require different kinds of knowledge about words. An example of words that require different kinds of knowing would be words of measurement (*inch, mile*), which have specific meanings, versus words whose meaning is relative (*hot, cold*). An example of word users requiring different kinds of knowledge would be a chemist's versus an artist's understanding of the word *yellow*.

This concept has implications for the process of choosing which words to teach and for determining the depth of word knowledge required for each of them. If we recognize that learning words is a process of knowledge accrual (we learn something about a word and gradually add more knowledge), then as teachers the decision is to determine how much we need to teach initially. Proctor et al. (2009) found that, even though the quantity of words known is predictive of reading comprehension, for the bilingual and monolingual fifth-grade students they studied, depth of word knowledge was also significant. In the subject areas, we clearly need to spend extended time on important concepts (*triangle, democracy*), but in literacy instruction, teachers are often concerned about which words to teach prior to reading an instructional reading passage and how much to teach about the words.

> If we recognize that learning words is a process of knowledge accrual (we learn something about a word and gradually add more knowledge), then as teachers the decision is to determine how much we need to teach initially.

Beck, McKeown, and Kucan (2002) have been leaders in promoting the idea of three levels of word importance—level 3 words being the content-area concepts that need extended time and level 2 being words that are suitable for instruction. Level 1 words are the most basic words (*clock, baby)* that usually do not require instruction in school. Many teachers seem comfortable using this designation in determining which words to teach from a reading selection.

Vaughan et al. (2009) extend this idea of heterogeneity to different ways of teaching—in their case to the use of graphic organizers, discussion, and video in seventh-grade social studies classes. The regular education and EL students in their study successfully learned the target vocabulary and were able to improve comprehension of the social studies material.

Word lists. The concepts of polysemy and heterogeneity have also been important to the search for lists of common academic vocabulary words whose meaning does not change across disciplines.

Hiebert and Lubliner (2008) describe academic vocabulary as consisting of four components: content-specific words (for example, the word *equator*), school-task words (the term *learning log*), literary vocabulary (words such as *flustered* or *rambunctious*), and general academic vocabulary (words like *features* and *reasons*). This latter type of vocabulary—words that are neither polysemous nor heterogeneous—would comprise the set of academic vocabulary words that could be taught across disciplines. This basic approach has been prevalent since the 1980s in tertiary education with EL students.

Word lists have been around in education since the middle of the nineteenth century. Word lists rest on the concept that teaching a core set of words that cut across disciplines benefits students and saves instructional time. However, the effectiveness of teaching any specific list and the conditions under which it is best taught have yet to be determined.

Some researchers have been compiling such words or including them in more comprehensive lists (Biemiller 2004; Hiebert, 2005; Lawrence, Snow, & White, 2009; Marzano, 2004). However, Hyland & Tse (2007) have argued that not all the words on Coxhead's (2000) Academic Word List (AWL) have the same meaning across disciplines (for example, *plot* in relation to graphs in science and math, and *plot* in relation to story grammar in English). Townsend (2009) addressed this issue by using a multimodal, multidimensional language workshop approach to successfully teach middle school EL students the sixty most common words on the AWL. Researchers have compiled other lists of words from existing databases, based on criteria like semantic relatedness, for teachers to use at specific grade levels (Biemiller, 2005; Hiebert, 2005).

Multidimensionality

Multidimensionality refers to the idea that words have multiple dimensions—for example, cognitive and affective dimensions (such as the conceptual meaning and the connotations of a word). The implication is that there is not just one way to know or to learn a word. One could argue that multidimensionality also includes all the other dimensions of how a word works—polysemy, heterogeneity, semantic relatedness in all its forms, and so on. Scott, Nagy, and

Flinspach (2008) suggest that metacognitive awareness, or word consciousness, as outlined in section one, is needed to address the issue of polysemy in relation to the use of common words in the content areas, where words (such as *right* in *right angle*) take on new meanings. As students engage in the new literacies, they may encounter many words that have several meanings, and they may experience the possibilities of learning words in different ways. It is clear that modern technologies not only provide, but may require, that multiple dimensions be addressed in the teaching and learning of vocabulary—that we look not only at the nature of words themselves, but also at vocabulary instruction and word learning more generally.

What We Have Learned About the Potential of Technology for Vocabulary Learning

There are many ways to look at the question of what we have learned about the potential of technology for vocabulary learning. To begin, it is important to recognize that technology is not singular, but in fact represents myriad approaches to instruction that change as rapidly as the technologies themselves change. During the 1980s, for example, technology referred primarily to various software programs that were used to supplement the predominant classroom instruction. Thus, the term *computer-assisted instruction* (CAI) was coined. Today, CAI is not limited to software but can include the Internet as the source of supplemental instruction. Further, new models of technology integration allow for an expanded view of technology in the classroom. In addition to their presence as a support outside the parameters of the actual lesson, hyperlinks to video clips, podcasts, and blogs are being used within the lesson itself, both by teachers and their students (Sylvester & Greenidge, 2009; Tan & Guo, 2009). Most recently, researchers have begun to study the ways in which digital learning environments can be used effectively to support students' vocabulary learning.

While some teachers include little or no technology at all in their instruction, research indicates that many teachers integrate technology into their practice in a wide variety of ways (Blachowicz et al., 2009; Karchmer, 2001; Labbo & Reinking, 1999; Watts-Taffe & Gwinn, 2007). Some use published vocabulary-building programs so that students get individualized exposure and practice with new words. Some search Google Images for visuals to support the large-group instruction of individual words. Some manipulate digital text so that when their students come across words that are likely to be unknown, they can click on an embedded hyperlink to a visual image or verbal definition at the moment it's needed. Others teach their students how to use online dictionaries and thesauri as "just in time" resources during both reading and writing.

In addition to considering the multidimensionality of technology in the teaching and learning process, we need to remember, as suggested earlier, the multidimensionality of vocabulary learning itself: vocabulary learning includes learning individual word meanings, learning strategies for independent word learning, and developing word consciousness. In each of these dimensions, new technologies offer new possibilities and potential challenges for teaching and learning.

Individual Word Meanings

Most of the research on the role of technology in vocabulary learning has focused on the effects of particular software programs on vocabulary growth. In a recent best-evidence synthesis, Slavin and his colleagues (2009) reviewed the research on the effects of instructional technology (IT) on K–6 reading instruction as part of a larger look at effective elementary reading instruction. They reviewed thirteen studies focusing on first grade and thirty-one studies focused on second through sixth grade. Although the first-grade studies did not report results for vocabulary, Slavin and his colleagues found that notable effects on comprehension were more the exception than the rule. In grades 2 through 6, results of vocabulary subtests were often reported along with comprehension. Here again, large-scale evidence that typical supplementary CAI programs lead to improved word knowledge was not found. Across all grade levels, approaches showing the most promise were those categorized as other than simply CAI.

Other studies have focused on the effects of vocabulary hyperlinks in digital text, allowing for instant access to visual and verbal supports for word learning (Procter, Dalton, & Grisham, 2007).

Mostow and his colleagues (2003) found vocabulary gains as a result of a computer-based reading tutor that includes speech recognition and feedback, verbal and graphic vocabulary information, and embedded questions. Although it is impossible to know from their study which of these supports, if any, was the most effective, they point to promising possibilities. Studies of students' use of vocabulary links indicate that they are useful but often underutilized. It also appears that teacher mediation is an important consideration in maximizing resources such as these for student learning (Dalton, Pisha, Eagleton, Coyne, & Deysher, 2002; MacArthur & Haynes, 1995).

As noted elsewhere (Blachowicz, Fisher, Ogle, & Watts-Taffe, 2006), we believe that one of the most important questions before us as a community of educators is this: what are the connections between learning from technology and the type of classroom instruction that occurs in advance or in tandem? Studies conducted by Koren (1999), working with second-language learners, and by Pawling (1999), working with high school students, suggest the importance of active inferencing and metacognition among students.

At the same time, Dalton and Proctor (2009) warn of the potential for cognitive overload when students are confronted with too much information in multimedia format, prompting these additional questions: how much and what types of information are helpful rather than hurtful to word learning (and comprehension, more generally), and what new strategies do students need in order to make the most of the new resources for word learning afforded them by technology?

> Dalton and Proctor (2009) warn of the potential for cognitive overload when students are confronted with too much information in multimedia format.

Word-Learning Strategies

Dalton and Proctor (2009) suggest that new word-learning strategies are needed within the context of digital text, specifically as related to online "reading to learn" or Internet inquiry. They point out that within the context of Internet inquiry, words are used in multiple ways: to convey content information, to link to related information, and to inform about the resources and navigation tools specific to particular websites. For hyperlinked text, students are required to understand the meaning of the word within the text currently on the screen, as well as its meaning in relation to its linked destination. Currently, there is virtually no research on the strategies that students use related to these issues or the strategies they should be taught to use.

Word Consciousness and a Language-Rich Environment

As outlined in the first section, wide reading and immersion in a language-rich environment are tremendously important to students' vocabulary development. With the first decade of the 21st century behind us, it is clear that a language-rich environment must include both the texts and the associated language of this new century. Digital reading and writing, multimedia texts (websites, blogs, discussion boards, multimedia presentations, and so on) are an integral part of a language-rich environment. Further, students require instruction in the vocabulary of this new environment. Words such as *search engine, website, link,* and *navigate* comprise a new vocabulary of reading, writing, and thinking.

Within this expanded, language-rich environment, technology affords tremendous opportunities for increased word consciousness. Studies indicate that students are motivated and engaged by technology use and that this spills over into their interest in new words encountered in digital environments.

Making the "Best of the Best" and Keeping Our Eyes Open

Earlier in this chapter, we discussed what we know about teaching vocabulary generally. As we close this section, we want to emphasize the concept of making the "best of the best." In other words, we advocate integrating new technologies into vocabulary instruction in ways that reflect research-based best practice in vocabulary development in general. A computer program or website that simply provides a definition is unlikely to be as useful as more textured, in-depth information about a word, offered in a way that fosters connections with prior knowledge and builds semantic relationships.

> In other words, we advocate integrating new technologies into vocabulary instruction in ways that reflect research-based best practice in vocabulary development in general.

In addition, much of what we need to know about how best to utilize technology with our students is as yet unknown. We will learn it as we try different approaches and keep our eyes open to the ways our students respond, the kinds of support that are most helpful, and the unexpected challenges that arise. As with other dimensions of instruction, the role of the teacher is paramount. Slavin and his colleagues state at the end of their review of the effects of technology on reading growth that "what matters for student achievement are approaches that fundamentally change what teachers and students do together every day." (2009, p. 1453).

What Teachers and Researchers Can Do

Researchers and teachers know a lot about good vocabulary instruction. In the preceding pages, we have provided updates on the general landscape of vocabulary instruction, some essentials of effective instruction, and some new ways of thinking about the dimensions of word meaning that may help us tailor our instruction to different learners, as well as ways in which technology can enrich this learning. Although we don't yet know enough about how teachers can make the most of this knowledge in the classroom instructional program, we know enough to establish some general guidelines.

Based on the research, it is our belief that teachers need to infuse vocabulary instruction across their curricula. To do this, teachers must do the following:

- Ensure that the classroom is full of accountable talk, listening, reading, and writing. The more we foster the use of new and exciting vocabulary, the more it becomes part of the fabric of our students' school. The teacher's role is to provide scaffolding, feedback, and opportunity for word encounters and use.

- Intentionally teach individual words—words from literacy materials, content materials, current events, and so forth. This teaching should include both grade-appropriate high-frequency words and content and academic words. Providing definitional, contextual, and usage instruction and feedback, along with discussion and use, are critical for deep learning.

- Build and strengthen the students' *word-learning strategies* and understanding of the generative elements of words, such as roots and affixes, in ways that give them the ability to learn new words independently. Lessons need to include working through context and word parts to make sure students understand the process of using these clues to meaning. References can be brought into the process for prediction testing as well.

- Develop word consciousness by introducing categories of word relations—synonyms, antonyms, connotation, and so forth. Also, understanding the ways words "mean," as described in the section on teaching to all children, can enlarge students' awareness of the richness and flexibility of vocabulary. You can build interest further with games, Word Wizard, or other motivating techniques.

- Use the engaging nature of technology to make word investigations more profitable and involving.

Along with many other reading educators and researchers, we have called for careful research conducted in classrooms to document the ways in which teachers effectively orchestrate the essentials of vocabulary instruction (Blachowicz et al., 2009; Graves, 2006). Recently, there have been attempts to rethink these models (Baumann, Ware, & Edwards, 2007; Carlo, August, & Snow, 2005; Lubliner & Smetana, 2005). Only by providing rich case studies of research in action in the classroom, and by documenting its effect on learners, will we be able to advance to our next state of knowledge about vocabulary instruction.

This is an exciting time to be digging deep into vocabulary instruction, and we think this topic will show great strides and continue to be on the "hot list" for years to come.

References

Anderson, R. C., Wilson, P., & Fielding, L. (1988). Growth in reading and how children spend their time outside of school. *Reading Research Quarterly, 23*(3), 285–303.

Baumann, J. F., Edwards, E. C., Boland, E., Olejnik, S., & Kame'enui, E. J. (2003) Vocabulary tricks. Effects of instruction in morphology and context on fifth grade students' ability to derive and infer word meaning. *American Educational Research Journal, 40*(2), 447–494.

Baumann, J. F., Edwards, E. C., Font, G., Tereshinski, C. A., Kame'enui, E. J., & Olejnik, S. (2002). Teaching morphemic and contextual analysis to fifth-grade students. *Reading Research Quarterly, 37*(2), 150–176.

Baumann, J., Font, G., Edwards, D. C., & Boland, E. (2005). Strategies for teaching middle grade students to use word parts and context clues to expand vocabulary. In E. H. Hiebert & M. L. Kamil (Eds.), *Teaching and learning vocabulary: Bringing research to practice* (pp. 179–205). Mahwah, NJ: Lawrence Erlbaum Associates.

Baumann, J. F., & Kameenui, E. J. (2004). *Reading vocabulary: Research to practice.* New York: Guilford Press.

Baumann, J. F., Ware, D., & Edwards, E. C. (2007). Bumping into spicy, tasty words that catch your tongue: A formative experiment on vocabulary instruction. *The Reading Teacher, 61*(2), 108–122.

Beck, I. L., McCaslin, E. S., & McKeown, M. G. (1980). *The rationale and design of a program to teach vocabulary to fourth-grade students.* Pittsburgh, PA: University of Pittsburgh Learning Research and Development Center.

Beck, I. L., & McKeown, M. G. (1991). Conditions of vocabulary acquisition. In R. Barr, M. L. Kamil, P. B. Mosenthal, & P. D. Pearson (Eds.), *Handbook of reading research, Volume II* (pp. 789–814). New York: Longman.

Beck, I. L., McKeown, M. G., & Kucan, L. (2002). *Bringing words to life: Robust vocabulary instruction.* New York: Guilford Press.

Beck, I. L., McKeown, M. G., & Omanson, R. C. (1987). The effects and uses of diverse vocabulary instructional techniques. In M. G. McKeown & M. E. Curtis (Eds.), *The nature of vocabulary acquisition* (pp. 147–163). Hillsdale, NJ: Lawrence Erlbaum Associates.

Becker, W. C. (1977). Teaching reading and language to the disadvantaged—what we have learned from field research. *Harvard Educational Review, 47,* 518–543.

Biemiller, A. (2005). Size and sequence in vocabulary development: Implications for choosing words for primary grade vocabulary instruction. In E. H. Hiebert & M. Kamil (Eds.), *Teaching and learning vocabulary: Bringing research to practice* (pp. 223–242). Mahwah, NJ: Erlbaum.

Biemiller, A. (2004). Teaching vocabulary in the primary grades: Vocabulary instruction needed. In J. F. Baumann & J. Kame'enui (Eds.), *Vocabulary instruction: Research to practice* (pp. 28–40). New York: Guilford Press.

Blachowicz, C. L. Z., Bates, A., Berne, J., Bridgman, T., Chaney, J., & Perney, J. (2009). Technology and at-risk young readers in their classrooms. *Reading Psychology, 30*(5), 387–411.

Blachowicz, C. L. Z., & Fisher, P. J. (2010). *Teaching vocabulary in all classrooms* (4th ed.). Boston, MA: Allyn & Bacon.

Blachowicz, C. L. Z., Fisher, P. J., Ogle, D., & Watts-Taffe, S. (2006). Vocabulary: Questions from the classroom. *Reading Research Quarterly, 41*(4), 524–539.

Blachowicz, C. L. Z., & Obrochta, C. (2005). Vocabulary visits: Developing content vocabulary in the primary grades. *The Reading Teacher, 59,* 262–269.

Blachowicz, C. L. Z., Obrochta, C., & Fogelberg, E. (2005). Literacy coaching for change. *International Reading Association, 62*(6), 55–58.

Blachowicz, C. L. Z., Watts-Taffe, S., & Fisher, P. (2006). *Integrated vocabulary instruction: Meeting the needs of diverse learners in grades 1–5.* Naperville, IL: Learning Point Associates.

Blachowicz, C. L. Z., & Zabroske, B. (1990). Context instruction: a metacognitive approach for at-risk readers. *Journal of Reading, 33*(7), 504–508.

Blanton, W., & Moorman, G. (1990). The presentation of reading lessons. *Reading Research and Instruction, 29*(3), 35–55.

Buikema, J. L., & Graves, M. F. (1993). Teaching students to use context clues to infer word meanings. *Journal of Reading, 36,* 450–457.

Carlisle, J. (2007). Fostering morphological processing, vocabulary development, and reading comprehension. In R. K. Wagner, A. E. Muse, & K. R. Tannenbaum (Eds.) *Vocabulary acquisition: Implications for reading comprehension* (pp. 78–103). New York: Guilford Press.

Carlo, M. S., August, D., McLaughlin, B., Snow, C. E., Dressler, C., Lipman, D. N., Lipman, D. N., . . . White, C. E. (2004). Closing the gap: Addressing the vocabulary needs of English-language learners in bilingual and mainstream classes. *Reading Research Quarterly, 39*(2), 188–215.

Carlo, M. S., August, D., & Snow, C. E. (2005). Sustained vocabulary-learning strategies for English language learners. In E. H. Hiebert & M. Kamil (Eds.), *Teaching and learning vocabulary: Bringing research to practice* (pp. 137–153). Mahwah, NJ: Lawrence Erlbaum Associates.

Cassidy, J., & Cassidy, D. (2005). What's hot, what's not. *Reading Today, 23*(3), 1.

Cassidy, J., & Cassidy, D. (2009). What's hot, what's not. *Reading Today, 26*(6), 3.

Coxhead, A. (2000). A new academic word list. *TESOL Quarterly, 34*(2), 213–238.

Dalton, B., Pisha, B., Eagleton, M., Coyne, P., & Deysher, S. (2002). *Engaging the text: Reciprocal teaching and questioning strategies in a scaffolded learning environment.* Final report to the U.S. Department of Education, Office of Special Education Programs. Peabody, MA: Center for Applied Special Technology.

Dalton, B., & Proctor, C. P. (2009). The changing landscape of text and comprehension in the age of new literacies. In J. Coiro, M. Knobel, C. Lankshear, & D. Leu (Eds.), *Handbook of research on new literacies* (pp. 297–324). New York: Routledge.

Dressler, C., & Kamil, M. L. (2006). First- and second-language literacy. In D. August & T. Shanahan (Eds.), (2006). *Developing literacy in second-language learners: Report of the National Literacy Panel on Language-Minority Children and Youth* (pp. 197–238). Mahwah, NJ: Lawrence Erlbaum Associates.

Durkin, D. (1978–1979). What classroom observations reveal about reading comprehension instruction. *Reading Research Quarterly, 14,* 481–533.

Elley, W. B. (1988). Vocabulary acquisition from listening to stories. *Reading Research Quarterly, 24,* 174–187.

Farstrup, A., & Samuels, S. J. (2008). *What the research has to say about vocabulary instruction.* Newark, DE: International Reading Association.

Fukkink, R. G., & de Glopper, K. (1998). Effects of instruction in deriving word meaning from context: A meta-analysis. *Review of Educational Research, 68*(4), 450–469.

Graves, M. F. (2006). *The vocabulary book.* New York: Teachers College Press.

Graves, M. F., & Watts-Taffe, S. M. (2002). The place of word consciousness in a research-based vocabulary program. In A. E. Farstrup and S. J. Samuels (Eds.) *What research has to say about reading instruction* (3rd ed., pp. 140–165). Newark, DE: International Reading Association.

Hart, B., & Risley, T. R. (1995). *Meaningful differences in the everyday experience of young American children.* Baltimore: Brookes.

Hiebert, E. H. (2005). In pursuit of an effective, efficient, vocabulary curriculum for elementary students. In E. H. Hiebert & M. Kamil (Eds.), *Teaching and learning vocabulary: Bringing research to practice* (pp. 243–263). Mahwah, NJ: Lawrence Erlbaum Associates.

Hiebert, E. H., & Kamil, M. L. (Eds.) (2005). *Teaching and learning vocabulary: Bringing research to practice.* Mahwah, NJ: Lawrence Erlbaum Associates.

Hiebert, E. H., & Lubliner, S. (2008). The nature, learning, and instruction of general academic vocabulary. In A. E. Farstrup and S. J. Samuels (Eds.), *What research has to say about vocabulary instruction* (pp. 106–129). Newark, DE: International Reading Association.

Hyland, K., & Tse, P. (2007). Is there an academic vocabulary? *TESOL Quarterly, 41*(2), 235–253.

Jitendra, A. K., Edwards, L. L., Sacks, G., & Jacobson, L. A. (2004). What research says about vocabulary instruction for students with learning disabilities. *Exceptional Children, 70,* 299–322.

Karchmer, R. A. (2001). The journey ahead: Thirteen teachers report how the Internet influences literacy and literacy instruction in their K–12 classrooms. *Reading Research Quarterly, 36*(4), 442–466.

Kieffer, M. J., & Lesaux, N. K. (2007). Breaking down words to build meaning: Morphology, vocabulary, and reading comprehension in the urban classroom. *The Reading Teacher, 61*(2), 134–144.

Kieffer, M. J., & Lesaux, N. K. (2008). The role of derivational morphology in the reading comprehension of Spanish-speaking English language learners. *Reading and Writing: An Interdisciplinary Journal, 21*(8), 783–804.

Kim, J. S., & White, T. G. (2008). Scaffolding voluntary summer reading for children in grades 3 to 5: An experimental study. *Scientific Studies of Reading, 12*(1), 1–23.

Koren, S. (1999). Vocabulary instruction through hypertext: Are there advantages over conventional methods of teaching? *Teaching English as a Second or Foreign Language, 4*(1), 1–13.

Labbo, L. D., & Reinking, D. (1999). Negotiating the multiple realities of technology in literacy research and instruction. *Reading Research Quarterly, 34*(4), 478–492.

Lawrence, J., Snow, C. E., & White, C. (2009, April). *Results from year two of word generation.* Paper presented at the annual meeting of the American Educational Research Association, San Diego, CA.

Lubliner, S., & Smetana, L. (2005). The effects of comprehensive vocabulary instruction on Title I students' metacognitive word-learning skills and reading comprehension. *Journal of Literacy Research, 37,* 163–199.

MacArthur, C. A., & Haynes, J. B. (1995). Student assistant for learning from text (SALT): A hypermedia reading aid. *Journal of Learning Disabilities, 28*(3), 50–59.

Malabonga, V., Kenyon, D. M., Carlo, M, August, D., & Louguit, M. (2008). Development of a cognate awareness measure for Spanish-speaking English language learners. *Language Testing,* 25, 495–519.

Marzano, R. J. (2004). *Building background knowledge for academic achievement: Research on what works in schools.* Alexandria, VA: Association for Supervision & Curriculum Development.

McCutchen, D., Logan, B., & Biangardi-Orpe, U. (2009). Making meaning: Childrens' sensitivity to morphological information during word reading. *Reading Research Quarterly, 44,* 360–376.

Mostow, J., Aist, G., Buckhead, P., Corbett, A., Cuneo, A., Eitelman, S., . . . Tobin, B. (2003). Evaluation of an automated reading tutor that listens: Comparison to human tutoring and classroom instruction. *Journal of Educational Computing Research, 29*(1), 61–117.

Nagy, W. E. (2005). Why vocabulary instruction needs to be long-term and comprehensive. In E. H. Hiebert & M. L. Kamil (Eds.), *Teaching and learning vocabulary: Bringing research to practice* (pp. 27–44). Mahwah, NJ: Lawrence Erlbaum Associates.

Nagy, W. (2007). Metalinguistic awareness and the vocabulary-comprehension connection. In R. K. Wager, A. E. Muse, & K. R. Tannenbaum (Eds.), *Vocabulary acquisition: Implications for reading comprehension* (pp. 52–77). New York: Guilford Press.

Nagy, W., Berninger, V. W., & Abbott, R. D. (2006). Contribution of morphology beyond phonology to literacy outcomes of upper elementary and middle-school students. *Journal of Educational Psychology, 98,* 134–147.

Nagy, W., Berninger, V. W., Abbott, R. D., Vaughan, K., & Vermeulen, K. (2003). Relationship of morphology and other language skills to literacy skills in at-risk second-grade readers and at-risk fourth-grade writers. *Journal of Educational Psychology, 95,* 730–742.

Nagy, W. E., & Scott, J. A. (2000). Vocabulary acquisition. In R. Barr, M. L. Kamil, P. B. Mosenthal, & P. D. Pearson (Eds.), *Handbook of reading research* (Vol. 3, pp. 269–284). New York: Longman.

National Reading Panel. (2000). *Report of the National Reading Panel: Teaching children to read.* Washington, DC: National Academy Press.

Ogle, D. (1986). K W L: A teaching model that develops active reading of expository text. *Reading Teacher, 39,* 564–570.

Padak, N., Newton, E., Rasinski, T. & Newton, R. M. (2008). Getting to the root of word study: Teaching Latin and Greek word roots in elementary and middle grades. In A. E. Farstrup & S. J. Samuels (Eds.) *What research has to say about vocabulary instruction* (pp. 6–31). Newark, DE: International Reading Association.

Pawling, E. (1999). Modern languages and CD-ROM based learning. *British Journal of Educational Technology, 30,* 163–176.

Petty, W., Herold, C., & Stohl, E. (1967). *The state of knowledge about the teaching of Vocabulary* (Cooperative Research Project No. 3128). Champaign, IL: National Council of Teachers of English. (ERIC Document Reproduction Service No. ED 012 395)

Proctor, C. P., Dalton, B., & Grisham, D. (2007). Scaffolding English language learners and struggling readers in a universal literacy environment with embedded strategy instruction and vocabulary support. *Journal of Literacy Research, 39,* 71–93.

Proctor, C. P., Uccelli, O., Dalton, B., & Snow, C. (2009). Understanding the depth of vocabulary online with bilingual and monolingual students. *Reading and Writing Quarterly, 25,* 311–333.

Ryder, R. J., & Graves, M. F. (1994). Vocabulary instruction presented prior to reading in two basal readers. *Elementary School Journal, 95,* 139–153.

Scott, J. A., Jamieson-Noel, D., & Asselin, M. (2003). Vocabulary instruction throughout the day in twenty-three Canadian upper-elementary classrooms. *Elementary School Journal, 103,* 269–268.

Scott, J. A., Nagy, W. E., & Flinspach, S. L. (2008). More than merely words: Redefining vocabulary learning in a culturally and linguistically diverse society. In A. E. Farstrup & S. J. Samuels (Eds.), *What research has to say about vocabulary instruction* (pp. 182–210). Newark, DE: International Reading Association.

Slavin, R. E., Lake, C., Chambers, B., Cheung, A., & Davis, S. (2009). Effective reading programs for the elementary grades: A best-evidence synthesis. *Review of Educational Research, 79,* 1391–1466.

Stahl, S., & Fairbanks, M. (1986). The effects of vocabulary instruction: A model-based meta-analysis. *Review of Educational Research, 56,* 72–110.

Swanborn, M. S. L., & de Glopper, K. (1999). Incidental word learning while reading: A meta-analysis. *Review of Educational Research, 69,* 261–285.

Sylvester, R., & Greenidge, W. (2009). Digital storytelling: Extending the potential for struggling writers. *The Reading Teacher, 63*(4), 284–295.

Tan, L., & Guo, L. (2009). From print to critical multimedia literacy: One teacher's foray into new literacies practices. *Journal of Adolescent & Adult Literacy, 53*(4), 315–324.

Townsend, D. (2009). Building academic vocabulary in after-school settings: Games for growth with middle school English-language learners. *Journal of Adolescent and Adult Literacy, 53,* 242–251.

van Kleek, A. V., Stahl, S. A., Bauer, E. B (2003). *On reading storybooks to children: Parents and teachers.* Mahwah, NJ: Erlbaum.

Vaughan, S., Martinez, L. R., Linan-Thompson, S., Reutebach, C. K., Carlson, C. D., & Francis, D. J. (2009). Enhancing social studies vocabulary and comprehension for seventh-grade English language learners: Findings from two experimental studies. *Journal of Research on Educational Effectiveness, 2,* 297–324.

Walsh, K. (2003). Basal readers: The lost opportunity to build the knowledge that propels comprehension. *American Educator, 21*(1), 24–27.

Watts, S. M. (1995). Vocabulary instruction during reading lessons in six classrooms. *Journal of Reading Behavior, 27*(3), 399–424.

Watts-Taffe, S., & Gwinn, C. B. (2007). *Integrating literacy and technology: Effective practice for grades K–6.* New York: Guilford Press.

Maureen McLaughlin

Maureen McLaughlin, EdD, is a professor of reading education and chairperson of the Reading Department at East Stroudsburg University of Pennsylvania. She earned her doctorate in reading and language development at Boston University. Prior to her tenure at the university, McLaughlin spent fifteen years as a classroom teacher, reading specialist, and department chair in a public school system.

McLaughlin served as a member of the board of directors of the International Reading Association from 2005–2008 and received its Outstanding Teacher Educator in Reading Award in 2010. She is the author of numerous publications about the teaching of reading, reading comprehension, and content-area literacies, including *Guided Comprehension in the Primary Grades* and *Guided Comprehension in Grades 3–8.* Her latest book is *Content Area Reading: Teaching and Learning in an Age of Multiple Literacies.*

A frequent speaker at international, national, and state conferences, McLaughlin is a consultant to school districts and universities throughout North America. Her research interests include reading comprehension and critical literacy.

In this chapter, McLaughlin begins with a discussion of theory that addresses constructivist beliefs; the roles of teachers, students, and text; and the nature of comprehension instruction. Next, she explains the Guided Comprehension Model, which connects theory and practice. She then explores critical literacy, an approach that enables readers to comprehend at deeper levels.

Chapter 10

Teaching Reading Comprehension: Theory Into Practice

Maureen McLaughlin

As literacy professionals, we share the common goal of teaching students to become active, strategic readers who successfully comprehend text. Of course, as teachers, we have varied roles in this process. We need to be active readers ourselves. We need to teach students how to activate their background knowledge and motivate them to engage them in reading, writing, and discussion. We also need to explicitly teach students a repertoire of comprehension strategies they can use as needed while reading.

Teaching students how to comprehend is the focus of this chapter. It begins with a discussion of theory that addresses constructivist beliefs; the roles of teachers, students, and text; and the nature of comprehension instruction. Next, I explain the Guided Comprehension Model, which connects theory and practice. Finally, I explore critical literacy, an approach that enables readers to comprehend at deeper levels.

Theory: What Research Has to Say About Reading Comprehension

Reading comprehension has been the focus of renewed interest in the 2000s. A variety of texts that support research-based comprehension practices (for example, Block, Gambrell, & Pressley,

2002; Block & Parris, 2008) and a number of volumes about teaching reading comprehension strategies (such as Harvey & Goudvis, 2007; McLaughlin, 2010, 2011; McLaughlin & Allen, 2009) have been published. Numerous publications explore how readers comprehend online text (Coiro & Dobler, 2007; Coiro, Knobel, Lankshear, & Leu, 2008). This research purports that comprehension is a multifaceted process. Factors such as constructivist beliefs; the roles of teachers, readers, and text; and the type of instruction are important factors in the construction of meaning.

Reading Comprehension as a Constructivist Process

In reading comprehension, constructivism is reflected in schema-based learning development, which suggests that learning takes place when new information is integrated with what is already known. The more experience learners have with a particular topic, the easier it is for them to make connections between what they are learning and what they know (Anderson, 1994, 2004; Anderson & Pearson, 1984). Of course, if students have limited or no background knowledge, teachers can provide it in a variety of ways. For example, they can read related texts aloud, share pictures, visit websites with students, or show video clips.

The social constructivist nature of comprehension suggests that readers refine their understanding by negotiating meaning with others. This typically occurs through discussion. The social nature of constructing meaning reflects Vygotsky's (1978) principle of social mediation.

Online reading comprehension is also constructivist in nature. In that context, students actively create meaning based on their personal paths to inquiry and discovery (El-Hindi, 1998; Schmar-Dobbler, 2003). This conclusion is also supported by researchers' beliefs that online reading comprehension is a problem-based inquiry process (Coiro, Knoebel, Lankshear, & Leu, 2008; Leu, Kinzer, Coiro, & Cammack, 2004).

The Role of Teachers in Comprehension Instruction

Influential teachers are highly valued participants in the reading process. They know the importance of every student having successful literacy experiences. It is the teacher's knowledge that makes a difference in student achievement (International Reading Association, 2000).

The teacher's role in the reading process is to create experiences and environments that introduce, nurture, and extend students' abilities to engage with text. This requires that teachers engage in explicit instruction, which includes modeling, scaffolding, facilitating, and participating (Au & Raphael, 1998).

When using explicit instruction, teachers introduce text by helping students activate their prior knowledge about a given topic, make connections, and set purposes for reading. Explicit instruction involves directly teaching students, often through a multiple-step process that promotes scaffolding. When teachers scaffold instruction, they gradually release responsibility to the students. For example, when teaching students to summarize, teachers may begin by explaining and modeling summarizing. At this point, they provide full support to students. In the next step, teachers may guide students as they summarize in small groups or with partners. In this stage, teachers offer support as needed. Finally, teachers may encourage students to practice summarizing independently. At this point, teachers provide little or no support. As the teachers move from full support to providing support as needed to providing little or no support, students take on more and more responsibility.

> When teachers scaffold instruction, they gradually release responsibility to the students.

Both reading researchers and professional organizations have delineated the characteristics of influential reading teachers (International Reading Association, 2000; Ruddell, 1995, 2004). The following characterization of such reading teachers integrates their ideas.

Influential reading teachers believe that all children can learn. They differentiate instruction and know that motivation and multiple kinds of text are essential elements of teaching and learning. They understand that reading is a social constructivist process that functions best in authentic situations. They teach in print-rich, concept-rich environments.

These teachers have in-depth knowledge of various aspects of literacy, including reading and writing. They teach for a variety of purposes, using diverse methods, materials, and grouping patterns to focus on individual needs, interests, and learning styles. They continually monitor student learning and adjust teaching as needed to ensure the success of all learners. They also understand the strategies good readers use and can teach students how to use them. Influential teachers use strategies that provide formative feedback to monitor the effectiveness of teaching and student performance.

The Role of Readers in the Comprehension Process

Reading researchers have reported that much of what we know about comprehension is based on studies of good readers (Duke & Pearson, 2002; Pressley, 2000). They describe good readers as active participants in the reading process, who constantly monitor the relation between the goals they have set and the text they are reading. They also use a repertoire of comprehension strategies to facilitate the construction of meaning. Researchers believe that using such strategies helps students become metacognitive readers (Palincsar & Brown, 1984; Roehler & Duffy, 1984)—readers who can think about and monitor their own thinking while reading.

Good readers read both narrative and expository texts and have ideas about how to figure out unfamiliar words. They use their knowledge of text structure to efficiently and strategically process text. This knowledge develops from experiences with different genres and is correlated with age or time in school (Goldman & Rakestraw, 2000). These students spontaneously generate questions at different points in the reading process for a variety of reasons. They know that they use questioning in their everyday lives and that it increases their comprehension. These readers are problem solvers who have the ability to discover new information on their own.

Good readers read widely, which provides exposure to various genres and text formats, affords opportunities for strategy use, increases understanding of how words work, provides bases for discussion and meaning negotiation, and accommodates students' interests. They monitor their comprehension and know when they are constructing meaning and when they are not. When comprehension breaks down due to lack of background information, difficulty of words, or unfamiliar text structure, good readers know and use a variety of "fix up" strategies. These include rereading, changing the pace of reading, using context clues, cross-checking cueing systems, and asking for help. These readers are able to select the appropriate strategies and to consistently focus on making sense of text.

The Role of Text in Comprehension Instruction

Students benefit from engaging daily with multiple types and levels of text. Experience in reading multiple genres provides students with knowledge of numerous text structures and improves their text-driven processing (Goldman & Rakestraw, 2000). Transacting with a wide variety of genres—including biography, historical fiction, legends, poetry, and brochures—enhances students' motivation and increases their comprehension (Gambrell, 2001).

When leveled text is used, teachers scaffold learning experiences, and students receive varying levels of support, depending on the purpose and instructional setting. From a reading assessment perspective, we typically think of texts as having three different levels: independent, instructional, and frustration. We provide independent-level or easy text when students are working on their own in literacy centers or on routines. Students can read texts at this level with no teacher support. We use instructional-level text or "just right" text when students are engaged in guided reading. Students can read text at this level with some assistance from the teacher. We do not encourage students to read frustration-level text, but we can share texts at more challenging levels in several ways, including through teacher read-aloud.

The Nature of Reading Comprehension Instruction

Research supports the conclusion that the explicit instruction of comprehension strategies increases students' comprehension (Duke & Pearson, 2002). Explicit instruction typically involves a multiple-step process, during which teachers gradually release responsibility to students. Research suggests that comprehension strategy instruction should begin in primary grades (Hilden & Pressley, 2002; McLaughlin, 2003).

Research also shows that students need different kinds and amounts of reading comprehension instruction (Duke & Pearson, 2002). As teachers, we understand this. We know that we have students of differing capabilities in our classes, and we strive to help them comprehend to the best of their abilities. For many years, we referred to this as "teaching to students' individual needs." Today we describe it as differentiating instruction.

Differentiation enables us to accommodate the diversity of students' needs and create multiple pathways to learning during comprehension instruction (Tyner & Green, 2005). To develop environments that promote differentiated instruction, Gibson and Hasbrouck (2008) suggest that we do the following:

- Embrace collaborative teaching and learning.
- Use explicit strategy instruction.
- Establish consistent routines and procedures.
- Scaffold student learning.
- Increase student engagement.
- Teach students how to learn, as well as what to learn.
- Change the way teaching occurs.

We know that comprehension is a social constructivist process, so it is only logical that inviting students to work in collaborative settings will enrich and refine their understanding. This supports differentiated instruction in a variety of ways. For example, when teachers engage students in guided reading, the students read text at the same level and negotiate meaning with others of similar reading abilities.

Working collaboratively with other teachers enables educators to refine their understanding and expand their knowledge of various students and teaching methods. For example, when classroom teachers collaborate with the teachers of English learners, they may gain a deeper understanding of how to differentiate comprehension instruction for these learners. This may result in the classroom teachers employing instructional techniques the English language teachers recommend. This, in turn, may result in further collaboration with grade-level or content-area teachers.

Explicitly teaching comprehension strategies affords teachers opportunities to observe students in various stages of learning. This knowledge offers further insights into students' interests and abilities, which contributes to differentiation. Engaged readers read widely for enjoyment and are motivated to read for different purposes, use prior knowledge to construct meaning, and participate in social interactions (Baker & Wigfield, 1999). Promoting engagement encourages students to become more active, strategic readers.

> Explicitly teaching comprehension strategies affords teachers opportunities to observe students in various stages of learning.

Teachers can change how instruction occurs by differentiating a number of instructional components to support students as they gain competence and confidence in learning. These include *content*, the information being taught; *process*, the way in which the information is taught; and *product*, how the students demonstrate their learning (Tomlinson, 1999). For example, if we were teaching struggling readers about a topic, such as oceans, we could provide texts and other resources, such as scaffolded outlines, at a variety of levels (content); to support students' learning, we could teach in a variety of settings—whole class, small group, trios, pairs, and individual—and provide support as needed (process); and when demonstrating what students have learned, we could invite them to represent their thinking in a variety of ways—speaking, writing, sketching, dramatizing, singing, and creating projects (product).

Although each of the topics discussed in this section plays a prominent role in the construction of meaning, comprehension instruction is also influenced by other research-based factors. Examples of these include engagement theory (Casey 2008/2009; Guthrie & Wigfield, 1997), context (Cambourne, 2002; Lipson & Wixson, 2009), fluency (Rasinski, 2010; Samuels, 2002), and vocabulary (Blachowicz, Fisher, Ogle, & Watts-Taffe, 2006; Pearson, Hiebert, & Kamil, 2007).

Practice: Teaching Reading Comprehension

The Guided Comprehension Model is a framework for teaching reading comprehension strategies that incorporates explicit instruction, teacher-guided small groups, and independent centers and routines (McLaughlin & Allen, 2009). The delineation of the model demonstrates how various aspects of theory, including differentiated instruction, can be put into practice when teaching comprehension strategies.

Guided Comprehension is a context in which students learn and employ comprehension strategies in a variety of settings using multiple levels and types of text (McLaughlin & Allen, 2009). We know that readers use a repertoire of comprehension strategies when constructing meaning. The strategies featured in the Guided Comprehension Model (McLaughlin & Allen, 2009) include the following:

- Previewing—Activating background knowledge, predicting, and setting purposes for reading

- Self-questioning—Generating questions to guide reading

- Making connections—Relating reading to self, text, and others

- Visualizing—Creating mental pictures while reading

- Knowing how words work—Understanding words through strategic vocabulary development, including the use of graphophonic, syntactic, and semantic cueing systems to figure out unknown words

- Monitoring—Asking, "Does this make sense?" and adapting strategic processes to accommodate the response

- Summarizing—Synthesizing important ideas

- Evaluating—Making judgments about text content and author's craft

Guided Comprehension is a three-stage process focused on explicit instruction, application, and reflection. In stage one, teachers explicitly instruct students in a whole-group setting using a five-step process: explain, demonstrate, guide, practice, and reflect. In stage two, students apply the strategies in three settings: teacher-guided small groups, student-facilitated comprehension centers, and student-facilitated comprehension routines. Students' placement in the small groups is dynamic and evolves as their reading abilities increase. Students also have access to a variety of leveled texts in the centers and routines. In stage three, teachers and students engage in reflection and goal setting.

The Guided Comprehension Model is designed to help teachers and students think through reading as a strategy-based process. The research-based model integrates the following:

- Explicit instruction of comprehension strategies

- Leveled texts

- Dynamic assessment

> The Guided Comprehension Model is designed to help teachers and students think through reading as a strategy-based process.

- Scaffolded instruction (varying levels of teacher support, with gradual release of responsibility to students)

- Various genres and text types

- Reading, writing, and discussion

- Strategy instruction and application in a variety of settings

- Guided practice, independent practice, and transfer of learning in multiple settings

- Reflection and goal setting

The model progresses from explicit teaching to independent practice and transfer. Reflection is prevalent in all stages, and informal assessment permeates every aspect of the model, facilitating the gathering of information about student progress and continually informing teaching and learning.

Differentiation of instruction occurs in multiple ways in Guided Comprehension. For example, in the content of the lessons, students use leveled texts to accommodate their abilities. This provides students of all reading levels with access to information about a given topic. Further, the process of teaching—the way the information is taught—is varied to accommodate students' needs. For example, teachers may supplement content with visual cues, such as pictures or video clips, to accommodate students who are English learners. Finally, the products that represent students' understanding vary in Guided

Comprehension. Discussion and written response are often thought of as typical modes of representation, but in Guided Comprehension, students also have opportunities to sketch, sing, dramatize, integrate technology, and create projects to represent their thinking.

The Stages of Guided Comprehension

There are three stages in the Guided Comprehension Model. Stage one focuses on explicit comprehension instruction. Stage two provides opportunities to practice comprehension strategies in three settings: teacher-guided small groups, Guided Comprehension centers, and routines. Stage three involves teacher-facilitated whole-group reflection and goal setting: reflecting on performance, sharing products, and setting new goals.

Stage one: explicit instruction. This stage features a five-step process for explicit strategy instruction. Explicit instruction typically occurs in a whole-class setting, because all students need to learn how to use the strategies. On occasion, explicit instruction takes place in small groups. For example, teachers might choose to explicitly teach the strategies to a small group of English learners or struggling readers before teaching them to the whole group. This would enable those students to have prior knowledge of the strategies when they were being taught to the whole class.

Types and levels of text vary in this stage. The texts selected need to be engaging and work well when demonstrating particular strategies. The level of the texts used in this stage varies because the teacher is doing the reading. Texts the teacher reads may range from an independent or easy level to more challenging levels. During explicit instruction, students receive full teacher support as the teacher reads, explains, and demonstrates. The teacher engages in scaffolding—the gradual release of responsibility—during the *guide* and *practice* steps. The following details the five steps of explicit instruction.

1. Explain the strategy. Focus on how the strategy works and how it contributes to comprehension. Invite students to make connections to their background knowledge. For example, when introducing self-questioning, explain the strategy, describe the process, and provide an example. Next, ask students how they use questioning in their lives to help make connections to their background knowledge. This creates a contextual framework for the strategy. During this step, explain to the students the strategy application that will help them learn how to use the strategy. For example, if we are using Question-Answer Relationships (QAR) (Raphael, 1986) to teach the students how to engage in self-questioning, we will explain that strategy application at this point.

2. *Demonstrate the strategy.* Demonstrate strategies by reading a selection aloud and using a think-aloud (Davey, 1983) and a visual to share ideas with students. Begin by introducing the text and encouraging them to make connections. While thinking aloud, orally explain precisely what is triggering your thoughts and how it is affecting your understanding. This often leads to the development of personal connections, questions for clarification, and refined predictions. When using a think-aloud to demonstrate strategies, explain your thinking so students have a clear idea of the cognitively active process readers experience as they transact with text. For example, when demonstrating self-questioning, teachers can read a section of text and think aloud about the questions they generate to guide their reading. They can state the questions, explain how the ideas occurred, and share the responses that are predicted. If the strategy requires a written or sketched response, also model that during this step. For example, when using QAR, students may orally respond or complete a response form, so demonstrate how to do both during this time.

3. *Guide students to apply the strategy.* Read the next section of the text aloud, and invite students to work with partners to apply the strategy just demonstrated. For example, if we explained and demonstrated self-questioning and QAR, we would then read aloud a portion of the text and guide students to work with partners to generate different types of questions related to the text. Next, we would discuss the questions the paired students created and read aloud another section of text.

4. *Practice the strategy.* Monitor as students work independently to practice the strategy within the whole-group setting. Continue reading segments of the text with reduced teacher support, or invite the students to read independent-level text on their

own. In either case, the students independently use the strategy, which in this case is self-questioning. During this step, differentiate instruction by providing additional scaffolding for those students who need more support and by releasing the task to those students who are ready to use it. The goal is to ensure that students know the strategy and the process for using it. Ultimately, the students develop a repertoire of strategies that they can use as needed when they are reading on their own.

5. *Reflect on strategy use.* Encourage students to reflect on how using the strategy helped them understand the text. Invite students to share their reflections in small groups or with the whole class. Finally, discuss how they can use the strategy when they are reading on their own.

Throughout stage one of Guided Comprehension, students' learning is scaffolded. When students learn how the strategy works and experience a demonstration, they have our total support. When they engage in guided practice, they have our support as necessary. When they apply the strategy independently in the practice step, our support is reduced and the students are in control. We also use multiple authentic assessments in this stage. These include observation, discussion, sketching, and informal writing.

We can use explicit instruction to teach our students a wide variety of strategy applications, including the concept of definition map (Schwartz & Raphael, 1985), K-W-L (Ogle, 1986), and Bookmark Technique (McLaughlin & Allen, 2009). Procedures such as these provide students with numerous opportunities to learn and use comprehension strategies as they think their way through text.

Stage two: teacher-guided small groups and student-facilitated centers and routines. Once the small groups are formed according to approximate reading levels and the appropriate text is matched to students' abilities, the teacher meets with one or more guided small groups every day. During this time, students practice using comprehension strategies while reading instructional-level or just-right text. These books are at the students' approximate reading levels as determined by running records or similar assessments. In this setting, students receive support as needed from the teacher. The goal is for students to read the text silently, although younger students may whisper read. During this step, teachers also complete running records when students appear able to move to a different level. Teachers can conduct informal fluency checks by inviting individual students to whisper read a segment of text. During this part of stage two, teachers use the following four-part small-group format.

1. Review the strategy. Review previously taught strategies, and focus on the strategy taught in stage one. Introduce the text, provide an overview of the text structure, and focus on essential vocabulary.

2. Guide students to apply the strategy. Guide the students to apply the strategy taught in stage one, as well as previously taught strategies, as they read a section of the instructional-level text. Begin by introducing the text and encouraging students to make connections. Prompt the students to construct personal meanings. Incorporate word study as needed. Scaffold as necessary, gradually releasing support as students become more proficient. Encourage discussion and repeat this process with other sections of text.

3. Practice the strategy. Practice by inviting students to work in pairs or individually to apply the strategies as they read sections of the text (silently or in whisper tones). Encourage students to record their thinking in their Guided Comprehension journals or on graphic organizers.

4. Reflect on strategy use. Reflect by inviting students to share ways in which the strategies helped them understand the text. Discuss the text and ways in which the students can apply the strategies when reading independently in the comprehension centers and routines.

When students are not in a guided reading group, they work in student-facilitated comprehension centers or routines. In these settings, teachers differentiate texts by providing a variety of levels to accommodate students' independent or easy reading levels. This means students can read the texts without teacher assistance. Products are also often differentiated, encouraging students to complete tasks of varying levels of complexity using a variety of modes of representation.

Comprehension centers provide purposeful, authentic settings for students to integrate and apply comprehension strategies. Students may work in small groups, with partners, or on their own when they are engaged in the centers. Students also practice their comprehension strategies while participating in comprehension routines. Comprehension routines are habits of thinking and organizing that facilitate reading and response in authentic contexts. Examples of these include literature circles and cross-age reading experiences. These are independent settings. This implies that students are knowledgeable about the strategies and routines, are provided with texts at their independent levels, and have ample time for practicing and transferring these processes.

Stage three: teacher-facilitated whole-group reflection and goal setting. In stage three of the Guided Comprehension Model, the students gather to reflect on the comprehension strategies they have learned, how they used the strategies to understand text, and how well they can use the strategies independently. This stage follows a three-step process: share, reflect, and set new goals.

When students share, they typically meet in small groups, trios, or pairs to show and discuss strategy applications, writing, and projects they created during the lessons. Then students are invited to share some examples with the whole class. Next, students reflect on what they have learned about using strategies and how they will continue to use them in their reading. Finally, the students discuss whether the current goals have been met and set new goals as necessary.

The ultimate goal of Guided Comprehension is to help students develop a repertoire of strategies they can use as needed when reading. In this model, explicit instruction, guided and independent practice, and numerous opportunities for engagement support student learning.

Comprehending at Deeper Levels

Current thinking about reading suggests that in addition to strategy instruction, we should teach our students to comprehend at deeper levels—levels that require readers to understand beyond the information on the printed page and to critically analyze the author's message (Luke & Freebody, 1999; McLaughlin & DeVoogd, 2004, 2011; Serafini, 2003.) In *critical literacy*, an approach that promotes deeper comprehension, readers are active participants in the reading process. They move beyond passively accepting the text's message to question, examine, or dispute the power relations that exist between readers and authors. Critical readers ponder what the author wants them to believe, take action, and promote fairness between people. Critical literacy focuses on the problem and its complexity. It addresses issues of power and promotes reflection, action, and transformation (Freire, 1970).

> Critical readers ponder what the author wants them to believe, take action, and promote fairness between people.

Reading from a critical perspective involves thinking beyond the text to understand such issues as why the author wrote about a particular topic, why he or she wrote from a particular perspective, and why some ideas about the topic were included and others were not. For example, to demonstrate reading from a critical approach to students who are learning about World War II, we could invite the students to engage in the juxtapositioning of texts. Students could read a variety of novels or expository texts that represent different perspectives in discussion circles. Viewpoints might include the following: victims of the Holocaust, victims of the Japanese American internment, soldiers from countries that fought in the war, American and Japanese survivors of the bombing of Pearl Harbor, and political leaders such as Winston Churchill. Students in each group would read about and discuss one perspective and then share what they have learned with the class through a method of their choosing. Following that, everyone would discuss the multiple perspectives, question each viewpoint, and take action based on what they have learned.

Becoming critically literate means that we do not passively accept information imparted by others, but rather question the source of the ideas and examine who is represented and who is marginalized. Then we take action. When we consider the vast amount of information to which today's students have access, we realize that they, too, need to question. They need, as Pearson (2001) notes, to comprehend with a critical edge.

Working to ensure that students understand what they read and can, in fact, comprehend at deeper levels is a noble goal for every literacy professional. As we know ever so well, it will take time and effort to make such a goal a reality, but in the end, it will be wonderfully rewarding to observe our students comprehending to their greatest potentials.

References and Resources

Anderson, R. C. (1994). Role of reader's schema in comprehension, learning, and memory. In R. B. Ruddell, M. R. Ruddell, & H. Singer (Eds.), *Theoretical models and processes of reading* (4th ed., pp. 469–482). Newark, DE: International Reading Association.

Anderson, R. C. (2004). Role of reader's schema in comprehension, learning, and memory. In R. B. Ruddell, M. R. Ruddell, & H. Singer (Eds.), *Theoretical models and processes of reading* (5th ed., pp. 594–606). Newark, DE: International Reading Association.

Anderson, R. C., & Pearson, P. D. (1984). A schema-theoretic view of basic processes in reading comprehension. In P. D. Pearson, R. Barr, M. L. Kamil, & P. Mosenthal (Eds.), *Handbook of reading research* (pp. 225–253). New York: Longman.

Au, K. H., & Raphael, T. E. (1998). Curriculum and teaching in literature-based programs. In T. E. Raphael & K. H. Au (Eds.), *Literature-based instruction: Reshaping the curriculum* (pp. 123–148). Norwood, MA: Christopher-Gordon.

Baker, L., & Wigfield, A. (1999). Dimensions of children's motivation for reading and their relations to reading activity and reading achievement. *Reading Research Quarterly, 34,* 452–481.

Blachowicz, C. L., Fisher, P., Ogle, D. M., & Watts-Taffe, S. (2006). Vocabulary: Questions from the classroom. *Reading Research Quarterly, 41*(4), 524–539.

Block, C. C., Gambrell, L. B., & Pressley, M. (2002). *Improving comprehension instruction: Rethinking research, theory, and classroom practice.* San Francisco: Jossey-Bass.

Block, C. C., & Parris, S. R. (2008). *Comprehension instruction: Research-based practices* (2nd ed.). New York: Guilford Press.

Cambourne, B. (2002). Holistic, integrated approaches to reading and language arts instruction: The constructivist framework of an instructional theory. In A. E. Farstrup & S. J. Samuels (Eds.), *What research has to say about reading instruction* (3rd ed., pp. 25–47). Newark, DE: International Reading Association.

Casey, H. K. (2008/2009). Engaging the disengaged: Using learning clubs to motivate struggling adolescent readers and writers. *Journal of Adolescent & Adult Literacy, 52*(4), 284–294.

Coiro, J., & Dobler, E. (2007). Exploring the online reading comprehension strategies used by sixth-grade skilled readers to search for and locate information on the Internet. *Reading Research Quarterly, 42,* 214–257.

Coiro, J., Knobel, M., Lankshear, C., & Leu, D. J. (2008). *Handbook of research on new literacies.* Mahwah, NJ: Erlbaum.

Davey, B. (1983). Think-aloud—demonstrating the cognitive processes of reading comprehension. *Journal of Reading, 27,* 44–47.

Duke, N. K., & Pearson, P. D. (2002). Effective practices for developing reading comprehension. In A. E. Farstrup & S. J. Samuels (Eds.), *What research has to say about reading instruction* (3rd ed., pp. 205–242). Newark, DE: International Reading Association.

El-Hindi, A. E. (1998). Beyond classroom boundaries: Constructivist teaching with the Internet. *The Reading Teacher, 51*(8), 694–700.

Freire, P. (1970). *Pedagogy of the oppressed.* New York: Continuum.

Gambrell, L. B. (2001). *It's not either/or but more: Balancing narrative and informational text to improve reading comprehension.* Paper presented at the forty-sixth annual Convention of the International Reading Association, New Orleans, LA.

Gibson, V., & Hasbrouck, J. (2008). *Differentiated instruction: Grouping for success.* New York: McGraw-Hill.

Goldman, S. R., & Rakestraw, J. A. (2000). Structural aspects of constructing meaning from text. In M. L. Kamil, P. D. Pearson, & R. Barr (Eds.), *Handbook of reading research: Vol. 3* (pp. 311–335). Mahwah, NJ: Lawrence Erlbaum Associates.

Guthrie, J. T., & Wigfield, A. (Eds.). (1997). *Reading engagement: Motivating readers through integrated instruction.* Newark, DE: International Reading Association.

Harvey, S., & Goudvis, A. (2007). *Strategies that work: Teaching comprehension for understanding and engagement.* York, ME: Stenhouse.

Hilden, K., & Pressley, M. (2002, December). *Can teachers become comprehension strategies teachers given a small amount of training?* Paper presented at the fifty-second annual meeting of the National Reading Conference, Miami, FL.

International Reading Association. (2000). *Excellent reading teachers: A position statement of the International Reading Association.* Newark, DE: Author.

Leu, D. J., & Kinzer, C. K. (2000). The convergence of literacy instruction with networked technologies for information and communication. *Reading Research Quarterly, 35*(1), 108–127.

Leu, D. J., Kinzer, C. K., Coiro, J. L., & Cammack, D. W. (2004). Toward a theory of new literacies emerging from the Internet and other information and communication technologies. In R. B. Ruddell & N. J. Unrau (Eds.), *Theoretical models and processes of reading* (5th ed., pp. 1570–1613). Newark, DE: International Reading Association.

Lipson, M. Y., & Wixson, K. K. (2009). *Assessment and instruction of reading and writing difficulties: An interactive approach* (4th ed.). Boston: Allyn & Bacon.

Luke, A., & Freebody, P. (1999, August). Further notes on the four resources model. *Reading Online.* Accessed at www.readingonline.org/research/lukefreebody .html on September 26, 2010.

McLaughlin, M. (2003). *Guided Comprehension in the primary grades: A framework for curricularizing strategy instruction.* Paper presented at the fifty-third annual meeting of the National Reading Conference, Scottsdale, AZ.

McLaughlin, M. (2010). *Content area reading: Teaching and learning in an age of multiple literacies.* Boston: Allyn & Bacon.

McLaughlin, M. (2011). *Guided Comprehension in the primary grades* (2nd ed.). Newark, DE: International Reading Association.

McLaughlin, M., & Allen, M. B. (2009). *Guided Comprehension in grades 3–8* (2nd ed.). Newark, DE: International Reading Association.

McLaughlin, M., & DeVoogd, G. (2004). *Critical literacy: Enhancing students' reading comprehension.* New York: Scholastic.

McLaughlin, M., & DeVoogd, G. (2011). Critical literacy as comprehension: Understanding at deeper levels. In D. Lapp & D. Fisher (Eds.), *The handbook of research on teaching the English language arts* (3rd ed., pp. 278–282). New York: Routledge.

Ogle, D. (1986). K-W-L: A teaching model that develops active reading of expository text. *The Reading Teacher, 39,* 564–570.

Palincsar, A. S., & Brown, A. L. (1984). Reciprocal teaching of comprehension-fostering and monitoring activities. *Cognition and Instruction, 1,* 117–175.

Pearson, P. D. (2001, February). *Comprehension strategy instruction: An idea whose time has come again.* Paper presented at the annual meeting of the Colorado Council of the International Reading Association, Denver, CO.

Pearson, P. D., Hiebert, E. H., & Kamil, M. L. (2007). Vocabulary assessment: What we know and what we need to learn. *Reading Research Quarterly, 42*(2), 282–296.

Pressley, M. (2000). What should comprehension instruction be the instruction of? In M. L. Kamil, P. B. Mosenthal, P. D. Pearson, & R. Barr (Eds.), *Handbook of reading research: Vol. 3* (pp. 545–561). Mahwah, NJ: Erlbaum.

Pressley, M. (2006, April). *What the future of reading research could be.* Paper presented at the International Reading Association Reading Research Conference, Chicago.

Raphael, T. (1986). Teaching children question-answer relationships, revisited. *The Reading Teacher, 39,* 516–522.

Rasinski, T. V. (2010). *The fluent reader: Oral and silent reading strategies for building fluency, word recognition, and comprehension* (2nd ed.). New York: Scholastic.

Roehler, L. R., & Duffy, G. G. (1984). Direct explanation of comprehension processes. In G. G. Duffy, L. R. Roehler, & J. Mason (Eds.), *Comprehension instruction: Perspectives and suggestions* (pp. 265–280). New York: Longman.

Ruddell, R. B. (1995). Those influential literacy teachers: Meaning negotiators and motivation builders. *The Reading Teacher, 48,* 454–463.

Ruddell, R. B. (2004). Researching the influential literacy teacher: Characteristics, beliefs, strategies, and new research directions. In R. B. Ruddell & N. J. Unrau (Eds.), *Theoretical models and processes of reading* (5th ed., pp. 979–997). Newark, DE: International Reading Association.

Samuels, S. J. (2002). Reading fluency: Its development and assessment. In A. E. Farstrup & S. J. Samuels (Eds.), *What research has to say about reading instruction* (3rd ed., pp. 166–183). Newark, DE: International Reading Association.

Schmar-Dobler, E. (2003). Reading on the Internet: The link between literacy and technology. *Journal of Adolescent and Adult Literacy, 47*(1), 80–85.

Schwartz, R., & Raphael, T. (1985). Concept of definition: A key to improving students' vocabulary. *The Reading Teacher, 39,* 198–205.

Serafini, F. (2003). Informing our practice: Modernist, transactional, and critical perspectives on children's literature and reading instruction. *Reading Online, 6*(6). Accessed at www.readingonline.org/articles/art_index.asp?HREF=serafini/index.html on September 27, 2010.

Tomlinson, C. A. (1999). *The differentiated classroom: Responding to the needs of all learners.* Alexandria, VA: Association for Supervision and Curriculum Development.

Tyner, B., & Green, S. E. (2005). *Small-group reading instruction: A differentiated model for intermediate readers, grades 3–8.* Newark, DE: International Reading Association.

Vygotsky, L. S. (1978). *Mind in society: The development of higher psychological processes* (M. Cole, V. John-Steiner, S. Scribner, & E. Souberman, Eds.). Cambridge, MA: Harvard University Press. (Original work published 1934)

Ruth Culham

Ruth Culham, EdD, began her career as a K–8 librarian before teaching grades 5–9, when she fell in love with teaching middle school students and was named Montana English Teacher of the Year. Culham also worked as a researcher and then a unit manager of the Assessment Program at Education Northwest.

The success of her book *6+1 Traits of Writing: The Complete Guide for Grades 3 and Up* opened the door to founding the Culham Writing Company, where she continues to write best-selling books and materials while conducting staff development on the traits of writing model. She also authored two award-winning staff development video series. She is the author of fourteen books, the most recent of which won the 2011 Teacher's Choice Award, and many related materials. She is currently authoring a new writing program—*Traits Complete*—for grades K–8.

In this chapter, Culham examines the writing-reading connection. She advocates the use of mentor texts in teaching writing. She then names the six traits of good writing, providing definitions, key qualities, and questions for teachers to ask themselves as they identify mentor texts to model the traits. She also suggests favorite authors of mentor texts for each trait.

Chapter 11

Reading With a Writer's Eye

Ruth Culham

There they were: nineteen ninth graders suited up for the first home football game, squeezed awkwardly into their seats for my seventh-period English class. "Put your helmets on your desks," I instructed, wondering how I was going to make it through the next testosterone-charged forty-five minutes. Surely the last thing on these young men's minds was writing.

There must have been some wisdom in scheduling the entire football team into the same English class at the end of the day. I just had no idea what it was. This group was a challenge to motivate on a typical day, so it was going to take superhuman powers to pull off something good—even sorta good—on a game day.

After several unsuccessful attempts to engage students with paired readings, a routine activity for writing workshop, I grabbed a treasured book from my shelf—an autographed copy of *Kavik the Wolf Dog* by Walt Morey—and I asked the students to suspend their writing for the moment. "Just listen," I said, hoping the book would do what I could not—focus and inspire my class. I began to read from chapter 1:

> Charlie One Eye lifted the squirming pup by the scruff of the neck, and looked at him. His careless grip pinched the pup's tender skin, and he wriggled and whimpered in protest. But the man studied him with no concern. The whimper turned

to a growl. Suddenly the pup twisted his head and sank tiny needle-sharp teeth in Charlie's thumb. (p. 1)

I read on. With each sentence, the mood became energized, like the feeling at a home game after a first-blood score. Motion ceased. Students who'd been squirming in their seats sat transfixed, hands gently wrapped around the top of their helmets, listening. Walt Morey accomplished more in five minutes than I'd been able to accomplish in twenty-five.

So I read on until the final bell. Though that was the sound my students had been living for just forty-five minutes earlier, they lingered a moment before Tracy broke the spell to ask, "Will you read more tomorrow?" I nodded, "Of course." And then suddenly he and his teammates were gone—leaving a tangle of chairs and desks as they chest-butted their way out the door.

Now this story by itself might be useful to extol the virtues of reading aloud to even the most reluctant students, or to illustrate how to survive a challenging teaching situation. What happened over the next week was what really mattered and sticks with me to this day. As I continued to read aloud a little every day, qualities of Walt Morey's writing began showing up in students' work. Students who never tried a lively introduction came up with some gems. Those who had trouble creating insightful details were churning them out right and left. A student who rarely wrote more than a sentence or two shared a whole page at the next writing circle. Everyone, it seemed, was writing under the influence of Walt Morey. Everyone was a noticeably better writer from having a front-row seat to his work.

Until then, I didn't understand the extent of the relationship between reading and teaching writing. I knew that students of all ages appreciate being read to. I knew they would agree to do disagreeable tasks if I rewarded them with more read-aloud time. I knew that even my most fidgety students would sit still and listen, soaking in the rhythm and cadence of well-written prose. But it didn't occur to me that reading aloud was "teaching" them something. If the kids liked it, and I liked doing it, that was enough. I took great pains to make sure my principal and colleagues didn't know just how much reading aloud I was doing. I wanted them to believe that what went on behind my closed doors was more rigorous and academic.

Today I know better. I know reading aloud is rigorous and academic. Some of the best teaching involves nothing more than a great book and a captive audience. There was a reason the freshman football players sat mesmerized by Walt Morey's words. They were learning how writing works—how it should open, how it should unfold, and what chords it should strike to fully engage readers. Resolute in this new understanding, I'd now encourage my principal and fellow teachers to watch my students fall under the spell of a great writer as I read aloud and how simple it is to use their words to teach. And I'd challenge them to read aloud their own favorite books any time they wanted to do a really good job teaching writing.

What the Research Says About the Writing-Reading Connection

> *Writing—the art of communicating thoughts to the mind—is the great invention of the world. . . . Great, very great, in enabling us to converse with the head, the absent, and the unborn, at all distances of time and space, and great not only in its direct benefits, but its great help to all other inventions.*
>
> —Abraham Lincoln

Thanks in great measure to research summaries about writing in recent years, such as *The Neglected "R": The Need for a Writing Revolution* (National Commission on Writing in American's Schools and Colleges, 2003), *Because Writing Matters* (National Writing Project & Nagin, 2004), and *Writing Next: Effective Strategies to Improve Writing of Adolescents in Middle and High Schools* (Graham & Perrin, 2007), we have volumes of reasons to accept writing as an essential communication tool and improving writing instruction as an essential task in schools. My freshman students were typical, it seems. Until they were inspired by the work of Walt Morey and the other writers they came to know, they weren't learning how to write because they didn't understand the importance of learning to write—and neither did I.

The importance of learning to write has since been explained and is best summed up by the National Commission on Writing in its 2003 report, *The Neglected "R"*: "American education will never realize its potential as an engine of opportunity and economic growth until a writing revolution puts language and communication in their proper place in the classroom. Writing is how students connect the dots in their knowledge" (p. 1). The report continues, "If students are to make knowledge their own, they must struggle with the details, wrestle with the facts, and rework raw information and dimly understood concepts into language they can communicate to someone else. In short, if students are to learn, they must write" (p. 9).

One of the most logical places to inspire that writing is through the reading students do in and out of class. In *Because Writing Matters* from the National Writing Project (2004), the authors address the reading-and-writing connection by citing the work of Gail E. Tompkins from *Literacy for the Twenty-First Century: A Balanced Approach* (2001). Tompkins argues that there are three reasons the two disciplines support each other: "(1) readers and writers use the same intellectual strategies, (2) the reading and writing processes are similar, and (3) children use many of the same skills in both reading and writing" (pp. 31–32). This well-documented report concludes that teaching reading and writing, blending one with the other, is fundamental to developing strong literacy skills.

The authors of the report *Writing Next*, Steve Graham and Dolores Perin (2007), also acknowledge the pivotal relationship between reading and writing. They present eleven essential elements to help students learn critical writing literacy skills. Number ten on their list is "study of models," which urges teachers to provide students with opportunities to read, analyze, and emulate models of good writing. Not only does their research support the use of reading to improve writing, it suggests a very specific way to accomplish that: using models. They state, "Students are encouraged to analyze these examples and to emulate the critical elements, patterns, and forms embodied in the models in their own writing" (p. 20). Models, whether they are fiction or nonfiction, print or

> Models, whether they are fiction or nonfiction, print or electronic, are what students should be turning to for examples of what good writing looks like in its many forms.

electronic, are what students should be turning to for examples of what good writing looks like in its many forms.

The fact that reading is crucial to improving writing is not a startling new discovery. Researcher Frank Smith (1994) noted, "Reading like a writer is collaborative learning, even though it might appear that the reader is alone. But reading like a writer means reading with the author, as if one were writing the text oneself" (pp. 195–196). In other words, the reader positions him- or herself to sit beside the author and study how the text is constructed and how it communicates. And there is no limit to the number of authors, past or present, from which we can choose to help us teach. Smith continues:

> Authors—even dead ones—have this tremendous advantage over live teachers; they always proceed at the pace of the individual learner, and are able to repeat their lessons as often as the learner wants, without any coercion, embarrassment or punitive threat. (Teachers have other important responsibilities, like encouraging learners to see themselves as writers, demonstrating how members of the writers' club engage in club activities, and putting apprentice writers in the company of authors). (p. 196)

Francine Prose (2007) echoes this belief when she writes about the connection between reading and writing, drawing from her own experience as a seasoned pro at both:

> Like most—maybe all—writers, I learned to write by writing, and, by example, by reading books. Long before the idea of a writer's conference was a glimmer in anyone's eye, writers learned by reading the work of their predecessors. They studied meter with Ovid, plot construction with Homer, comedy with Aristophanes; they honed their prose style by absorbing the lucid sentences of Montaigne and Samuel Johnson. And who could have asked for better teachers: generous, uncritical, blessed with wisdom and genius, as endless forgiving as only the dead can be? (pp. 2–3)

Writers use reading for inspiration. They mine their reading, and as they sluice the sludge from gold and precious gemstones, they use what they discover to adorn their own writing. How else

Writers use reading for inspiration. They mine their reading, and as they sluice the sludge from gold and precious gemstones, they use what they discover to adorn their own writing.

can writers come up with an idea, choose a structure to showcase that idea, arrive at the right tone, apply a rich vocabulary, craft good sentences, and use conventions to clarify and deepen meaning? Katie Wood Ray (1999) aptly points out that "really good writers can imagine all kinds of things to do with text, and this imagination comes from their sense of craft, a sense garnered over time from reading like writers and from writing themselves—trying out the crafts they have come to understand" (p. 48). She emphasizes, "Writing well involves learning to attend to the craft of writing, learning to do the sophisticated work of separating what it's about from how it is written" (p. 10). It is this very process of sorting out how language works that makes reading such a powerful tool in the teaching of writing.

How Mentor Texts Help Us Put Research Into Practice

Researcher Pilar Duran Escribano (1999) explains, "Reading puts the learner in touch with other minds so that he can experience the ways in which writers have organized information, selected words and structured arguments" (p. 62). We use these texts to show students the way. They are our co-teachers in the classroom. Lynne Dorfman and Rose Cappelli (2007), authors of *Mentor Texts: Teaching Writing Through Children's Literature, K–6,* define mentor texts as "pieces of literature that we can return to again and again as we help our young writers learn how to do what they may not yet be able to do on their own" (p. 2). How remarkable to contemplate using favorite texts over and over, learning more from them at every read. Perhaps this is why every August for the past twenty-eight years, I pull out my copy of *To Kill a Mockingbird,* and read it again. It's still teaching me.

So where do we find these mentor texts? The answer is simple: everywhere. Mentor texts can be found in good classrooms and beyond. Newspapers, magazines, signs, play lists, menus, brochures, forms, directions, and letters are good candidates, as are electronic forms of text. Finding the right texts requires learning how to see reading through the eyes of the writer and matching the needs of the writer to the strengths of the text.

Donald Hall and Donald Emblen (1994), two renowned poets, writers, and writing teachers, might say it best: "Reading well precedes writing well. Of all the ancestors claimed by a fine piece of prose, the most important is the prose from which the writer learned his craft. Writers learn craft not by memorizing rules about restrictive clauses, but by striving to equal a standard formed from reading" (p. xxi).

> Mentor texts can be found in good classrooms and beyond. . . . Finding the right texts requires learning how to see reading through the eyes of the writer and matching the needs of the writer to the strengths of the text.

As I discovered when I observed the influence of Walt Morey's work on my students, the mentor text motivates, inspires, and gives students the courage to write. Writing is not for the faint of heart. It's hard to write well. It's a challenge to know what to say and how to say it clearly, and it takes courage. But it's important because, as Frank Smith (1994) so wisely notes:

> Not only can a piece of writing communicate thought from writer to reader, but also the act of writing can tell the author things that were not known (or not known to be known) before the writing began. Thus we might build a boat to learn more about how boats are built, or climb a hill without knowing in advance the view that will be attained or even the route that we will be able to take. Writing can extend both our imagination and our understanding. (p. 1)

Students of every age need opportunities to learn from their writing, too.

Mentor Texts and the Traits of Writing

We are cups, constantly and quietly being filled. The trick is, knowing how to tip ourselves over and let the beautiful stuff out.

—Ray Bradbury

Noticing what a professional writer does, naming it, and showing students how to do it in their own work are essential to their success. Good writing happens over time, with lots of practice, lots of support, and lots of models. The traits (ideas, organization, voice, word choice, sentence fluency, and conventions) give you the language to move students forward, step by step. Mentor texts give you the fuel to keep them going. It's a perfect match.

The traits are an assessment model that, over twenty years of development and implementation, has found its way into the lexicon of many, many writing teachers. Acknowledging that using a shared vocabulary can be helpful across the grades and over time, these teachers find the traits easy to understand and blend into their writing program—be it highly structured or more informal.

In trait-based classrooms, students learn what ideas, organization, voice, word choice, sentence fluency, and conventions are and how they appear in their own and other's work. Good teachers begin with simple examples, such as a step-by-step list to teach primary writers about organization, for instance, and build to more complex and thoughtful examples, such as an essay based on deductive logic to teach secondary writers. Teachers use the traits to select mentor texts so students marinate in rich materials that will, in turn, inspire good writing.

First conceived as an assessment model, the traits have proven to be much more. Because the traits are known to many teachers and well documented (Arter, Spandel, Culham & Pollard, 1994), their use in instruction became the next logical application. Students learn which areas in their writing need the most attention from the assessment. Then they can turn to mentor texts to see the moves authors made in those areas and make changes in their own writing.

Though the traits allow us to look analytically at different qualities of writing, teaching a trait is still a big instructional challenge. It's hard to imagine, for instance, how a teacher might teach "ideas." It's a huge conceptual task at any grade. However, it is possible to teach students how to find a topic or focus the topic so it is narrow and manageable by showing them how an author accomplishes these difficult writing moves in published texts. In Gordon Korman's hilarious book *No More Dead Dogs* (2002), he takes his big idea— students who don't want to write on an assigned topic—and spins it out in a clever, original story that focuses on the actions of one student and his teacher.

Imagine the daunting task of teaching students how to organize text. Now imagine how much easier it would be to teach students about different nonfiction text types by examining how the author of *Scaredy Squirrel* (2006), picture-book author Melanie Watt, constructs her writing using various different nonfiction text structures such as lists, schedules, and comparison-contrast charts. Students see examples of different organizational formats and can try applying them in their own writing.

The secret to teaching writing turns out to be breaking the traits into smaller, more manageable parts and finding strong examples of what each part looks like as it appears in fiction and nonfiction texts. These parts are called "key qualities," and every trait has four that are easy to understand and easy to teach. Specific lessons that zero in on different aspects of each trait make teaching writing more systematic and helpful for student writers. If students are taught the key qualities of the traits each year, they develop a deep understanding of how writing works. That understanding shows up in the strong pieces of writing they create themselves.

> The secret to teaching writing turns out to be breaking the traits into smaller, more manageable parts and finding strong examples of what each part looks like as it appears in fiction and nonfiction texts.

One of the best methods of teaching students these key qualities is through mentor texts. Teachers identify the key qualities in the materials already available in the classroom and use them as models for instruction. Whether in novels, nonfiction books, magazines, newspapers, and a myriad of other resources, it just makes sense to show students, for example, the difference it makes for the reader when they create sentences of varying lengths in their writing. By selecting passages from a variety of sources that show different sentence patterns in action, students see firsthand why their own sentences would work more effectively if they were varied, too. They learn the writing technique from the mentor text and the effect it has to make their own writing clear for the reader.

Over time, teachers can identify every one of the key qualities in different reading selections and use them as models. It starts simply, such as finding a passage from *Because of Winn Dixie* (2000) by Kate

DiCamillo that has an insightful and empathic voice that creates a connection to the audience, one of the key qualities of voice:

> "Come on, Winn-Dixie," I said to the dog.
>
> I started walking and he followed along behind me as I went out of the produce department and down the cereal aisle and past all the cashiers and out the door.
>
> Once we were safely outside, I checked him over real careful and he didn't look that good. He was big, but skinny; you could see his ribs. And there were bald patches all over him, places where he didn't have any fur at all. Mostly, he looked like a big piece of old brown carpet that had been left out in the rain.
>
> "You're a mess," I told him. "I bet you don't belong to anybody."
>
> He smiled at me. He did that thing again, where he pulled back his lips and showed me his teeth. He smiled so big that it made him sneeze. It was like he was saying, "I know I'm a mess. Isn't it funny?"
>
> It's hard not to immediately fall in love with a dog who has a good sense of humor. (pp. 11–12)

Once students have been exposed to exquisite writing such DiCamillo's passage, teachers can name the trait in focus and zero in on a key quality to show students the writer's technique and why it works so effectively. When we work with reading with this kind of precision, it becomes a much easier task for students to apply the writer's moves to their own writing. The mentor text teaches students how to make their writing stronger.

> By keeping an eye and an ear out for the best writing, and taking time to mark and file it by key quality for use when developing and presenting lessons, teachers develop a rich and diverse collection of mentor texts to inspire the best writing from students.

By keeping an eye and an ear out for the best writing, and taking time to mark and file it by key quality for use when developing and presenting lessons, teachers develop a rich and diverse collection of mentor texts to inspire the best writing from students. In this way, reading and writing serve each other well—working hand in hand, seamlessly.

In the section that follows, I provide a thorough definition of each trait along with its four key qualities—characteristics of each trait that provide teachers with specific skills to assess for and teach. There are short explanations of each key quality designed to help teachers identify mentor text passages that illustrate each so they can be used in writing instruction. In addition, I provide a short list of questions teachers should ask themselves when looking for mentor texts to model each trait and learn new techniques for applying it. Finally, I suggest favorite authors of mentor texts for each trait, for primary, intermediate, and middle school.

The Traits and Their Definitions

Seeking definitive definitions for the traits of writing is an ongoing quest. As researchers and teachers have sought to clarify and refine their meanings, the trait names have not changed since first conceived in 1985. Simply put, they are the ideas, organization, voice, word choice, sentence fluency, and conventions of writing. The feature of presentation was added later as a bonus element to address the physical appearance of the writing, but the core traits have remained the same over time and across the grades.

Ideas

We don't want him [the writer] to describe every ride at Disneyland, or tell us that the Grand Canyon is awesome, or that Venice has canals. If one of the rides at Disneyland got stuck, if somebody fell into the awesome Grand Canyon, that would be worth hearing about.

—William Zinsser

The ideas trait concerns the piece's content—its central message and the details that support that message. The piece shows strength in ideas when its topic is clear and narrow, and its details are specific, interesting, and accurate. Because the writer knows what he or she wants to say and anticipates the reader's questions, the piece is focused, well developed, and full of original thinking. To accomplish this, the writer must apply the key qualities of this trait with skill and confidence.

Finding a topic. The writer offers a clear, central theme or a simple, original story line that is memorable.

Focusing the topic. The writer narrows the theme or story line to create a piece that is clear, tight, and manageable.

Developing the topic. The writer provides enough critical evidence to support the theme and shows insight on the topic. Or he or she tells the story in a fresh way through an original, unpredictable plot.

Using details. The writer offers credible, accurate details that create pictures in the reader's mind, from the beginning of the piece to the end. Those details provide the reader with evidence of the writer's knowledge about and/or experience with the topic.

Questions to consider when choosing mentor texts for ideas. "What should I write about?" is one of the most frequently asked questions in the writing classroom, no matter the age of the writer. We can use mentor text to answer that question and show how to work effectively with an idea to inform and intrigue the reader. When browsing the bookstore or library for books, magazines, or other print materials to use when teaching about ideas, ask yourself the following questions:

- Is the material on a topic I like? A topic my students like? A theme I want to cover? A content standard I have to cover?

- Did the writer have something new to say about the topic? Does he or she zero in on a small part of a big idea?

- Has the author thought deeply about what my students need to know? Is the content convincing, interesting, and accurate?

- Will the writing create pictures in my students' minds? Do details draw upon the five senses? Do they support the book's main topic? Are they original?

Favorite Authors

Primary: Lisa Rowe Fraustino, *The Hickory Chair*

Intermediate: Christopher Paul Curtis, *The Watsons Go to Birmingham–1963*

Middle School: Suzanne Collins, *The Hunger Games*

High School: Harper Lee, *To Kill a Mockingbird*

Organization

Writing allows us to turn . . . chaos into something beautiful, to frame selected moments, to uncover and celebrate the organizing patterns of our existence.

—Lucy McCormick Calkins

Organization is the internal structure of the piece. Writing that is well organized unfolds logically from beginning to end. It starts with an introduction that creates a sense of anticipation. It continues by presenting information in the right doses and at the right moments so the reader never loses sight of the main idea. Transitions from one point to the next are strong. It concludes with an ending that leaves the reader with a thing or two to ponder. To accomplish this, the writer must apply the key qualities of the organization trait with skill and confidence.

Creating the lead. The writer grabs the reader's attention from the start and leads him or her into the piece naturally. He or she entices the reader, providing a tantalizing glimpse of what is to come.

Using sequence words and transition words. The writer includes a variety of carefully selected sequence words (such as *later*, *then*, and *meanwhile*) and transition words (such as *however*, *also*, and *clearly*), which are placed wisely to guide the reader through the piece by showing how ideas progress, relate, and/or diverge.

Structuring the body. The writer creates a piece that is easy to follow by fitting details together logically. He or she slows down to spotlight important points or events, and speeds up when he or she needs to move the reader along.

Ending with a sense of resolution. The writer sums up his or her thinking in a natural, thoughtful, and convincing way. He or she anticipates and answers any lingering questions the reader may have, and leaves the reader thinking, providing a strong sense of closure.

Questions to consider when choosing books for organization. If the ideas are not laid out in a way that enables the reader to easily engage with them, it's a problem. There are many, many ways to organize text. Sharing mentor texts that represent a variety of organizational techniques can help writers make good choices. Whether you're considering fiction or nonfiction, ask yourself the following questions as you make your selections:

- Does the author give me something interesting to think about right from the start? Do I want to keep reading?

- In the body of the book, does the author use a variety of sequence words, such as *later, then,* and *meanwhile,* and transition words such as *however, because, also,* and *for instance?* Does he or she clearly connect ideas from sentence to sentence and from paragraph to paragraph?

- Is it easy to follow the author's points? Are the details well placed? Does the organization support the book's main idea?

- Is the ending satisfying? Has the author wrapped up all the loose ends and left me with something to think about?

Favorite Authors

Primary: Stephen T. Johnson, *Alphabet City*

Elementary: Gary Paulsen, *Puppies, Dogs, and Blue Northers*

Middle School: PJ Haarsma, *The Softwire: Virus on Orbis 1*

High School: Gene Luen Yang, *American Born Chinese*

Voice

The idea is to write it so that people hear it and it slides through the brain and goes straight to the heart.

—Maya Angelou

Voice is the tone and tenor of the piece—the personal stamp of the writer. It's the force behind the words that proves a real person is speaking and cares about what is being said. Skilled writers engage the reader with voice. They have a solid handle on their audience and purpose for writing, and they choose an appropriate voice—cheerful or melancholy, humorous or serious, confident or uncertain, confrontational or conciliatory, whimsical or authoritative, and so on. To accomplish this, the writer must apply the key qualities of the voice trait with skill and confidence.

Establishing a tone. The writer cares about the topic, and it shows. The writing is expressive and compelling. The reader feels the writer's conviction, authority, and integrity.

Conveying the purpose. The writer makes clear his or her reason for creating the piece. He or she offers a point of view that is appropriate for the mode (narrative, expository, or persuasive), which compels the reader to read on.

Creating a connection to the audience. The writer speaks in a way that makes the reader want to listen. He or she has considered what the reader needs to know and the best way to convey it by sharing his or her fascination, feelings, and opinions about the topic.

Taking risks to create voice. The writer expresses ideas in new ways, which makes the piece interesting and original. The writing sounds like the writer because of his or her use of distinctive, just-right words and phrases.

Questions to consider when choosing mentor texts for voice. When you feel the little hairs on your neck stand up as you're reading, when you laugh out loud, when you find yourself thinking, "Yes, that's exactly how it would have happened," that's voice in action. Look for books and materials that stand out and are expressive, and ask yourself the following questions:

- Can I name the primary voice (for example, fun-loving, irritated, knowledgeable, suspenseful, convincing)? Is the writing expressive? Can I internally hear the voice of the author even as I read the passage silently? Does it sound like the author cares about the topic?

- Is the purpose of the writing clear—to entertain, inform, explain, or maybe persuade? Does the author strike the right tone and have a clear point of view?

- Has the author thought about audience, and, if so, has he or she captured the right voice for that audience? Will my students know how the author feels about the book's main topic?

- Is the writing interesting, fresh, and original? Has the author tried something different from what I've seen before in books for children?

Favorite Authors

Primary: Jerome Ashford Frame, *Yesterday I Had the Blues*

Elementary: Kate DiCamillo, *The Tale of Despereaux*

Middle School: Sharon Draper, *The Battle of Jericho*

High School: Sherman Alexie, *The Absolutely True Diary of a Part-Time Indian*

Word Choice

The craft of writing itself can be inspiring. It is intoxicating to play around with language, to hear the music of what we say, to see more clearly as we speak, to follow the unexpected paths where words take us.

—Donald Murray

Words are like building blocks. By selecting just the right nouns, verbs, adjectives, adverbs, and every other kind of word with care, writers construct a message. If that message is solid, they spark the imagination, create images, and connect—on many levels—with the reader. Good word choice brings clarity to the writer's ideas. Word choice is the workhorse trait: writers use it to transform the ordinary into the extraordinary, the mundane into the spectacular. They use it to move, enlighten, and inspire the reader. To accomplish this, the writer must apply the key qualities of the word choice trait with skill and confidence:

Applying strong verbs. The writer uses many "action words," giving the piece punch and pizzazz. He or she has stretched to find lively verbs that add energy to the piece.

Selecting striking words and phrases. The writer uses many finely honed words and phrases. His or her creative and effective use of literary techniques such as alliteration, similes, and metaphors makes the piece a pleasure to read.

Using specific and accurate words. The writer uses words with precision. He or she selects words the reader needs in order to fully understand the message. The writer chooses nouns, adjectives, adverbs, and so forth that create clarity and bring the topic to life.

Choosing words that deepen meaning. The writer uses words to capture the reader's imagination and enhance the piece's meaning. There is a deliberate attempt to choose the best word over the first word that comes to mind.

Questions to consider when choosing mentor texts for word choice. Words can grab our attention right from the get-go and make the message clear and interesting, or they can bog us down. Look for mentor texts that contain "just right" words that express precisely what the writer wants to convey. Ask yourself the following questions:

- Are the plenty of vivid action words—for example, *scurry* rather than *run?* Do those words give the writing punch and pizzazz?

- Has the author chosen words that sound just right? Does he or she use compound adjectives, alliteration, assonance, onomatopoeia, idioms, and other word-play techniques?

- Will the words help my students create pictures in their minds? Or are they more likely to confuse them? Has the author chosen the best words possible for the grade I teach? For the subjects I teach?

- Is there evidence that the author really thought about the words he or she selected? Will those words capture my students' imagination and engage them in the text?

Favorite Authors

Primary: Rick Walton, *Bullfrog Pops*

Elementary: Pam Muñoz Ryan, *Becoming Naomi Leon*

Middle School: Tony Earley, *The Blue Star*

High School: Ursula LeGuin, *Wizard of Earthsea*

Sentence Fluency

Avoid run-on sentences they are hard to read.

—William Saffire

Sentence fluency is concerned with how words and phrases flow through a piece of writing. It is achieved by paying close attention to the ways individual sentences are crafted and groups of sentences are combined. When skilled writers read their drafts, they hear passages that sing out and those that don't. They check for natural starting and stopping points. They listen for the way the words sound as they flitter and flow within and among sentences. That is why sentence fluency is often called the auditory trait. Writers "read" for it with the ear to hear the rhythm and flow as much as the eye to see how sentences are constructed. To accomplish this kind of fluency, the writer must apply the key qualities of the sentence fluency trait with skill and confidence:

Crafting well-built sentences. The writer carefully and creatively constructs sentences for maximum impact. Transition words such as *but, and*, and *so* are used successfully to join sentences and sentence parts.

Varying sentence types. The writer uses various types of sentences (simple, compound, and/or complex) to enhance the central theme or story line. The piece is made up of an effective mix of long, complex sentences and short, simple ones.

Capturing smooth and rhythmic flow. The writer thinks about how the sentences sound. He or she uses phrasing that is almost musical. If the piece were read aloud, it would be easy on the ear.

Breaking the "rules" to create fluency. The writer diverges from standard English to create interest and impact. For example, he or she may use a sentence fragment, such as "All alone in the forest," or a single word, such as "Bam!" to accent a particular moment or action. He or she might begin with informal words such as *well*, *and*, or *but* to create a conversational tone, or he or she might break rules intentionally to make dialogue sound authentic.

Questions to consider when choosing mentor texts for sentence fluency. The way the sentences flow across the page, their sturdy construction that helps to convey meaning are what make a piece fluent. It may require a second or third reading in order to notice the artistry in action because good writing looks so simple. It's not, of course; it's anything but. When a passage in a book or other text reads smoothly, ask yourself the following questions to determine if it could be used as a mentor text:

- Does it contain sentences of different lengths that begin in different ways? Has the author used conjunctions such as *but, and,* and *so* to connect parts of sentences?

- Does it contain different types of sentences from simple to complex? Does the author intermingle sentence types? Does he or she use particular types of sentences to enhance the book's main topic?

- Is it easy to read aloud? Do individual sentences flow? Do paragraphs flow? Does the entire book flow?

- Are the sentences grammatically correct—or has the author intentionally broken the rules for impact? Does the author use fragments, exclamations, and interjections with style and purpose? Does the dialogue sound natural?

Favorite Authors

Primary: Jane Yolen, *Owl Moon*

Elementary: Karen Hesse, *Out of the Dust*

Middle School: Randa Abdel-Fattah, *Does My Head Look Big in This?*

High School: Gary Paulsen, *Nightjohn*

Conventions

Grammar is not essential for comprehension. . . . But writing that is ungrammatical confounds our expectations. Like unconventional spelling and punctuation, it makes writing more difficult to anticipate, although it is rarely the cause of it being incomprehensive.

—Frank Smith

Conventions are the editing standards we apply to a piece of writing to make it mechanically correct and, therefore, easy to read. Writers edit for conventions because they care about their work. They want their reader to be able to follow their writing effortlessly and become immersed in their ideas, which can only happen if the reader is not bogged down by unintentional errors. To accomplish this, the writer must apply the key qualities of the conventions trait with skill and confidence.

Checking spelling. The writer spells sight words, high-frequency words, and less familiar words correctly. When he or she spells less familiar words incorrectly, those words are phonetically correct. Overall, the piece reveals control in spelling.

Punctuating effectively and paragraphing accurately. The writer handles basic punctuation skillfully. He or she understands how to use periods, commas, question marks, and exclamation marks to enhance clarity and meaning. Paragraphs are indented in the right places. The piece is ready for a general audience.

Capitalizing correctly. The writer uses capital letters consistently and accurately. A deep understanding of how to capitalize dialogue, abbreviations, proper names, and titles is evident.

Applying grammar and usage. The writer forms grammatically correct phrases and sentences. He or she shows care in applying the rules of standard English. The writer may break from those rules for stylistic reasons, but otherwise abides by them.

Questions to consider when choosing mentor texts for conventions. When conventions are used skillfully, they go unnoticed by the reader. So teachers need to show different conventions in action to inspire students and get them to try new and creative ways of applying them. When considering mentor texts for conventions, ask yourself the following questions:

- Does the writing contain plenty of good examples of common spelling rules? Has the author used standard English spelling, or has he or she chosen to subvert it for a good reason? Does the book contain a lot of words that my students typically misspell?

- Are there many good examples of common capitalization rules? Does it contain a lot of words that my students typically neglect to capitalize or capitalize incorrectly? Has the author used standard English capitalization, or has he or she chosen to subvert it for a good reason?

- Are there many good examples of common punctuation rules? Has the author not only used punctuation correctly but also creatively for stylistic reasons—to highlight a point, set a pace, or emphasize a word or phrase, for example?

- Are there many good examples of common grammar and usage rules? Does the author use homophones, synonyms, antonyms, and other special words? Does he or she follow standard rules—such as subject-verb agreement and verb tense consistency—or break them for stylistic reasons such as through the use of regional dialogue?

Favorite Authors

Primary: Robin Pulver, *Punctuation Takes a Vacation*

Elementary: Michael Dahl, *If You Were a Verb*

Middle School: Kate Klise, *Regarding the Trees*

High School: Walter Dean Myers, *Slam!*

Reading With a Writer's Eye

Learning how to read with the writer's eye takes practice, but it is worth it. I was lucky to have a copy of *Kavik the Wolf Dog* on my shelf when my lesson went into a tailspin. It provided wise words to put my class back on course. Thank goodness for Walt Morey that day and the days that followed. His ideas, organization, voice, word choice, and sentence fluency began to permeate my students' pieces. And he is just one of a never-ending supply of writers who can inspire students. Their words and ideas are everywhere.

We read for many purposes, and surely one of those purposes is to study the moves of authors and to discover a new technique, a new way of saying something, or a new perspective on a familiar theme. Each time we are inspired by reading and try what we learn in our own writing, we grow. And grow. And who knows where that will take us—and our students.

References and Resources

Abdel-Fattah, R. (2007). *Does my head look big in this?* New York: Orchard Books.

Alexie, S. (2009). *The absolutely true diary of a part-time Indian.* New York: Little, Brown.

Arter, J., Spandel, V., Culham, R., & Pollard, J. (1994). *Study findings on the integration of writing assessment & instruction: School centers for classroom assessment final report, 1992–93.* Portland, OR: Northwest Regional Educational Laboratory.

Bradbury, R. (1990). *Zen and the art of writing.* Santa Barbara, CA: Capra.

Calkins, L. M. (1994). *The art of teaching writing* (new edition). Portsmouth, NH: Heinemann.

Collins, S. (2008). *The hunger games.* New York: Scholastic.

Curtis, C. P. (1995). *The Watsons go to Birmingam--1963.* New York: Delacorte.

Dahl, M. (2007). *If you were a verb.* Minneapolis, MN: Picture Window Books.

DiCamillo, K. (2000). *Because of Winn Dixie.* Cambridge, MA: Candlewick.

DiCamillo, K. (2003). *The tale of Despereaux.* Cambridge, MA: Candlewick.

Dorfman, L. R., & Cappelli, R. (2007) *Mentor texts: Teaching writing through children's literature, K–6.* Portland, ME: Stenhouse.

Draper, S. (2005). *The battle of Jericho.* New York: Simon Pulse.

Earley, T. (2008). *The blue star.* New York: Little, Brown.

Escribano, P. D. (1999). *Teaching writing through reading: a text-centred approach.* Accessed at http://www.aelfe.org/documents/text1-Duran.pdf on October 23, 2009.

Frame, J. A. (2003). *Yesterday I had the blues.* Berkeley, CA: Tricycle.

Fraustino, L. R. (2001). *The hickory chair*. New York: Arthur A. Levine Books.

Graham, S., & Perin, D. (2007). *Writing next: Effective strategies to improve writing of adolescents in middle and high schools: A report to Carnegie Corporation of New York*. Washington, DC: Alliance for Excellent Education.

Haarsma, PJ. (2008). *The softwire: virus on orbis 1*. Cambridge, MA: Candlewick.

Hall, D., & Emblen, D. L. (1994) *A writer's reader* (7th ed.). New York: Longman.

Hesse, K. (1997). *Out of the dust*. New York: Scholastic.

Johnson, S. T. (1995). *Alphabet city*. New York: Viking.

Klise, K. (2005). *Regarding the trees*. New York: Harcourt Children's Books.

Korman, G. (2002). *No more dead dogs*. New York: Hyperion.

Lee, H. (1960). *To kill a mockingbird*. Philadelphia: Lippincott.

LeGuin U. (1968). *A wizard of earthsea*. Berkeley, CA: Parnassus Press.

Lincoln, A. (February 11, 1859). Second lecture on discoveries and inventions. A speech for the Phi Alpha Society of Illinois College at Jacksonville. In *The Collected Works of Abraham Lincoln* (Vol. 3, pp. 356–363). Piscataway, NJ: Rutgers University Press.

Muñoz-Ryan, P. (2004) *Becoming Naomi Leon*. New York: Scholastic.

Murray, D. (1985). *A writer teaches writing*. Boston: Houghton Mifflin.

Myers, W. D. (1996). *Slam!* New York: Scholastic.

National Commission on Writing in American's Schools and Colleges. (2003). *The neglected "R": The need for a writing revolution*. Washington, DC: College Entrance Examination Board.

National Writing Project (NWP), & Nagin, C. (2003). *Because writing matters*. San Francisco: Jossey-Bass.

Paulsen, G. (1993). *Nightjohn*. New York: Bantam Doubleday Books for Young Readers.

Paulsen, G. (1996). *Puppies, dogs, and blue northers*. New York: Harcourt Brace.

Prose, F. (2007). *Reading like a writer: A guide for people who love books and for those who want to write them*. New York: Harper Perennial.

Ray, K. W. (1999). *Wondrous words: Writers and writing in the elementary classroom*. Urbana, IL: National Council Teachers of English.

Saffire, W. (1990). *Fumblerules*. New York: Doubleday.

Smith, F. (1994). *Writing and the writer* (2nd ed.). Hillsdale, NJ: Lawrence Erlbaum Associates.

Tompkins, G. (2001). *Literacy for the twenty-first century: A balanced approach* (2nd ed.). Upper Saddle River, NJ: Merrill Education.

Truss, L. (2006). *Eats, shoots & leaves: Why, commas really do make a difference!* New York: Putnam Juvenile.

Walton, R. (1999). *Bullfrog pops!* Layton, UT: Gibbs Smith.

Watt, L. (2006). *Scaredy squirrel.* Toronto, Ontario, Canada: Kids Can.

Yang, G. L. (2006). *American born Chinese.* New York: First Second Books.

Yolen, J. (1987). *Owl moon.* New York: Philomel.

Zinsser, W. (2001). *On writing well* (2nd ed.). New York: HarperCollins.

Richard T. Vacca

Richard T. Vacca, PhD, is a professor emeritus at Kent State University, where he directed the Reading and Writing Center and coordinated the Masters of Arts in Teaching program. He also taught at Northern Illinois University and the University of Connecticut. He is a coauthor of *Content Area Reading: Literacy and Learning Across the Curriculum* and *Reading and Learning to Read*. In addition to his many other publications, he has been an author of literature and language arts books for students in grades 6–12. Vacca has also made scholarly presentations throughout the United States, Canada, Europe, and Asia. He was a member of the Board of Directors of the College Reading Association and the International Reading Association (IRA) and served as the president of the IRA. During his tenure there, he founded the Adolescent Literacy Commission and served as that body's first cochair. He is a member of the Reading Hall of Fame.

Maryann Mraz

Maryann Mraz, PhD, is an associate professor in the Department of Reading and Elementary Education at the University of North Carolina Charlotte. She is the author or coauthor of over forty books, chapters, articles, and instructional materials on literacy education, including *Content Area Reading: Literacy and Learning Across the Curriculum* and *The Literacy Coach's Companion*. Her work has been published in *Reading Research and Instruction, Literacy Research and Instruction, The Reading Teacher, Reading and Writing Quarterly,* and other periodicals. She is an elected member of the Board of the Association of Literacy Educators and Researchers. She provides professional development training to teachers and literacy coaches and frequently presents her work at national literacy conferences.

In this chapter, Vacca and Mraz explore the appropriate roles content-area teachers play in the reading and literacy development of their students, and effective content-area reading practices.

Chapter 12

Content-Area Reading Instruction

Richard T. Vacca and Maryann Mraz

Since the 1930s, the slogan "It works, if you work it" has been embraced by individuals throughout the world in self-help programs. During the same era, another popular slogan quickly became the catchphrase of educators interested in helping students read more effectively in content areas: "Every teacher is a teacher of reading." Far from being embraced, however, this slogan has been misinterpreted and often dismissed by content-area teachers who do not view themselves as "teachers of reading." In this chapter, we explore (1) the appropriate roles content-area teachers play in the reading and literacy development of their students, and (2) the state of the art and research in effective content-area reading practices. In doing so, we underscore the notion that content-area reading works only if students and teachers "work it."

Classrooms in today's schools encompass a wide range of learners, including competent, unsure, and struggling readers. However, scoring well on standardized reading tests doesn't necessarily guarantee that students who are identified as competent readers will effectively use reading to learn in a discipline. Conversely, a struggling or unsure reader is capable of learning effectively with academic texts with the instructional support of caring and knowledgeable teachers. In this chapter, we contend that many learners, regardless of their level of general reading ability, have not learned how to *think with text* (Vacca, Vacca, & Mraz, 2011). Content-area reading involves more than saying words on a printed page or screen or selecting snippets of information to answer questions on homework assignments. Students must learn how to think with text by becoming engaged, confident, and strategic in their study of discipline-related texts. This is where all teachers can play a pivotal role in the literacy development of their students.

William S. Gray (1919, 1925) is recognized as one of the early pioneers in content-area reading and is associated with the ill-fated mantra, "Every teacher is a teacher of reading." Although the theoretical underpinnings and research support for content-area reading are as relevant today as they were in Gray's era, content-area reading instruction is still not readily incorporated into classroom practices, despite the attention given it by literacy researchers and educators. Why is this the case?

Literacy processes, such as reading and writing, remain an important means of facilitating conceptual development and learning in content-area classrooms. Yet preservice and inservice teachers alike tend to resist taking content-area reading coursework (Maimon, 1997), even though it is a requirement in most teacher certification programs. The culture and organization of schools, particularly in an era of accountability and high-stakes testing, continue to influence the way teachers view their roles, think about instruction, and resist the use of content-area reading practices (Ratekin, Simpson, Alvermann, & Dishner, 1985). The irony behind such resistance is that content-area teachers genuinely value the role that reading plays in learning but fail to attend to reading in their own instructional practices (O'Brien & Stewart, 1992). Yet the responsibility for teaching students to use reading to learn is a shared one, belonging to all teachers in all subjects.

Content-area teachers have historically viewed their primary responsibility as preparing students to learn the important concepts and principles underlying their disciplines—and this is as it should be. However, there is often a disconnect in the way content-area teachers think about developing concepts through literacy processes such as reading. Assigning texts to read as part of the ebb and flow of classroom practice is at best a starting point, not an endpoint, for learning in the content areas. Content-area reading teachers are not primarily responsible for the direct teaching of reading skills—skills that are best taught by qualified reading professionals. However, all content-area teachers have an important functional role to play in showing students how to use literacy processes, such as reading and writing to think and learn with text.

> All content-area teachers have an important functional role to play in showing students how to use literacy processes such as reading and writing to think and learn with text.

Past and Present Practices

Content-area reading has been the focus of research and practice for nearly a century. For many years, it was associated with how learners use reading skills and strategies to comprehend academic text in various content areas. Since the 1990s, however, this concept has broadened to include a wide array of language processes. The term *content literacy* is widely used in lieu of *content-area reading* to refer to students' ability to use reading, writing, talking, listening, and viewing to learn content in a given discipline (Vacca, 2002). Most recently, the concept of disciplinary literacy has influenced the way researchers and educators think about literacy and learning in content areas (Buehl & Moore, 2009; Lee, 2004; Moje, 2007; Moje, Overby, Tysvaer, & Morris, 2008; Shanahan & Shanahan, 2008). Each subject area, or discipline, poses unique challenges in terms of purposes for reading, vocabulary, and texts. Discipline literacy focuses on showing students how to learn with discipline-specific texts so that they can understand the concepts related to that discipline.

From Reading and Study Skills to Cognitive Learning Strategies

Early in the history of content-area reading, research reflected an emphasis on the identification of reading and study skills associated with each of the content areas (Gray, 1925; McCallister, 1930). For the most part, researchers from the early beginnings of content-area reading concluded that, while there are skills common to all academic disciplines, some of these skills hold special relationships to achievement in each of them. Artley (1944), for example, studied the relationship between general reading ability and reading skills specific to social studies. He found that the ability to read generally is related to the ability to read social studies. However, he also concluded that there are specific factors associated with reading social studies that may not be associated with other content areas, like mathematics or science. In other words, a historian reads historical text somewhat differently from the way scientists or mathematicians read text in their respective disciplines. Even though the historian, scientist, and mathematician have developed general reading ability, how they adapt that ability to think with texts in their fields of study is essential to learning content-specific concepts.

As content-area reading research and practice continued to develop, reading researchers moved beyond the identification of reading and skills in each of the content areas to the study of various instructional frameworks that would make a difference in students' ability to learn content through reading. Two distinctly different instructional frameworks for content-area reading emerged: (1) a *direct instructional framework*, in which reading skills and strategies are taught apart from the content-area classroom, with the expectation that students transfer these skills and strategies to actual content-area learning situations (Simpson, 1929; Salisbury, 1934); and (2) a *functional instructional framework*, in which reading and study skills are embedded within the context of content-area instructional routines, utilizing texts that are an integral part of disciplinary learning. A functional approach is rooted in the assumption that reading skills and strategies are best taught by content-area teachers within the context of authentic learning situations (Herber, 1970; Leggitt, 1934; Vacca, Vacca, & Mraz, 2011).

Even though the majority of students learn to read in elementary school with some degree of proficiency, they must learn how to adapt reading and thinking strategies to meet the conceptual and textual demands inherent in each discipline they study.

Hal Herber's *Teaching Reading in Content Areas* (1970) was the first comprehensive textbook on content-area reading instruction. This was a seminal work, supporting a functional approach to instruction, and its guiding principle is as powerful today as it was more than forty years ago: content determines process. This means that, even though the majority of students learn to read in elementary school with some degree of proficiency, they must learn how to adapt reading and thinking strategies to meet the conceptual and textual demands inherent in each discipline they study.

Beginning in the 1970s, there was a major shift away from reading as a skill-centered process to reading as a cognitive learning process. Researchers and practitioners were concerned with how readers come to know, and with the plans and strategies text learners use to construct meaning. Numerous investigations were initiated to better understand the role of cognitive and metacognitive processes in reading and to validate reading strategies grounded in cognitive and metacognitive principles. Metacognition involves the ability to control one's own cognitive activities (Brown, Bransford, Ferrara, & Campione, 1983) and is closely related to strategic learning. Good readers are strategic readers and are metacognitively aware, knowledgeable about their own reading processes, and in control of reading and learning activities. Strategic learners know what, how, when, and why it is important to monitor what they are reading and to regulate their use of comprehension strategies.

A major impact on the development of present-day content-area reading practices has been research related to schema theory, text structure, engagement, and self-efficacy.

- Readers, for example, are in a better position to understand what they are reading whenever they use schema—prior knowledge—to construct meaning. Prior knowledge reflects the experiences, conceptual understanding, attitudes, values, and skills a learner brings to reading.

- Cognitive researchers have shown that text structure is crucial to learning and memory (Kintsch, 1977; Meyer & Rice, 1984). The skilled reader searches for the structure of idea relationships in informational text and can readily differentiate important ideas from less important ideas in the material (Meyer, Brandt, & Bluth, 1980; Taylor, 1980). Skilled readers identify text patterns in informational text that represent various types of logical connections among ideas (Meyer, 1975; Vacca, Vacca, & Mraz, 2011).

- Engaged learners are cognitively active, not passive, in the construction of meaning. They actively "work" with text to make meaning. They are motivated and confident in their ability to think and learn with text.

From Content-Area Reading to Disciplinary Literacy

Some researchers and practitioners contend that content-area reading practices place too great an emphasis on generic literacy strategies that may not be applicable to specific disciplines. The rationale for disciplinary literacy suggests, however, that using literacy to learn in a discipline is inextricably related to content knowledge and thinking. Doug Buehl (2009), a long-time advocate of content-area reading and a former social studies teacher, contends that middle and high school teachers must focus not only on what students should know and be able to do, but also on how "experts within a discipline read, write, and think" (p. 535). He advocates for continued research on discipline-specific literacy practices, which seem to be "an especially fertile ground for determining how to mentor students to read, write, and think through the lens of a mathematician, biologist, musician, historian, artist, novelist, and so forth" (p. 537).

Elizabeth Moje and her colleagues (2008) provide a comprehensive discourse on the theory, research, and pedagogical practices supporting instructional approaches to disciplinary literacy. They underscore the relationship between content knowledge and thinking. To develop content knowledge in a discipline, students need to acquire the thinking processes that are valued and used by that discipline. Shanahan and Shanahan (2008) also concluded, based on preliminary research, that disciplinary experts from different content fields use a different array of reading processes to think and learn with text.

> To develop content knowledge in a discipline, students need to acquire the thinking processes that are valued and used by that discipline.

Whether it's called content-area reading, content literacy, or disciplinary literacy, the driving principle behind each of these instructional concepts is as applicable today as it was during Herber's time: content determines process. The structure, vocabulary, and conceptual demands of a discipline-specific text determine how a reader will think with, make sense of, and learn from that text. A functional approach to literacy and learning in content areas strongly suggests that teachers must have a solid understanding of the thinking processes within a discipline so that they can effectively adapt and modify general literacy strategies, tailoring them to meet the conceptual and textual demands of the content under study. In the remainder of this chapter, we describe many potentially useful instructional strategies and practices that support thinking and content knowledge development.

Thinking With Text

Students who know how to think with text are confident in their ability to understand what they read. Confident learners are neither passive nor clueless. Unsure learners, on the other hand, may attempt half-hearted searches for isolated bits and pieces of information to answer questions on a homework assignment or find ways to avoid academic reading altogether. Developing a high level of self-efficacy in all students is an important dimension of content-area reading instruction that is sometimes overlooked.

Self-Efficacy and Confidence

Confident learners exhibit a high level of self-efficacy in situations that require them to think deeply about what they are reading. They approach text with the expectation that they will be successful. As a result, they bring a sense of control to classroom activities that require thinking and learning with text. Moreover, confident readers are more self-motivated and persistent than unsure learners in their efforts to think with text in ways not demonstrated by students with low levels of self-efficacy.

Bandura (1986) explains that self-efficacy refers to "people's judgment of their abilities to organize and execute courses of action required to attain designated types of performance" (p. 391). Self-efficacy is not as concerned with the skills and strategies students bring to content-area reading situations, but rather focuses on students' estimations of their ability to apply whatever skills and strategies they bring to learning. Jinks and Lorsbach (2003) describe self-efficacy as "what we believe we can do with whatever skill we have, rather than our actual ability or skill" (p. 115). Unfortunately, when students doubt their ability to read successfully, especially in an academic context, their effort is often minimal, and they question their ability to succeed as readers. Often, unsure readers are disengaged, lack intrinsic motivation, and are more likely to be influenced by extrinsic motivators such as rewards (Guthrie & Davis, 2003).

In discussing strategies for improving self-efficacy, Putnam (2009) draws a powerful analogy to running a marathon race. He notes that many of us would doubt our ability to run a marathon in the same way that students who struggle with reading doubt their ability to think and learn with text in content areas. He suggests several strategies that content-area teachers can easily incorporate into their instructional repertoire. These include making provisions for student choice, providing explicit strategy instruction, and offering positive feedback.

Make provisions for student choice. In beginning a training program for a marathon, Putnam points out, it is important to run the right route. Running too difficult a route can easily discourage a novice runner in training. Likewise, using a single text for all content-area reading assignments—for example, a difficult textbook—discourages readers who have experienced failure in the past and believe the same thing will happen again. Providing students with text alternatives—and choice in the texts they use for disciplinary learning—gives them a sense of control over the situation and promotes motivation.

Provide explicit strategy instruction. As Putnam explains, runners who are in training work on more efficient methods for improving overall performance—for example, improving posture and stride length. All readers, likewise, can benefit from explicit instruction in the use of strategies. These strategies develop good habits of thinking that facilitate content knowledge through reading. Whether it involves showing students how to read purposefully by generating questions or how to take notes while reading, explicit strategy instruction is essential for raising students' level of self-efficacy and engagement.

Provide positive feedback. According to Putnam, positive feedback improves students' belief in their ability to handle reading tasks with competence, which in turn increases self-efficacy. Content-area teachers prop up students' confidence in their ability to handle disciplinary literacy tasks by first acknowledging something that the student did well, then identifying an area in which there is room for improvement, and finally acknowledging another area of strength. This approach is sometimes known as "sandwiching" feedback.

Self-Efficacy and Engagement

Self-efficacy and engagement go hand in hand in the content-area classroom. If students believe, for example, that they have a good chance to succeed at a disciplinary literacy task, they are likely to exhibit a willingness to engage in reading or writing to complete it. When readers become self-motivated, they perceive that they have some level of control over their reading, they apply appropriate strategies in order make complex reading tasks more manageable, and they display a high level of engagement in their reading experiences.

In order to think and learn with text, students need to approach reading in a purposeful manner and attend to the task. Assigning them a text for homework or in-class discussion won't necessarily guarantee that they will want to read it attentively or purposefully. The opposite may be the case. Students with low self-efficacy become discouraged with the task even before they start, or disengage quickly if the text holds no inherent interest. An engaged reader, however, knows how to make personal connections with the text. From an instructional perspective, teachers are in a better position to increase students' motivation if they activate prior knowledge and provoke thinking about a topic before, during, and after a text assignment.

> Teachers are in a better position to increase students' motivation if they activate prior knowledge and provoke thinking about a topic before, during, and after a text assignment.

For example, a strategy such as questioning the author (QtA) shows students the importance of asking questions not only before but also during and after reading (Beck, McKeown, Hamilton, & Kucan, 1997). When readers struggle with text, they often do not have a clue about generating questions, let alone interacting with the author. The QtA strategy shows students how to read text closely, as if the author were there to be challenged and questioned. QtA places value on the quality and depth of students' responses to the author's intent. Good readers monitor whether the author is making sense by asking questions such as "What is the author trying to say here?" "What does the author mean?" "So what?" "What is the significance of the author's message?" "Does this make sense with what the author told us before?" and "Does the author explain this clearly?"

QtA is but one of many generic literacy strategies that may be adapted to meet the conceptual and textual demands of discipline-specific text. In the next section, we look at strategy-based learning through the use of several generic literacy strategies that may be useful in content-area reading situations. Keep in mind, however, that content determines process. Some strategies may have limited utility in a content area. How a teacher adapts the strategies that follow makes all the difference in whether or not they work to facilitate thinking with text.

Strategy-Based Learning

Students, particularly those who struggle with literacy learning, benefit from instructional strategies that provide scaffolds to support their comprehension. For teachers, providing instructional scaffolds means understanding the diverse learning needs of students and then modeling or leading students through strategies that will both engage them and lead them toward the understanding of content-area concepts (Vacca, Vacca, & Mraz, 2011).

Explicit strategy instruction is a key mechanism for providing the learning scaffolds that students need in content-area classrooms. Traditional approaches to teaching content-area concepts tend to be passive and often rely on definition-based approaches in which the teacher gives students a list of terms to be memorized or list of definitions to look up in a glossary (Taylor, Mraz, Nichols, Rickelman, & Wood, 2009). Similarly, "blind" instruction directs students on how to follow the steps and procedures of a given strategy but doesn't necessarily teach students the rationale for using it.

Explicit strategy instruction provides the instructional support students need to become aware of, use, and develop control of learning strategies and to develop an understanding of problem-solving techniques they can apply independently, across content-area texts (Pearson, 1982). Explicit strategy instruction involves the following steps:

1. Awareness and explanation of the strategy—Explaining a strategy to students helps them to develop a rationale for its use; to become more aware of what the strategy is, how and when to use it, and why it is important to use. A give-and-take exchange between teacher and students lays the groundwork for building learners' self-confidence: "Why is this strategy useful?" "What is the payoff for students?" "How does it improve learning?"

2. Demonstration of the strategy—Once students understand the rules and procedures associated with a reading strategy, the teacher models the use of the strategy through think-alouds. Think-alouds allow the teacher to share with students the thinking processes that a disciplinary expert uses to make the strategy work (Davey, 1983).

3. Strategy practice—To build confidence in the use of the strategy, the teacher provides students with an easy text or two to practice the strategy and discuss how they will use it to think with text.

4. Strategy application—Once students have had several "try-outs" with the strategy, the teacher encourages its application by framing an assignment so that students will have to use the strategy to think with text.

Strategy instruction can occur *before* reading, *during* reading, and *after* reading (B-D-A). The B-D-A instructional framework allows teachers to incorporate explicit strategy instruction throughout lessons involving content literacy and learning. During the "before" reading phase of a lesson, a teacher can emphasize one or more of the following:

- Arousing curiosity about the topic to be read

- Building and activating prior knowledge

- Introducing key vocabulary and concepts

- Evoking predictions and creating anticipation for reading

- Defining problems to be solved through reading

- Eliciting student-generated questions about the material prior to assigning a text reading

The before-reading phase is a time for teachers to consider how students will connect previous lessons, as well as their experiences, to the lesson about to be presented. By activating prior knowledge and generating interest in a text, teachers can create an instructional context in which students will read with purpose (Heffernan, 2003; Vacca, Vacca, & Mraz, 2011).

While teachers effortlessly recognize the important sections of a text assignment, most students do not. Instead, students tend to treat every passage and paragraph within a content-area text with equal importance. They struggle to discern key points from supporting information. Explicit strategy instruction applied during reading can help to bridge the gap between students and texts so that students learn how to respond actively to the reading and identify key ideas. After-reading strategies can create a structure for refining students' understanding of emerging concepts. Ideas encountered before and during reading can be clarified and extended in the after-reading phase of the lesson (Vacca, Vacca, & Mraz, 2011).

A lesson using the B-D-A framework does not necessarily take place in a single class session; several class meetings may be needed to complete the lesson and achieve its objectives. The complexity of the material, students' familiarity with the topic, the amount of guidance they need to comprehend a given text, and the teacher's own professional judgment determine which components will be emphasized during a particular lesson. All of the components of a B-D-A lesson do not receive the same emphasis in a given reading assignment, and a single strategy may span one or more sections of the B-D-A framework. The following strategies (marked with a B, D, or A) can be used to engage students in active and purposeful reading.

Anticipation Guides (B, A)

An anticipation guide is a series of statements to which students respond before reading the text. Their value lies in the discussion that takes place among students about their varying before-reading points of view. Through this discussion, students' prior knowledge about the topic—as well as their misconceptions—is revealed. It is important for teachers to remain open to a wide range of responses as students present their understandings, attitudes, and beliefs. When constructing an anticipation guide, teachers first determine the major ideas in a text that a student will read. Then, teachers write short, declarative statements that reflect those ideas in a manner that will elicit prediction and discussion (Schell, 2008). Students should be given time to think through each statement independently before comparing their responses, either with a partner or in a small group. Before reading the text selection, the teacher should synthesize the students' responses to the anticipation guide statements, illuminating both points of agreement and areas of difference. During reading, the students should reevaluate their anticipation guide responses in light of the information presented in the text. After reading, students may contrast their original predictions and responses with information in the text (Vacca, Vacca, & Mraz). Figure 12.1 shows an anticipation guide created for a middle-school science class as part of a unit on earthquakes.

Major Ideas	Before	After
1. The noise heard during an earth-quake is the sound of the earth moving and buildings shaking.	_____	_____
2. During the San Francisco earth-quake, soldiers blew up buildings to stop fire from spreading.	_____	_____

Figure 12.1: Earthquake anticipation guide. Continued →

3. Shockwaves start above the earth's surface.	_____	_____
4. Earthquakes usually occur along faults in the earth's crust.	_____	_____
5. The moon has earthquakes.	_____	_____

Story Impressions (B)

The story impression strategy uses clue words associated with the events, setting, and characters of a story to help readers predict the story prior to reading (McGinley & Denner, 1987). Story impressions can be particularly useful as a before-reading strategy with historical fiction or some other literary selection. By using fragments from the story, students are able to form an impression of how events may unfold or characters interact. The chain of clue words triggers students' impressions and prompts them to anticipate in writing the text they will read. The selected clue words are sequenced with arrows or lines to form a descriptive chain. Students write their predictive story based upon their impressions from the clues in that chain. Figure 12.2 applies the story impression strategy to Linda Sue Park's Newbery-Award-winning book *A Single Shard* (2001), which tells the story of a homeless twelfth-century Korean boy who agrees to apprentice with a local potter in order to pay back the debt incurred after breaking a treasured box. While the predicative story that the students produced is not expected to be identical to the story they will read, the story impression can serve to activate students' background knowledge and pique their interest in reading the text.

Word Study Strategies (D, A)

A strong connection has been established between vocabulary knowledge and effective reading comprehension (Anderson & Freebody, 1981; Thompson, 1999). When students are not familiar with many of the words they encounter in a text, they inevitably have difficulty understanding what they read. Information texts used in content-area classes tend to bring with them more challenging

Story Chain	Story Prediction
Korea scavenge pottery broken collecting tradition robbery shard journey family	While on a journey to Korea for vacation, a yearly family tradition, an old man is involved in a robbery. Thieves break an antique piece of pottery on his head and steal his money and passport so he isn't able to find a way home. He has to scavenge for food and collect money from kind strangers in order to survive. While asking for help in a public market, he discovers on the ground a shard of metal, which turns out to be gold. Instead of stealing the piece of gold, he returns it to a local shop owner, who is so impressed by his honesty that he helps him get back home.

Figure 12.2: Story impression: *A Single Shard,* by Linda Sue Park.

vocabulary demands than narrative or literacy texts (Pearson, Hiebert, & Kamill, 2007). Explicit strategy instruction of vocabulary concepts improves students' comprehension of a text (Bromley, 2007). Teaching concepts and the relationships between them involves providing students with multiple opportunities to connect concepts to prior knowledge and to define, clarify, and extend their word knowledge throughout a unit of study. Graphic organizers, which are tools for accomplishing this task, come in a variety of forms and can help students anticipate and synthesize concepts presented in a text and understand the connections among words. A graphic organizer displays key concepts from a text in a format that illustrates the connection between them. For example, network tree diagrams can be used to depict the hierarchical relationships among concept words, and timelines can be used to display the chronology of a series of events.

Word sorts can also provide students with opportunities to understand how words are related by classifying them into categories based upon students' understanding of their meanings. To implement a word sort, the teacher identifies the key words from a unit of study and invites students to sort them into logical arrangements of two or more categories. Students can work in pairs or small groups to complete the strategy; this affords them opportunities to learn from one another while examining words together (Gillet & Kita, 1979). The purpose of word sorting is to group words into categories that represent the shared features of the concepts presented. Students' prior knowledge, their evolving understanding of meanings as a result of reading the text, and their connection of new concepts to those previously learned all contribute to the thinking process involved in completing a word sort.

Words sorts may be either open or closed. In a closed sort, students are given the categories in which they are to sort the words. By contrast, open word sorts allow for more divergent thinking and inductive reasoning. Categories for grouping are not known in advance; students are asked to identify relationships and meaning patterns among content-area terms without having an initial structure from which to work. Both types of word sorts can be adapted to any content area (Vacca, Vacca, & Mraz, 2011).

Semantic Feature Analysis (D, A)

The semantic feature analysis (Johnson & Pearson, 1978) can help students to understand relationships among words and expand and retain content-area concepts. Using a chart or grid, students are asked to analyze similarities and differences among related concepts. To implement a semantic feature analysis, a topic is selected, and concepts related to that topic are then listed vertically on the semantic feature-analysis chart. Next, features or properties potentially associated with each concept are listed horizontally across the top of the chart. Students are asked to analyze each word according to the features or properties listed to determine whether or not a feature is associated with a given word. If a feature is associated with a word, students indicate it by writing an X in the corresponding cell. If a feature is not associated with the word, students leave the cell empty. Students may write a question mark (?) if they are uncertain about the relationship of a particular feature to the word being analyzed. These questions can serve as catalysts for further reading and study (Vacca, Vacca, & Mraz, 2011). Figure 12.3 shows a semantic feature analysis used in a high school science class astronomy unit.

	Moons in Orbit	Rings	Bigger Than Earth	Rocky Surface	Water	Volcanoes
Mercury				X		X
Venus				X		X
Earth	X			X	X	X
Mars	X			X		X
Jupiter	X	X	X			
Saturn	X	X	X			
Uranus	X	X	X			
Neptune	X	X	X			

Figure 12.3: Semantic feature analysis: Planets in the solar system.

Discussion Web (A)

Discussion webs can be a useful after-reading strategy to engage students in thoughtful deliberations about a text they have read. An alternative to teacher-dominated discussion, discussion webs invite students to consider different sides of an issue or topic before drawing conclusions (Alvermann, 1991). At the center of the discussion web is a text-related question for students to consider. Students are asked to respond to the question from multiple points of view, rather than advocating for a particular position.

The discussion cycle begins with students first thinking about the ideas they want to contribute to the discussion, based on a text they have read. Students start discussing their ideas with a partner and then team with a second set of partners to articulate differences in perspectives and responses to the reading and to work toward a consensus about the topic being addressed. Finally, a spokesperson is selected from each group of four to share ideas and conclusions with the entire class.

Figure 12.4 (page 288) depicts a discussion web developed in a high school government class studying the branches of government. The question in the center of the web was central to the students' reading and was posed in such a way that it reflected more than one point of view. Students explored the possible pros and cons inherent

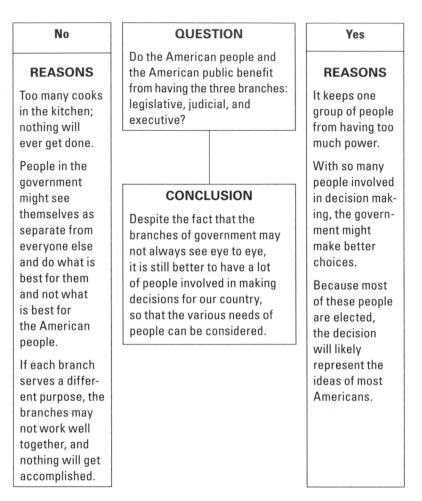

No	QUESTION	Yes
REASONS	Do the American people and the American public benefit from having the three branches: legislative, judicial, and executive?	**REASONS**
Too many cooks in the kitchen; nothing will ever get done.		It keeps one group of people from having too much power.

CONCLUSION

No / REASONS:
Too many cooks in the kitchen; nothing will ever get done.

People in the government might see themselves as separate from everyone else and do what is best for them and not what is best for the American people.

If each branch serves a different purpose, the branches may not work well together, and nothing will get accomplished.

CONCLUSION
Despite the fact that the branches of government may not always see eye to eye, it is still better to have a lot of people involved in making decisions for our country, so that the various needs of people can be considered.

Yes / REASONS:
It keeps one group of people from having too much power.

With so many people involved in decision making, the government might make better choices.

Because most of these people are elected, the decision will likely represent the ideas of most Americans.

Figure 12.4: Discussion web on the three branches of government.

in the question and then worked together to draw a conclusion based on their discussion.

It Works, If You Work It

The current educational environment presents a multitude of challenges for teachers. Students bring an ever-widening set of experiences and learning needs with them to their classrooms. Standards of literacy continue to increase, as the technological requirements of the 21st-century workplace demand higher levels of literacy sophistication. Teachers must continually seek to implement literacy learning processes and strategies that will help their students to comprehend text in any given subject area. Meanwhile, policy initiatives continue to emphasize teacher accountability, as measured by high-stakes test scores.

Reading is not an isolated skill that students master in elementary school and then simply apply in their middle and secondary years. Students need ongoing instruction that will help them develop a self-efficacy for learning, a high level of engagement with subject areas, and an understanding of strategies that can help them to solve literacy challenges. When it comes to content-area reading, by selecting effective strategies and offering explicit instruction to students on why, how, and when to apply those strategies, content-area teachers can "work it" in ways that facilitate learning across the curriculum.

References

Alvermann, D. E. (1991). The discussion web: A graphic aid for learning across the curriculum. *The Reading Teacher, 45*(2), 92–99.

Anderson, R. C., & Freebody, P. (1981). Vocabulary knowledge. In J. Guthrie (Ed.). *Comprehension and teaching: Research reviews* (pp. 77–117). Newark, DE: International Reading Association.

Artley, A. S. (1944). A study of certain relationships existing between general reading comprehension and reading comprehension in a specific subject matter area. *Journal of Educational Research, 37,* 463–473.

Bandura, A. (1986). *Social foundations of thought and action: A social cognitive theory.* Englewood Cliffs, NJ: Prentice Hall.

Beck, I. L., McKeown, M. G., Hamilton, R. L., & Kucan, L. (1997). *Question the author: An approach for enhancing student engagement with text.* Newark, DE: International Reading Association.

Bromley, K. (2007). Nine things every teacher should know about words and vocabulary instruction. *Journal of Adolescent and Adult Literacy, 50*(7), 528–537.

Brown, A. L., Bransford, J. W., Ferrara, R. F., & Campione, J. (1983). Learning, remembering, and understanding. In J. Flavell and E. Markham (Eds.), *Handbook of child psychology* (pp. 393–451). New York: Wiley.

Buehl, D. (2009). Linking research to practice in disciplinary instruction: An interview by David Moore. *Journal of Adolescent and Adult Literacy, 52*(6), 535–537.

Davey, B. (1983). Think aloud: Modeling the cognitive processes of reading comprehension. *Journal of Reading, 27,* 44–47.

Gillet, J., & Kita, M. J. (1979). Words, kids, and categories. *The Reading Teacher, 32,* 538–542.

Gray, W. S. (1919). The relation between study and reading. *Proceedings of the Annual Meeting of the National Education Association.* Washington, DC: National Education Association.

Gray, W. S. (1925). *Summary of investigations related to reading,* Supplementary Educational Monographs, No. 28. Chicago: University of Chicago Press.

Guthrie, J. T., & Davis, M. H. (2003). Motivating struggling readers in middle school through an engagement model of classroom practice. *Reading & Writing Quarterly, 19,* 59–85.

Hefferman, N. (2003). Helping students read better: The use of background knowledge. *English Teacher, 6,* 62–65.

Herber, H. L. (1970). *Teaching reading in content areas.* Englewood Cliffs, NJ: Prentice Hall.

Jinks, J., & Lorsbach, A. (2003). Introduction: Motivation and self-efficacy belief. *Reading & Writing Quarterly, 19,* 113–118.

Johnson, D. D., & Pearson, P. D. (1984). *Teaching reading vocabulary.* New York: Holt, Rinehart, & Winston.

Lee, C. D. (2004 Winter/Spring). Literacy in the academic disciplines and the needs of adolescent struggling readers. *Voices in Urban Education (VUE),* Winter/Spring 2004, 14–19.

Leggitt, D. (1934). Measuring progress in working skills in ninth grade civics. *School Review, 42,* 676–687.

Maimon, L. (1997). Reducing resistance to content area literacy courses. In W. M. Linek & E. G. Sturtevant (Eds.), *Exploring literacy: The nineteenth yearbook of the College Reading Association* (pp. 267–281). Platteville, WI: College Reading Association.

McCallister, J. M. (1930). Guiding pupils' reading activities in the study of content subjects. *Elementary School Journal, 31,* 271–284.

McGinley, W. J., & Denner, P. R. (1987). Story impressions: A pre-reading/writing activity. *Journal of Reading, 31,* 248–253.

Meyer, B. J. F. (1975). *The organization of prose and its effect in memory.* Amsterdam: North-Holland.

Meyer, B. J. F., & Rice, E. (1984). The structure of text. In P. D. Pearson (Ed.), *Handbook of reading research* (pp. 319–352). New York: Longman.

Meyer, B. J. F., Brandt, D. M., & Bluth, G. J. (1980). Use of top-level structure in text: Key for reading comprehension of ninth-grade students. *Reading Research Quarterly, 15,* 72–103.

Moje, E. B. (2007). Developing socially just subject-matter instruction: A review of the literature on disciplinary literacy. In N. L. Parker (Ed.), *Review of research in education.* (pp. 1–44). Washington, DC: American Educational Research Association.

Moje, E., Overby, M., Tysvaer, N., & Morris, K. (2008). The complex world of adolescent literacy: Myths, motivations, and mysteries. *Harvard Educational Review, 78*(1), 107–154.

O'Brien, D. G., & Stewart, R. A. (1992). Resistance to content area reading: Dimensions and solutions. In E. Dishner, T. Bean, J. Readence, & D. Moore (Eds.), *Reading in the content areas: Improving classroom instruction* (3rd ed.). Dubuque, IA: Kendall-Hunt.

Park, L. S. (2001). *A single shard.* New York: Yearling.

Pearson, P. D. (1982). *A context for instructional research and reading comprehension* (Technical Report No. 230). Urbana: University of Illinois Center for the Study of Reading.

Pearson, P. D., Hiebert, E. H., & Kamil, M. (2007). Vocabulary assessment: What we know and what we need to learn. *Reading Research Quarterly, 42*(2), 282–296.

Putnam, M. (2009) Running the race to improve self-efficacy. *Kappa Delta Pi Record, 45,* 53–57.

Ratekin, N., Simpson, M., Alvermann, D., & Dishner, E. (1985). Why teachers resist content reading instruction. *Journal of Reading, 32,* 396–401.

Salisbury, R. (1934). A study of the transfer effects of training in logical organization. *Journal of Educational Research, 28,* 241–254.

Schell, E. M. (2008). Empowering readers of social studies. In D. Lapp, J. Flood, & N. Farnan (Eds.), *Content area reading and learning* (pp. 271–302). New York: Lawrence Erlbaum Associates.

Shanahan, T., & Shanahan, C. (2008). Teaching disciplinary literacy to adolescents: Rethinking content-area literacy. *Harvard Educational Review, 78*(1), 40–59.

Simpson, R. G. (1929). The effect of specific training on ability to read historical materials. *Journal of Educational Research, 20,* 343–351.

Taylor, B. (1980). Children's memory of expository text after reading. *Reading Research Quarterly, 15,* 399–411.

Taylor, D. B., Mraz, M., Nichols, W. D., Rickelman, R. J., & Wood, K. D. (2009). Using explicit instruction to promote vocabulary learning for struggling readers. *Reading & Writing Quarterly, 25,* 205–220.

Thompson, R. A. (1999). Balancing vocabulary instruction with teacher-directed and student-centered activities. In S. Blair-Larson & K. Williams (Eds.). *The balanced reading program* (pp. 24–36). Newark, DE: International Reading Association.

Vacca, R. T. (2002). Making a difference in adolescents' school lives: Visible and invisible aspects of content area reading: In A.E. Farstrup & S. J. Samuels (Eds.), *What research has to say about reading instruction* (3rd ed., pp. 184–204). Newark, DE: International Reading Association.

Vacca, R. T., Vacca, J. L., & Mraz, M. (2011). *Content area reading: Literacy and learning across the curriculum* (10th ed.). Boston: Allyn & Bacon.

Peter Afflerbach

Peter Afflerbach, PhD, is a professor in the Reading Center at the University of Maryland. He teaches graduate and undergraduate courses in reading assessment and graduate courses in reading comprehension. He received his doctorate in reading psychology from the University at Albany. He is a former K–6 Chapter 1 Reading Program teacher, middle school remedial reading teacher, and high school English teacher.

Afflerbach's research interests include reading assessment, reading comprehension, and the verbal reporting methodology. He is the author of numerous books, including *Understanding and Using Reading Assessment, K–12.* He is coeditor of the *Handbook of Reading Research* (4th ed.) and editor of *Essential Readings in Assessment.* He has been published in numerous theoretical and practical journals, including *Reading Research Quarterly, Cognition and Instruction, Elementary School Journal, Journal of Reading, Journal of Reading Behavior, The Reading Teacher, Journal of Adolescent and Adult Literacy,* and *Language Arts.* He is coeditor of the academic research journal *Metacognition and Learning*, and he serves on the editorial advisory board of *Reading Research Quarterly.* Afflerbach has served as chair of the Literacy Assessment Committee of the International Reading Association, on the National Assessment of Educational Progress (NAEP) Reading Committee, and on the Common Core State Standards Review Panel. He was elected to the International Reading Association's Hall of Fame in 2009.

In this chapter, Afflerbach examines the different purposes and audiences for reading assessment, the formative and summative nature of assessment, and the focus of assessment. He then examines assessment validity and reliability in relation to how we develop confidence in our assessments of reading, accommodation of students, and successful professional development. He concludes with an overview of particular types of reading assessment.

Chapter 13

Assessing Reading

Peter Afflerbach

How can reading assessment accurately measure and describe students' strengths and needs? How does assessment help teachers understand and foster their students' reading development? This chapter focuses on the characteristics of effective reading assessment. The first section examines the different purposes and audiences for reading assessment. Then we will consider the formative and sum mative nature of assessment, as well as the focus of assessment. Next, we examine assessment validity and reliability in relation to how we develop confidence in our assessments of reading. We then consider accommodation of students in assessment, and teachers' professional development that is necessary for a successful reading assessment program. The chapter concludes with an overview of particular types of reading assessment.

The Three Purposes of Reading Assessment

Why do we assess reading? The overarching goal of reading assessment is to foster students' reading development. Thus, it is imperative to establish a direct link between reading assessment and students' reading growth, be it the development of phonemic awareness, the ability to critically evaluate a persuasive text, or the establishment of positive motivation to read. Helping all students become better readers involves a multitude of specific audiences and their needs for reading assessment (Farr, 1992). I propose that reading assessment is most effective when it is sensitive to the socially situated nature of schooling and to the needs of all legitimate assessment audiences and purposes (Afflerbach, Cho, Kim, & Clark, 2010).

The first and most common purpose of assessment is reporting: providing information that can inform instruction, certify student achievement, and demonstrate teacher and school accountability. A student's response to a teacher's question, the result of a quiz, work in relation to a performance-assessment rubric, or a standardized-test score all represent information that reports on the quality of students' learning.

It is less common to conceptualize reading assessment as serving the two additional purposes of teaching students about assessment and supporting student learning. However, there are distinct benefits to using assessment in this manner. Teaching students about assessment is a critical step on the path to independent reading. Self-assessment is a key aspect of metacognition (Baker & Brown, 1984; Veenman, Van Hoult-Wolters, & Afflerbach, 2006), and successful, independent reading requires the ability to self-assess. Accomplished student readers are able to set goals, monitor their progress toward goals, and determine the quality of their reading. Thus, helping developing readers learn to assess their own reading should be a focus in all reading assessment programs (Black & Wiliam, 1998).

> Teaching students about assessment is a critical step on the path to independent reading.

On a developmental continuum, entry into self-assessment may begin with questions that focus elementary student readers on monitoring their meaning making as they read. Students can learn to ask themselves, "Does that make sense?" and "How do I know?" at natural breaks in reading, such as at the ends of paragraphs and sentences. As readers develop the ability and inclination to self-assess, they perform increasingly complex tasks, such as managing the synthesis of information from different texts and monitoring their work in relation to a complex performance-assessment rubric. A focus on using reading assessments to teach self-reflection helps augment assessment that is done *to* and *for* students with assessment that is done *with* and *by* students (Afflerbach, 2002).

Teachers provide support when they give positive feedback to students (Johnston, 2004), such as focusing on student accomplishment and effort, or helping students build the connection between their ability to self-assess and reading independence. Teachers help contribute to students' positive self-esteem when they provide students with evidence of progress in reading. When we view reading assessment from a support perspective, we may examine our reading assessment systems and ask, "How do students interpret the assessment results and feedback that they receive in school?" and "Does our use of assessment to support students enhance their self-concepts in reading?" (Crooks, 1988). When reading assessment labels certain readers as "below average" or as having perpetual "needs improvement" or "low reading group" statuses, we are challenged to transform reading assessment into a supportive system that helps build or repair self-esteem related to reading (Stanovich, 1986).

A carefully planned reading assessment program serves the three distinct purposes—reporting, teaching, and supporting—within the constraints of school time and funding. A strategic approach to developing reading assessment can identify those assessment materials and procedures that serve these multiple purposes. Consider the following example of reading assessment within the subject of vocabulary.

> A carefully planned reading assessment program serves the three distinct purposes—reporting, teaching, and supporting—within the constraints of school time and funding.

Students sort index cards, each containing a single word in their evolving sight-word vocabularies, into the categories "I don't know," "I am getting to know," and "I definitely know." This process (that the teacher models and teaches) serves the three purposes. It reports on students' vocabulary growth as students show the progression of their learning of each word from "I don't know" to "I definitely know." It fosters students' ability to accurately self-assess as they determine the status of the words as they sort them. Finally, it supports students' positive self-concepts as readers by demonstrating both their ability to self-assess and their growing sight-word vocabulary.

The Audiences for Reading Assessment

Different audiences—students, teachers, parents, school administrators, elected officials, and the general public—require different types of reading assessment information. Table 13.1 outlines the purposes of reading assessment for various audiences (Afflerbach, 2007). Ideally, a reading assessment program provides all audiences with assessment information that suits their needs.

Table 13.1: Reading Assessment Audiences and Purposes

Audience	Purpose of Assessment
Students	To report on learning and communicate progress
	To provide support, motivation, and encouragement
	To teach about assessment and how to independently assess one's work and progress
	To build independence
Teachers	To determine the quality of student learning
	To inform instruction
	To construct grades and narrative reports
	To evaluate students
	To diagnose student strengths and weaknesses
Parents	To understand their children's achievements
	To help connect home and school efforts to support students
School Administrators	To determine instructional program effectiveness
	To prove school and teacher accountability
	To allocate school resources
Elected Officials	To establish accountability of schools
	To inform the public of school progress
	To determine funding
General Public	To demonstrate that tax dollars are well spent

Adapted from Afflerbach, P. (2007). Understanding and using reading assessment, K–12. Newark, DE: International Reading Association. Copyright © 2007 by the International Reading Association. Used with permission.

Teachers use assessment to determine and address students' individual needs and best match each student with instruction. Students use teacher feedback to develop positive self-concepts and independence, and to learn how to *do* assessment. Parents use report cards, test results, and information from parent-teacher conferences to better understand their children's accomplishments and challenges. Administrators use assessment information to determine program effectiveness, allocate resources, and prove accountability. Elected officials use this information to establish accountability, inform the public of progress, and determine funding. The general public wants to know that their tax dollars have been well spent.

Effective reading assessment programs include periodic checks for balance of attention to different audiences, because a delicate balance is needed to serve diverse audiences and provide useful information for all. For example, the federal demand for high-stakes testing in relation to adequate yearly progress (AYP) shapes curriculum and instruction, and it requires school districts to appropriate considerable resources to testing. When testing costs consume limited school resources, there may be several outcomes. First, the resources will not be available for the development and use of classroom assessment or for teachers' professional development to conduct effective forms of classroom assessment. Second, tests are most often temporally removed from the classroom reality of a student's understanding on a particular day, and they generally lack the degree of detail necessary to inform effective instruction. Thus, an over-focus on tests may deprive particular audiences of the assessment information they need. Understanding this situation can help schools and teachers develop strategies for advocating for a balance of useful assessment.

Types of Reading Assessment: Formative and Summative

A helpful distinction in assessment is between *formative* and *summative* reading assessments. Our understanding of the formative and summative functions of assessment helps us plan strategically for optimal use of assessment, and it helps us determine the relationships between different assessments.

Formative Assessment

Just as the act of reading involves constructing meaning, the act of reading assessment should result in constructing understanding of our students. Formative assessment helps us construct a dynamic and accurate mental model of the student. It provides evidence for our understanding of students' progress and challenges, and provides a means for continual updating and refining of this understanding. Formative assessments may derive from cumulative school records, test performances, portfolios of student work, teacher observations, reading inventories, and interviews with students. They inform the initial placement of students, for example, in a reading group; in this sense, they provide a tentative *claim* about the current status of the student's reading: his or her achievement level, skill and strategy development, and interests or motivation. Our understanding of each student should continue to be regularly refined and updated using an array of assessment information.

> Just as the act of reading involves constructing meaning, the act of reading assessment should result in constructing understanding of our students.

Teaching is enhanced through the practice of gathering and using continuous, formative reading assessment information. Reflective practitioners (Schon, 1990) are teachers who continually check on the appropriateness of their instruction. The information formative assessment yields is central to this reflective practice: it allows teachers to update their knowledge of the strengths and challenges individual students face and to adjust or maintain instruction. For example, as students read a science article, teacher questions and student responses provide an ongoing account of the nature of student understanding. The responses help the teacher construct an understanding of the effectiveness of the lesson. Without such information, instruction may be misdirected, redundant, or frustrating.

Vygotsky's (1978) portrayal of zones of proximal development further highlights the importance of formative assessment: serving as a guide through the zones and providing a consistent source of information that helps the teacher identify what a student can do and where the student might go next. The teacher who focuses on teaching reading comprehension strategies must have current and detailed information about how strategy use is developing within individual students to determine the instruction that is most appropriate for furthering their development. The teacher can request that students think aloud as they use reading strategies and can provide a checklist for appropriate strategy use. Each of these assessment sources informs subsequent teaching. As we consider a student's current level of achievement and the next anticipated level of achievement, formative assessment helps us both identify the instructional space and determine movement within it. Formative assessments help shape, or form, our thinking and related instruction for individual students.

Summative Assessment

In contrast, summative assessment has a decided product orientation with a goal of determining the state of students' learning after instruction. Typical opportunities for summative assessment occur at the end of a learning event, be it a lesson, chapter, unit, or end of a term like a marking period or academic year. The majority of summative assessments are focused on the end products of learning: for example, a student's cumulative knowledge of sound-symbol correspondences including single-letter sounds, short- and long-vowel sounds, and consonant blends. Or summative assessment may focus on a student's ability to establish literal and inferential understanding of stories following a reading comprehension strategy unit. As such, summative assessment can be characterized as serving the important purpose of providing summary statements of student learning. Summative assessment determines the attainment of learning benchmarks, certifies learning and performance, and demonstrates accountability.

An effective reading assessment program includes formative assessment that anticipates summative assessment performance. For example, formative assessment that is conducted as students work with letter tiles gives valuable information about how well a child is developing knowledge of sound-symbol correspondences. The assessment information describes the student's ongoing development with phonics and specifies which single letter and letter blends are known and which need further exposure and

An effective reading assessment program includes formative assessment that anticipates summative assessment performance.

learning. Instruction that is informed by this formative assessment helps teachers and students prepare for performance on summative assessments of sound-symbol correspondences. A single test on a single day is often used to measure accountability, but accountability is established through a carefully planned and executed reading assessment program that provides both formative and summative assessment information.

The Cognitive and Affective Foci for Reading Assessment

What do we assess when we assess reading? The assessment of reading is exceedingly, if not exclusively, focused on the development of students' reading skills and strategies (Afflerbach, Pearson, & Paris, 2008) and learning the content of texts. This focus is apparent in the array of assessments that inform us about students' phonemic awareness, phonics, fluency, vocabulary, and reading comprehension. Students are expected to become strategic and skillful readers. Thus, effective reading assessment focuses on the development of reading strategies and skills. Students use reading as a tool to learn and remember important content. Thus, effective reading assessment focuses on what students learn.

We know that the typical first grader is different from the typical sixth grader, and that the first grader must continue to develop strategies, skills, affect, and inclinations to be successful in later reading. As we consider the different learning that students experience, and the different types of reading that they encounter, we can determine that different educational goals require different assessments. Simple skills and strategies may be assessed with relatively simple assessments, while more complex skills and strategies may demand more complex assessments. When we want to know if a child has mastered the recognition, understanding, and use of a consonant blend (for example, /fl/) we can often quickly ascertain this with simple assessments that include flash cards, analysis of students' oral reading, and examination of student writing. In contrast, if we are interested in a student's ability to read three texts related to the Civil War and build

> As we consider the different learning that students experience, and the different types of reading that they encounter, we can determine that different educational goals require different assessments.

meaning across the three texts while determining the accuracy and trustworthiness of the information presented in each of the three texts, we need a performance assessment with relatively complex demands and scoring criteria.

Paris (2005) observes that reading skills and strategies are constrained or unconstrained in relation to students' ongoing reading development. Typically, skills and strategies related to decoding and reading aloud (for example, letter knowledge, phonics, and phonemic awareness) are constrained. Most students learn and master them in a relatively short time. Some children may have difficulty learning them, but assessing these constrained skills and strategies is relatively straightforward. In contrast, skills and strategies related to constructing meaning (comprehension and vocabulary) are less constrained. They typically require more time to assess. Questions and prompts related to reading comprehension assessment may have divergent, acceptable responses or performances. Higher-order thinking involves more unconstrained skills and strategies that contribute to reading for understanding. Thus, allowing divergent student responses and requiring complex reading material and reading performances will aid in the assessment of unconstrained skills. Such needs are addressed with extended constructed response items and performance assessments. The differentiation of constrained and unconstrained skills and strategies allows us to consider the relative complexity of the assessment content and form. Assessment of sound-symbol correspondences should not be needlessly complex, just as assessment of critical reading strategies requires some complexity.

While skill and strategy and the learning of course content are important foci for instruction and related assessment efforts, affective and social aspects of reading and reading development rarely receive assessment attention. Thus, we must determine if it is enough to assess only cognitive strategy and skill. Successful reading programs promote positive affect toward reading: students who consider themselves successful readers and who are motivated to read tend to do well in school (Stanovich, 1986). Reading teachers' most impressive successes may not be in moving a student from the 78th to the 93rd percentile in standardized, norm-referenced test performance, but in helping the reluctant reader become an enthusiastic reader and helping the reader who gives up at the first hint of difficulty develop into one who perseveres and succeeds. However, it is rare to find assessment that focuses on student motivation, self-concept, self-esteem, volition, or agency. If the collective wisdom of a school or district is that successful readers need positive motivation and healthy self-images, then assessment can help us better understand these important factors of student reader development. Assessment can focus students' motivation (Guthrie & Wigfield, 1997) and volition (Corno & Mandinach, 2004). Assessments and surveys include foci on students' self-concepts as readers (Chapman & Tunmer, 1995), their motivations and attitudes of reading (Gambrell, Palmer, Codling, & Mazzoni, 1996; McKenna & Kear, 1990), and reading interests (Hildebrandt, 2001).

The Validity of Reading Assessment: Construct and Consequential

Research, theory, and practice serve to continually update our best understanding of reading. As this understanding evolves, it is important to examine the relationship between the assessments we use and the *construct*, or model, of reading that we would assess. The close alignment of assessment with the construct of reading can increase the confidence we have in assessments, and in the inferences we make from assessment information. Thus, it is critical to determine if reading assessment reflects, thinly or robustly (Davis, 1998), all that reading is. Consider the 2009 framework of the National Assessment of Educational Progress (National Assessment Governing Board, 2008) that states reading is an active and complex process that involves the following:

- Understanding written text

- Developing and interpreting meaning

- Using meaning as appropriate to type of text, purpose, and situation

This definition reflects the ongoing evolution of how we conceptualize reading. Note that the definition focuses on *learning* and *remembering* text but adds the *use* of what is learned and remembered from reading. A legitimate inference from this definition is that reading assessment should include tasks in which students use what they have learned from reading. The definition broadens the parameters of *constructing* meaning to now include *using* the constructed meaning. The definition also assumes that the mechanics of reading, including the development of phonemic awareness, the derivation of sound-symbol correspondences, and reading at an appropriately fluent rate, are established and working well. Valid assessment will attend to these developmental differences and reflect the expectations of readers' growth as they progress across grades. Note that the definition has exclusive focus on cognitive skills and strategies. Thus, it is not one that would help guide the development and use of assessment that focuses on readers' affective development.

> Valid assessment will attend to developmental differences and reflect the expectations of readers' growth as they progress across grades.

A second important form of validity is *consequential validity*, a term that originated in relation to the consequences of high-stakes testing (Tittle, 1989). For example, test scores can have the consequence of reward or sanction for schools and teachers, and they influence student self-esteem and self-concept. When a school maintains a consistently positive test-score profile, it may benefit from increased funding, public recognition as a school of excellence, and the sense of accomplishment that is often associated with high test scores. In contrast, states and district education authorities may sanction schools with low test-score profiles, contributing to morale problems amongst the teaching corps, or to the decisions to adopt reading curriculum that serves as test preparation. These consequences of testing emerge regardless of students' reading achievement levels when they enter school or of the relative privilege or deprivation of students' home and community lives. Student self-esteem and self-concept tend to develop positively when assessment information is supportive and focused on student accomplishment, but when assessment information labels a student as "below average" or "failing," we should consider both the short-term and long-term consequences on developing readers' self-concepts and self-esteems.

It is important to think of consequential validity as an aspect of *any* type of assessment—our selection and development of assessments should always be informed, in part, by a thorough accounting of the possible positive and negative consequences of the assessments. For example, as assessment *reports*, is one consequence the timely provision of information that informs instruction? As assessment *teaches*, do students learn to self-assess as a consequence of teachers modeling assessment questions? As assessment *supports*, does each and every student build and maintain self-esteem as a consequence of reading assessment feedback? Attention to the consequences of assessment helps us take a proactive approach to developing the reading assessment program.

> It is important to think of consequential validity as an aspect of *any* type of assessment—our selection and development of assessments should always be informed, in part, by a thorough accounting of the possible positive and negative consequences of the assessments.

The Reliability of Reading Assessment

How is our reading assessment consistent? How does it accurately and reliably represent students' accomplishments and needs? Teacher expertise is necessary for reliable classroom assessment. The consistency with which a teacher implements assessment, gathers assessment data, interprets the data, and makes reasoned decisions based on the data reflects the reliability and usefulness of assessment. Formative assessment demands that teachers are supported in their efforts to become "evaluation experts" (Johnston, 1989) as they gather, interpret, and act with formative assessment information in classrooms. Thus, teachers need professional development to build the expertise that features in the reliable collection, interpretation, and use of assessment information. Using Running Records (Clay, 2002), conducting miscue analysis for diagnostic assessment of student reading, and then planning subsequent instruction typifies such expertise. A subtext for this chapter is the central role that teachers play in successful reading assessment. Assessment itself is central to reading program success, but many teachers are not adequately trained in the ways and means of effective assessment (Stiggins & Conklin, 1992). Consequently, there is an inattention to the importance of teacher-based classroom assessment, the need for initial training, and ongoing teacher professional development. The promise of classroom-based reading assessments will be more fully realized when teachers are supported in their efforts to develop assessment expertise.

Assessment and Attention to Individual Differences

A well-functioning reading assessment program informs us of progress and need in relation to each student's reading development. As well, reading assessment must attend to the needs of some students through accommodation. Legal designation and federal law require that particular students receive individualized instructional attention and accommodated assessment. Effective accommodations, most frequently researched in relation to testing, include linguistic modification (using clear and straightforward language in assessment prompts and directions) and the provision of additional time for students to participate in the assessment (Abedi, Lord, Hofstetter, & Baker, 2000; Stansfield, 2002; Stretch & Osborne, 2005).

While these accommodations are intended to help English learners (ELs) and students with special needs, the consideration of adequate time to complete an assessment and of clear language that communicates the purpose and demands of an assessment are requisite for any successful assessment. A related goal involves task analysis, in which we carefully analyze our assessments to determine what students must do to succeed, considering all of the procedural, declarative, and situational knowledge that an assessment item (or series of items) requires of students. While task analysis is resource consuming, it contributes to a reading assessment system that provides information that best informs our work with each and every student. In summary, the assessment accommodations that are made for particular students are worthy of our consideration for all students. For good practice, establish clear and comprehensible student assessment directions, instructions, and questions, and allocate sufficient time for students to meet assessment demands.

The Types of Assessment: Tools of the Trade

The focus on audience and purpose, the formative and summative nature of assessment, validity and reliability, and the object of our reading assessment help prepare for the selection and informed use of particular types of reading assessment—the tools of the trade. This section provides an overview of reading assessments that may prove useful for different purposes and audiences. While effective assessment is more than the matching of particular types of learning with particular types of assessment, I would like to present general guidelines for considering different types of assessment, along with representative strengths and corresponding uses of particular assessments.

Teacher Questioning

Questions are one of the most flexible and effective means of assessing students' reading development (Afflerbach, 2007). They can be scaled from relatively simple to increasingly complex, reflecting different types of thinking. We can ask young elementary students direct questions about literal comprehension ("What is the name of the team that Becky plays for?"), vocabulary ("Can you use *clue* in a sentence?"), and phonics ("What sound does the letter *h* make?"). Questions can also focus on the affective aspects of reading, including "Did you like the story? Why or why not?" Such questions show students that we are interested not only in their reading skills and strategy development, but also in what they think about the texts they read. As students further develop their reading prowess, questions can help us understand higher-order thinking in relation to reading ("Does the author provide sufficient evidence to support the claims she makes about global warming?"). Higher-order thinking depends on more basic thinking, so as we consider an arc of questions (Wolf, 1987) from simple to complex, we must remember that complexity builds on more basic understanding. Asking questions that require the synthesis, application, and critical evaluation of what is read must follow from the determination that students have established a literal understanding of text.

> Questions are one of the most flexible and effective means of assessing students' reading development.

Additionally, questions can teach. Posing questions can serve as a model of how to ask, what to ask about, and of encouraging particular types of thinking. A classroom teacher uses the question "What is a good prediction about the content of this chapter based on the title and first sentence?" to model, through thinking aloud, questions worth asking. The successful and independent student reader consistently asks questions of the current status of his or her work, progress toward goals, and challenges. Thus, asking appropriate questions helps developing readers begin the critical path to self-assessment ability.

Teacher Observation

Watching and listening are valuable, ever-available sources of reading assessment information. Teacher observation is authentic assessment, as it takes place as classroom reading events occur. Teachers can determine their need for observation, be it an update on student enthusiasm for reading, turn taking in a reading group, or demonstrated use of a particular reading strategy. Knowing what one is looking for is a key to effective observation. Reading inventories and running records offer a somewhat formalized approach to observation, as they help teachers begin the assessment routine with particular foci, be it students' sight-word knowledge, miscue analysis, fluency, and literal and inferential comprehension. Commercially published reading inventories require time and materials outside the curriculum, while running records (Clay, 2002) are more flexible and attainable when students are otherwise engaged in oral reading with classroom materials. Teacher observation is also valuable for assessing affective aspects of student learning. A student's level of motivation, reluctance, or enthusiasm for reading may be most apparent to the teacher who regularly observes students in the classroom. Using observation checklists, teachers and students can approach an assessment task with a preexisting schema for their assessment work.

Tests and Quizzes

There are many iterations of tests and quizzes across the school year. Tests and quizzes are normally given at the end of lessons, chapters, units, and marking periods and inform us of student attainment of learning goals and benchmarks. They may also provide valuable prereading information, as when we use a pretest to determine prior knowledge. Also, pretests can serve as formative assessments when their results lead to instruction that best prepares students to take summative tests. Given the considerable resources already dedicated to testing, my recommendation is that all teachers consider

> Given the considerable resources already dedicated to testing, my recommendation is that all teachers consider what tests can and cannot provide in terms of helping students grow as readers.

what tests can and cannot provide in terms of helping students grow as readers. Most tests are summative in nature, and, in general, the higher the stakes of the test, the less useful it is for informing classroom practice.

Multiple-choice questions and brief constructed-response items are often associated with tests and quizzes. While they are often overused in reading assessment, they do have value and utility. When we assess constrained skills (as discussed earlier in this chapter), including knowledge of phonics, sight words, and literal comprehension, multiple-choice reading assessment items may be suitable. In contrast, these items are limited in their abilities to describe students' higher-order thinking or to accommodate divergent student responses and performances. When using multiple-choice questions, it is imperative to determine a priori how well the assessment format accommodates the type of reading skill, strategy, or performance that is to be measured.

Portfolios

Portfolios allow for the establishment of student assessment routines over extended projects and time frames. They may encourage student involvement with assessment, and they help represent the detailed nature of student achievement. Portfolios, often associated with students' writing, can be used to store process and product assessment, as when students construct first drafts, revisions, edits, and final versions of their writing. Projects that demand the reading of multiple texts and student performances may benefit from portfolio assessment. For example, if students are required to read varied texts for a report on an African country, the portfolio can contain a student's list of resources, notes, interviews with experts, photos and graphics downloaded from the Internet, a reading response log, and drafts of a related writing or multimedia project.

Portfolios demand dedicated student involvement and so require that students learn both the means to establish and use portfolios and to appreciate their potential contributions to growth (Calfee & Perfumo, 1993). Portfolios should represent a psychological space as much as a physical space; while the portfolio holds documents, it should also present a series of ongoing opportunities for students to portray the complexity of learning, to demonstrate learning, and to learn and practice self-assessment. Students' responsibility for assessment is heightened with portfolios, and students benefit from instruction and modeling that illustrates the ways and means of successful portfolio development and assessment.

Performance Assessment

As students are asked to read and then use the knowledge they gain from reading, performance assessments should have a regular, central role in reading assessment. In school and out, we read to perform tasks. Performance assessments represent authentic assessment of students, their reading, and the tasks they undertake in relation to reading. When we ask students to create a class skit based on their readings of colonial America, they are employing constructed knowledge. When we ask students to critically evaluate the claims and evidence related to global warming, they perform in relation to what they read. When we ask students to perform a poem for an audience, they are employing their knowledge and proficiency in reading fluency.

Performance assessments consist of components that can serve both assessment and teaching roles. For example, a scoring rubric is used to assign a grade, but it can also be used to help students understand what is expected of them. Combined with samples of students' work and detailed scoring guides, performance assessments provide students with a roadmap to performance (Baxter & Glaser, 1998). Performance assessment can span a continuum of simple to complex: early readers may be asked to portray a character based on understanding a fairy tale, while accomplished readers can build models of chemical reactions based on their understanding of science texts. Performance assessment is demanding of students and teachers, and it is best used after careful consideration of the complexity and types of thinking that it demands of students. In all cases, performance assessment is appropriate for when we want to assess the application of knowledge gained from reading. Finally, performance assessment is notable for its transparency: students are encouraged to examine what they must do to earn particular grades or scores, and in doing so receive support for learning self-assessment.

A final, related point for all types of reading assessment is this: all reading assessment should be considered high-stakes assessment, because all assessment should make identifiable contributions to high-quality teaching and student learning. In the assessment litera-ture, and in our assessment conversations, we may encounter the distinction between *formal* and *informal* reading assessment. Johnston (1987) notes that labeling any assessment as *informal* places it at a disadvantage related to *formal* assessment, regardless of the quality and integrity of either. Consider the perspec-tive of a parent, an administrator, or legisla-tor. Given the choice of assessments (and the information that they provide to enhance the teaching and learning enterprise), would one choose formal or informal assessment information? I recommend that the terms *formal* and *informal* be retired, as they assign different a priori value to assessment information that is of supposed value. Why else is it collected and used?

> All reading assessment should be considered high-stakes assessment, because all assessment should make identifiable contributions to high-quality teaching and student learning.

Making Assessment Seamless

Reading assessment must be conducted with the goal of foster-ing students' reading development. Successful reading assessment is the result of valid and reliable measures that are integrated with the overall goals of schooling. Many schools and classrooms have an exclusive focus on cognitive skills and strategies, and, within this exclusive focus, tests drive many assessment efforts. It is important to determine the importance of both cognitive and affective growth in student reading and design assessments that account for each. Thus, how the construct of reading is conceptualized matters—it will provide a touchstone for examining curriculum and teaching goals. A smoothly functioning assessment system makes optimal combination of formative and summative reading assessment. The former anticipates the latter: ongoing classroom assessment helps teachers and their students focus on the reading development that summative assessment measures later.

If the goal of reading assessment is to foster students' reading development, then reading assessment must be useful to all those who have the ability to contribute to this effort. High-quality reading assessment reports on student success, as it supports students and teaches them how to *do* assessment. Ideally, assessments are combined in an effective reading assessment program that addresses all aspects of students' reading-related development, and ably serves all legitimate assessment audiences and purposes. School resources, including professional development, support it. Effective reading assessment programs are dynamic and flexible, and they are informed in an ongoing manner by relevant research in reading and assessment.

As instructional goals are set, it is important to consider the alignment between teaching, learning, and assessment. Too often, assessment operates from a top-down position, and tests drive curriculum; or assessment represents a series of afterthoughts— added to an instructional program because it is required, and not because it is tightly aligned with teaching goals and student learning. Optimally, assessment is seamless with teaching and learning, and it develops organically with curriculum.

References and Resources

Abedi, J., Lord, C., Hofstetter, C., & Baker, E. (2000). Impact of accommodation strategies on English language learners' test performance. *Educational Measurement: Issues and Practice, 19*, 16–26.

Afflerbach, P. (2002). Teaching reading self-assessment strategies. In C. C. Block & M. Pressley (Eds.), *Comprehension instruction: Research-based best practices* (pp. 96–111). New York: Guilford Press.

Afflerbach, P. (2007). *Understanding and using reading assessment, K–12.* Newark, DE: International Reading Association.

Afflerbach, P., Cho, B., Kim, J., & Clark, S. (2010). Classroom assessment of literacy. In D. Wyse, R. Andrews, & J. Hoffman (Eds.), *The international handbook of English, language and literacy teaching* (pp. 401–412). London: Routledge.

Afflerbach, P., Pearson, P. D., & Paris, S. (2008). Clarifying differences between reading skills and reading strategies. *The Reading Teacher, 61*, 364–373.

Baker, L., & Brown, A. L. (1984). Metacognitive skills and reading. In P. D. Pearson (Series Ed.), R. Barr, M. L. Kamil, & P. Mosenthal (Vol. Eds.), *Handbook of reading research: Vol. 1* (pp. 353–394). New York: Longman.

Baxter, G., & Glaser, R. (1998). Investigating the cognitive complexity of science assessments. *Educational Measurement: Issues and Practice, 17*(3), 37–45.

Black, P., & Wiliam, D. (1998). Inside the black box: Raising standards through classroom assessment. *Phi Delta Kappan, 80,* 139–148.

Calfee, R., & Perfumo, P. (1993). Student portfolios: Opportunities for a revolution in assessment. *Journal of Reading, 36,* 532–537.

Chapman, J., & Tunmer, W. (1995). Development of young children's reading self-concepts: An examination of emerging subcomponents and their relationship with reading achievement. *Journal of Educational Psychology, 87*(1), 154–167.

Clay, M. (2002). *An observation survey of early literacy achievement* (2nd ed.). Portsmouth, NH: Heinemann.

Corno, L., & Mandinach, E. (2004). What we have learned about student engagement in the past twenty years. In D. McInerney & S. Van Etten (Eds.), *Big theories revisited: Vol. 4. Research on sociocultural influences on motivation and learning* (pp. 299–328). Greenwich, CT: Information Age.

Crooks, T. (1988). The impact of classroom evaluation practices on students. *Review of Educational Research, 58,* 438–481.

Davis, A. (1998). *The limits of educational assessment.* Oxford, England: Blackwell.

Farr, R. (1992). Putting it all together: Solving the reading assessment puzzle. *The Reading Teacher, 46,* 26–37.

Gambrell, L., Palmer, B., Codling, R., & Mazzoni, S. (1996). *Motivation to read profile (MRP).* Instructional Resource No. 14. Athens, GA: National Reading Research Center.

Guthrie, J., & Wigfield, A. (1997). *Reading engagement: Motivating readers through integrated instruction.* Newark, DE: International Reading Association.

Hildebrandt, D. (2001). "But there's nothing good to read" (in the library media center). *Media Spectrum, 29,* 34–37.

Johnston, P. (1987). Teachers as evaluation experts. *The Reading Teacher, 40,* 744–748.

Johnston, P. (2004). *Choice words.* Portland, ME: Stenhouse.

McKenna, M., & Kear, D. (1990). Measuring attitude toward reading: A new tool for teachers. *The Reading Teacher, 43,* 626–639.

National Assessment Governing Board. (2008). *Reading framework for the 2009 National Assessment of Educational Progress* (Contract No. ED–02–R–0007). Washington, DC: U.S. Government Printing Office.

Paris, S. G. (2005). Reinterpreting the development of reading skills. *Reading Research Quarterly, 40*(2), 184–202.

Pellegrino, J., Chudowsky, N., & Glaser, R. (2001). *Knowing what students know: The science and design of educational assessment.* Washington, DC: National Academy.

Schon, D. (1990). *Educating the reflective practitioner: Toward a new design for teaching and learning in the professions.* San Francisco: Jossey-Bass.

Stanovich, K. (1986). Matthew effects in reading: Some consequences of individual differences in the acquisition of literacy. *Reading Research Quarterly, 21*(4), 360–407.

Stansfield, C. W. (2002). Linguistic simplification: A promising test accommodation for LEP students? *Practical Assessment, Research and Evaluation, 8*(7). Accessed at http://pareonline.net/getvn.asp?v=8&n=7 on February 28, 2010.

Stiggins, R., & Conklin, N. (1992). *In teachers' hands: Investigating the practices of classroom assessment.* Albany: State University of New York.

Stretch, L., & Osborne, J. (2005). Extended time test accommodation: Directions for future research and practice. *Practical Assessment, Research and Evaluation, 10*(8). Accessed at http://pareonline.net/genpare.asp?wh=4&abt=stretch on February 28, 2010.

Tittle, C. (1989). Validity: Whose construction is it in the teaching and learning context? *Educational Measurement: Issues and Practices, 8*, 5–13.

Veenman, M., Van Hout-Wolters, B., & Afflerbach, P. (2006). Metacognition and learning: Conceptual and methodological issues. *Metacognition and Learning, 1*, 3–14.

Vygotsky, L. S. (1978). *Mind in society: Development of higher psychological processes* (M. Cole, V. John-Steiner, S. Scribner, & E. Souberman, Eds.). Cambridge, MA: Harvard University Press.

Wolf, D. P. (1987, Winter). The art of questioning. *Academic Connections,* 1–7. Accessed at www.exploratorium.edu/IFI/resources/workshops/artofquestioning.html on February 28, 2010.

Rita M. Bean

Rita M. Bean, PhD, is professor emerita at the University of Pittsburgh. Prior to joining the university, she taught at the elementary level and also served as a K–12 reading supervisor. She served as a member of the International Reading Association board and was president of the College Reading Association. She has been published in many journals and books on the topics of reading curriculum and instruction, professional development, and the role of reading specialists/literacy coaches. Her newest book, *The Reading Specialist: Leadership for the Classroom, School, and Community* (2nd ed.), focuses on the role of the reading specialist, especially the leadership role. She has written chapters on literacy coaching and on the importance of professional development for teachers. Her current research focuses on the development and evaluation of early literacy reading programs, instruction for struggling readers, and the role of reading specialists/literacy coaches as change agents and in improving student learning. Bean received the Distinguished Teacher Award and the Distinguished Service Award from the University of Pittsburgh.

In this chapter, Bean addresses three big ideas gleaned from the research and literature on coaching: (1) a clear definition of coaching promotes clear expectations, (2) context for coaching matters, and (3) coach time spent with teachers is important.

Chapter 14

The Reading Coach: Professional Development and Literacy Leadership in the School

Rita M. Bean

Although past efforts to improve student learning have often focused on finding the right materials or programs, we have moved into an era in which the emphasis is on quality teaching. The federal government has developed policy that ties teacher performance ratings to their students' achievement, foundations are supporting school districts' efforts to develop performance pay scales, and districts are discussing ways to help teachers improve their classroom practices to improve student achievement.

At the same time, teaching is becoming more challenging with changing demographics in schools, for example, larger numbers of students of poverty, increased numbers of immigrants and English learners, and other students with needs that teachers may not be prepared to address. Concurrently, there is an increased emphasis on differentiating instruction to meet the needs of every student with accompanying accountability. One solution to improve teacher and teaching quality is job-embedded professional development from coaches who provide ongoing teacher support. Often the title of *coach* has a prefix descriptor: instructional, science, technology, literacy, or reading coach. Whatever the title, many coaches, from preschool through high school, are being asked to work with teachers to improve literacy instruction—specifically, helping students learn to read and write. Coaches are also being asked to work with content or academic discipline teachers to help students use literacy effectively as a means of learning the content.

> One solution to improve teacher and teaching quality is job-embedded professional development from coaches who provide ongoing teacher support.

In many ways, coaching has grown *topsy-turvy*: schools are employing literacy coaches; however, they are implementing coaching without a solid understanding of who should coach, how they should coach, and the conditions in schools that are necessary for coaching to be successful. As Taylor (2008) states, there continues to be a need for additional "rigorous empirical evidence of the effects of coaching on teachers' knowledge, teachers' practice, and students' learning" (p. 29). At the same time, there have been a number of studies, both small and large scale, whose results are helpful to those implementing such programs in schools and to coaches themselves.

In this chapter, I address three big ideas gleaned from the research and literature on coaching: (1) a clear definition of coaching promotes clear expectations, (2) context for coaching matters, and (3) time spent with teachers is important. In the beginning of each section, I describe relevant research findings, and at the end of each section, I discuss the implications for coaches and coaching.

Big Idea 1: A Clear Definition of Coaching Promotes Clear Expectations

A simple definition of *literacy coaching* might read as follows: *a set of activities in which an individual (coach) engages teachers in enhancing their instructional practices to improve student learning; a form of professional development for teachers.* However, such a definition does not account for the fact that those writing about coaching, designing school programs, doing the coaching, and being coached view the phenomenon differently. Bean (2009), for example, describes five general models of coaching: peer, resource, reflective, implementation-prescriptive, and implementation-goal oriented. Table 14.1 describes these various models and identifies qualifications generally required of those who serve as coaches. Obviously, the models require coaches to have different skills and knowledge, and, in addition, they create different relationships between the coach and the teachers with whom they work. In the *peer, resource,* and *reflective* models, coaches most often respond to teachers' requests and needs, although they may initiate a set of activities with specific teachers. In the *implementation* models, coaches, because of accountability demands, must be prepared to initiate activities with teachers, even though they will also respond to requests.

Table 14.1: Five General Models of Coaching

Coaching Model	General Description
Peer	Colleagues work with each other to provide support and feedback about instruction. All teachers can serve as coaches; one teacher may not be more expert than another.
Resource	An individual is assigned to support teachers' work in many different ways, such as by providing materials, problem solving, and providing feedback if asked. (In general, responding to teacher requests.) Often, the coach has some literacy expertise, for example, as a reading specialist.
Reflective	An individual is assigned to help teachers think about and reflect on their instructional practices to facilitate their work. This coach may have expertise in a specific area (literacy, science) or may be a subject-matter generalist who has expertise in instructional coaching.
Implementation-Prescriptive	An individual is assigned to support or facilitate the implementation of a specific instructional program, approach, or curriculum, such as Success for All. The coach must have specific knowledge of the program being implemented. The emphasis on fidelity of implementation may force the coach into an evaluative role.
Implementation-Goal Oriented	An individual works in a school where a specific framework or set of goals has been adopted and has the responsibility for facilitating implementation efforts. Because of the broad set of goals, teachers may have some choice in how to accomplish goals.

Certainly, working with teachers who request support requires a different set of skills than working with those who do not seek such support but are seen as needing help. Moreover, although those who write about coaching (Bean, 2009; Hasbrouck & Denton, 2005; Toll, 2007) indicate that it should not be evaluative in nature, because of the models' emphasis on "fidelity to implementation," teachers may view coaching as an attempt to evaluate their performance. When a majority of the teachers in a school have agreed to implement a specific program or set of goals, or when teachers agree with or believe in a specific initiative, it is easier for coaches to work collaboratively with them. In addition, all coaches must be skilled at being able to nudge or persuade teachers to make changes in their instructional practices.

Coaching differs in other dimensions than just the type of model. Coaches may be housed in the school and may have many responsibilities beyond coaching, or they may be external, assigned to a specific school to provide coaching only. Coaches can also be assigned to a small or large number of teachers or to one or more schools. Further, the context of the school and its interpretation of what coaches can or cannot do may differ.

Given the variability in how coaching may be defined, it should be obvious as to why research studies of the effectiveness of coaching may generate inconsistent results. For example, in an experimental study that investigated the impact of professional development with and without coaching on the classroom practices of early childhood teachers in 291 sites in four cities, Neuman and Cunningham (2009) found that there were significant improvements in language and literacy practices for teachers who received coursework plus coaching. In this study, coaches trained in what Neuman and Cunningham call a "diagnostic or prescriptive model of coaching" (p. 543) were randomly assigned to teachers who received sixty-four hours of individual one-on-one coaching; these coaches were not members of the staff, but made weekly visits to the various settings.

Garet et al. (2008) also investigated the impact of coaching in ninety schools in sixty districts (270 teachers) with equal numbers of schools assigned randomly to treatments. They reported no differences in teacher knowledge or practices between groups receiving professional development only and those receiving professional development plus coaching, although both of these groups exhibited significantly higher knowledge and more changes in instructional practices than did the control group. In this study, according to students' standardized tests, there was no effect of either treatment group on reading achievement. Current or retired educators from the school districts in the study conducted the coaching; these trained coaches were assigned to work half-time with teachers. However, although the professional development plus coaching group was coached on average for 61.5 hours, the range of coaching hours individual teachers received was as little as 1.2 hours to as many as 173 hours. Moreover, coaching was defined more broadly than it was in the Neuman and Cunningham (2009) study. Garet et al. (2008) indicate that coaching consists of four major activities: planning, observing and providing feedback, working in the classroom with teachers, and conducting grade-level meetings.

Why the differences in results? Garet et al. (2008) speculate that in their own study, perhaps too many teachers received too few hours of coaching or the coaches' knowledge was not sufficiently strong. Perhaps the intensive one-on-one coaching in the Neuman and Cunningham study (2009) was the contributing factor to changes in teacher practice. Readers of studies need to consider the many different ways in which coaching is defined and implemented in interpreting results. In sum, those involved in coaching initiatives might consider the following implications about the importance of establishing a clear definition of coaching: job description, expectations, and activities.

Job Description

It is critical to develop a job description that outlines coach qualifications and duties. There is a great deal of agreement that reading or literacy coaches must have expertise about literacy learning and prior experiences as a teacher and as an adult educator (International Reading Association, 2004, 2006; Frost & Bean, 2006); in fact, L'Allier and Elish-Piper (2006) found that there was greater improvement in student achievement when literacy coaches had reading endorsement. However, although coaches should have expertise, they should avoid being seen as experts who have all the answers. Rather, they should work with colleagues to generate solutions to problems.

Expectations

The expectations for coaching should be shared with principals and with teachers at each school. In other words, all involved must understand what coaches can and cannot do. For example, in their roles, coaches are not supervisors; they can visit classrooms to observe teachers and provide feedback, but rarely should they discuss specific evaluative information about a specific teacher with administrators. Toll (2004) states, "For coaching to be successful, it must be separated from supervision" (p. 6). Toll provides a number of tips for coaches, suggesting that when coaches talk with administrators about their activities, they summarize their work by grade level or department. For example, coaches might indicate that teachers at the fifth-grade level have identified reading vocabulary as an important focus and see the value of multiple exposures to words and the importance of helping students relate the new words to their own experiences. At the same time, the coach might indicate that there is a need for some modeling and coteaching to help teachers get a deeper understanding of how to use specific strategies in their daily instruction.

Activities

Coaches new to a school or to coaching can also behave in ways that clarify the nature of their work (Bean, 2009). They can initiate activities and seek responsibilities, such as scheduling introductory meetings with individual teachers to learn more about their students and needs, developing a list of professional resources and materials for teachers, and volunteering to help teachers with assessments.

Coaches must build a sense of trust and rapport. Coaching is built on trust, and although trust is built over time, new coaches begin this process by maintaining confidentiality. Anything an individual teacher says to a coach remains between them. Likewise, we must recognize that actions matter: teachers will develop respect for coaches when coaches have respect for them and acknowledge the many challenges that teachers face. As coaches in Carroll's study (2007) indicated, coaching is a "journey" or a "process." Coaching is not a one-shot event but involves working with teachers in multiple ways over time. As one coach explained, "We made a plan . . . had open communication. . . . Although things didn't always go as planned, we worked through it all together and she became a better teacher and I became a better coach because of our partnership" (Carroll, 2007, p. 79). Even if a school has a clear idea of what the expectations for coaching are, there is the important task of selecting a coach who can work effectively in that role.

> Actions matter: teachers will develop respect for coaches when coaches have respect for them and acknowledge the many challenges that teachers face.

Several organizations have written standards or position statements that assist those responsible for selecting coaches (IRA, 2004, 2006; Frost & Bean, 2006). Bean and Carroll (2006) identify several factors for administrators recruiting coaches to consider: the candidate should have an in-depth knowledge of literacy, be a master teacher, have the ability to work well with adults both individually and in groups, and have excellent interpersonal and communication skills. In other words, as stated by Bean and Carroll (2006), "literacy coaches . . . must not only demonstrate effective teaching abilities but also have the leadership skills that enable them to become effective change agents in schools" (p. 146).

Big Idea 2: The Context for Coaching Matters

Coaching does not occur in a vacuum. Within one district, there are schools where a districtwide coaching initiative is working effectively and others in which it is not (Camburn, Kimball, & Lowenhaupt, 2008). Moreover, conditions in a school significantly affect whether any coaching, regardless of model, is successfully implemented. Several key factors for effectiveness include the principal's understanding of and support for the coach and the coaching initiative; the culture of the school, including teachers' knowledge and attitude toward the innovation and coaching; and the goals the district sets for the coaching initiative.

As previously mentioned, one of the key factors leading to coaching success is the understanding and support of the principal.

Carroll (2007) found that coaches identified principal support as a critical ingredient; without their support, coaching was much less likely to be successful. For example, principals who had little understanding of coaching were more likely to ask coaches to assume responsibilities that took time away from their coaching—to substitute for teachers, handle administrative tasks, enter test scores, and gather, organize, and distribute materials. Even more detrimental to the coaching effort, some principals neither encouraged teachers to work with the coach nor adjusted scheduling to enable coaches to meet with individual teachers or groups of teachers. In their study of the principal's role in launching a coaching program, Matsumura, Sartoris, DiPrima Bickel, and Garnier (2009) found that principal leadership was significantly related to the frequency with which teachers talked with coaches and coaches observed teachers.

A broader issue related to school culture affects coaching. Leana and Pil (2006) label it "internal social capital": the interactions and relationships among teachers, administrators, and others that promote a common and shared vision within a school. Coaching seems to thrive in an environment of trust, one in which faculty norms include high expectations and a sense of collective responsibility for students, and a belief that they and their colleagues can make a difference in the educational lives of students. Atteberry, Bryk, Walker, and Biancarosa (2008), in their study of coaching in Literacy Collaborative schools, reported tremendous variability in coaching activities among and even within schools, even though coaches supporting this initiative received explicit and in-depth preparation. They reported that coaches tended to work more with teachers who had less preparation in early literacy, who engaged with their colleagues in a proactive manner, and who had a strong commitment to the school. Moreover, they found that school size accounted for much of the variation among schools; in other words, successful implementation of coaching relied upon a reasonable coach-to-teacher ratio.

Although principal support is essential, district factors can also influence the way coaching is implemented in a school. In their study of a coaching initiative in a large, decentralized urban district, Camburn et al. (2009) describe how developments at the district level and competing demands at school sites influence coaching. The tension between honoring district priorities and addressing the needs of the local schools created difficulties for some coaches who found themselves serving "two masters"—principals with their requirements and central office personnel and their dictates.

Coaches function as leaders in their school. As leaders, they help to set direction or establish goals for the literacy program, they have responsibility for "developing people," and they assist in redesigning the organization to accomplish goals (Leithwood, Louis, Anderson, & Wahlstrom, 2004, pp. 8–9). As leaders, coaches are responsible for building the leadership capacity of teachers. They lead, however, through influence, not authority. Coaches in the Bean et al. (2008) study often had leadership roles—chairing committees, writing proposals, leading professional development efforts, and being involved in decision making relative to changes in scheduling, materials, or grouping.

> As leaders, coaches are responsible for building the leadership capacity of teachers. They lead, however, through influence, not authority.

Implications for coaching about the importance of context include the following:

- Coaching programs will have a better chance of being accepted, valued, and successful in a school climate where there is a common vision or set of goals and where colleagues work together to establish a community of practice in which teachers are partners in change.

- Coaches must recognize the nuances of the context in which they work and differentiate their work accordingly. When conditions are conducive to coaching (supportive leadership, a sense of professional community), coaches can generally more quickly establish a positive relationship with teachers, one that enables them to focus on the ultimate goal of coaching—improving student learning. However, when conditions are not conducive to coaching, one of the major aspects of the coach's role is to help establish those necessary positive conditions for coaching. However, coaches must work with others in the school to establish such conditions.

- Building positive conditions for coaching should include working with the principal to establish an understanding of the coach's role and to gain the trust of the principal. The coach and principal should communicate on a regular basis, perhaps once a week. During that interaction, coach and principal can discuss coaching efforts as they relate to school goals, recognize what has been accomplished, and discuss short-term efforts for the following week or month. The coach and principal can each identify what is needed from the other to accomplish goals. For example, the principal will change the schedule so that teachers can meet together to discuss assessment results; the coach will prepare the assessment results so that teachers can use the planning time to make instructional decisions.

- By working with small groups of teachers, perhaps in grade-level or academic-discipline teams, coaches can facilitate teachers' sense of community. Sometimes, a more informal group relationship can be helpful. Thibodeau (2008), for example, writes about a study group that she led with a group of volunteer high school content teachers and the impact of that work on the classroom practices of the teachers. Walpole and Beauchat (2008) identify some key guidelines for leading study groups, including the importance of providing for choice and voice and helping participants make personal connections.

- Begin slowly (avoid the bull-in-a-china-shop approach). By serving as a resource for teachers or working with those who have indicated a need or willingness to be coached, others may see that coaching can be a positive source of professional support and improved instruction.

- Coaches must be effective communicators, which begins with active listening. Stephen Covey (1989), in his book *The Seven Habits of Highly Effective People*, states, "Seek first to understand, then to be understood" (p. 235). In other words, effective coaches try to understand not only what a teacher is saying, but the feelings that the teacher has about a specific topic or issue. When a teacher states, "I am having difficulty with classroom management," she may be frustrated, angry with herself or with her students, or just overwhelmed. Active listening enables coaches to set the stage for communicating empathy and reassuring the teacher that his or her concerns are valid and not an indication of incompetence. A coach's major task is to communicate with teachers in a way that is respectful, using language that is descriptive rather than judgmental. Figure 14.1 identifies six questions coaches might ask themselves as they think about the ways in which they communicate with teachers. (Consider the following resources to learn more about effective communication: Rodgers & Rodgers, 2007; Costa & Garmston, 2002; Johnson & Johnson, 2003.)

---

1. Am I an active listener? Do I listen to understand both the content of the message and the associated feelings or emotions?

2. Do I provide nonverbal indications of active listening? (Nodding in agreement, smiling, and encouraging elaboration)

3. Do I use strategies to make sure that I understand the words of the speaker? (Rephrasing or paraphrasing and asking speaker to clarify)

4. Do I build on what the speaker is saying? (Responding in a way that indicates I am listening)

5. Do I facilitate conversations that indicate the teacher and I are colearners or working together to solve a problem?

**Figure 14.1: Effective communication—
Questions for coaches to consider.**

- Coaches should consider how to facilitate understanding. For example, if the district proposes that specific instructional interventions be used in the schools, but those interventions don't seem to meet the needs of the students at a specific school, the coach and principal should address this concern. Is the concern a legitimate one? Can and will the principal modify the district mandate? Is there a need for the principal to raise this issue with central administration? Should the principal and coach meet with district personnel to address the issue? By providing opportunities to discuss an issue and for all to be heard, coaches can clarify misunderstandings and help those involved to understand all perspectives.

Big Idea 3: The Time Spent With Teachers Is Important

A number of studies have addressed questions about coaching activities—What are coaches doing in schools? And what should they be doing in schools? Often researchers study the time that coaches allocate to actual coaching as well as what coaches are doing with either individuals or groups of teachers (Atteberry et al., 2008; Bean et al., 2008; Deussen, Coskie, Robinson, & Autio, 2007; Roller, 2006; Zigmond, Bean, Kloo, & Brydon, 2011). What seems to be consistent across these studies is that coaches do a lot, and often they do not spend the majority of their time with teachers. Deussen et al. (2007) conducted a study of reading coaches in Reading First schools in five states. They found that these coaches worked with teachers who had little experience with coaching and spent on average only 28 percent of their time working with teachers, even though they had been asked to spend 60 to 80 percent of their time doing so. Deussen et al. (2007) identified five categories of coaches: data oriented, student oriented, managerial, those who worked with individual teachers, and those who worked with groups of teachers.

Likewise, Zigmond et al. (2011), in discussing data about how coaches in Reading First schools in Pennsylvania allocated their time, indicated that these coaches devoted little more than one-third of their effort to coaching (about fifteen hours a week or three hours a day in a forty-hour week). In this study, coaches on average divided their time almost equally between individual and group coaching. Zigmond et al. (2010) also indicated that although achievement improved in these Reading First schools, it was not possible in this evaluation study to determine what coaches do that makes a difference nor how the presence of coaches interacted "with other variables in the school that might also contribute to improving teaching and learning" (p. 28).

In a three-year study of coaching in a Head Start program, Shidler (2009) found that the three coaches spent more time in classrooms in years two and three than in year one; however, they found a relationship between time spent on-site coaching teachers and student outcomes only in year one, and then only on a single outcome measure, alphabet letter recognition. They found no significant relationship between time spent coaching and the gain scores on the Peabody Picture Vocabulary Test in any of the years. They indicate that there was more focused coaching in the initial year and make a valid point: rather than time spent in the classroom, the important factors to consider are the quality and type of interaction between coach and teacher. However, the study is limited in that it does not address specifically what coaches were doing as they worked with teachers or whether they were school-based coaches or coaches external to the school.

Even at the middle and high school levels, coaches are involved in many different activities. In a study of middle school coaches in 113 middle schools in Florida, Marsh et al. (2008) found that the majority of coaches spent less than half their time in the classroom assisting individual teachers. In that study, teachers and administrators indicated that coaches had a positive effect on instructional practice; however, the effect of coaching on student achievement was mixed, with significant gains for some cohorts but not for others. In the Pennsylvania High School Coaching Initiative, a reform model that focused on one-on-one instructional coaching in twenty-four high schools, researchers found differences in perceptions of teachers who were more intensively coached as compared with those who weren't (Brown et al., 2007). The intensively coached teachers felt that coaching changed the way they taught and that their knowledge of literacy strategies increased and deepened as a result of working with the coach; these intensively coached teachers also believed that coaching led to improved student achievement.

In Bean et al. (2010), an in-depth study of coaching in twenty schools, time spent coaching was related to achievement on the first- and second-grade standardized assessment measure. In schools identified as receiving *more* coaching (both individual and group), there were significantly more students identified as proficient and fewer identified as at risk than in schools identified as receiving *less* coaching. In schools identified as having more coaching, the average percent of coach time allocated to coaching was 44 percent, while in schools identified as having less coaching, the average percent of coach time allocated to coaching was 22 percent. On average, more time was spent working with individual teachers rather than groups, although there was variability across the coaches. A critical finding in the Bean et al. (2010) study, however, was the great variability in how coaches did their work. Some focused on observing in the classrooms while others did not observe at all. Others were more involved in modeling or co-teaching; most spent time talking with teachers, helping them to make instructional adjustments in their teaching. What seemed to be critical was that these coaches had explanations for why they focused on specific activities, some of which related to the needs of students or teachers, others related to the context in which they worked—they were not permitted to observe teachers until asked. In this study, teachers in schools in which coaches spent more time with them valued coaching more highly.

Likewise, L'Allier and Elish-Piper (2006) found that time spent with teachers mattered. In classrooms where teachers spent more time with coaches, students made higher average reading gains than did students in classrooms where literacy coaches spent the lowest percentage of time with teachers.

Few studies actually investigate the specifics of how coaches do their work and whether some activities are more productive than others. In other words, how essential is observing and providing feedback to individual teachers? What is the impact of modeling? What we can infer from the results of the studies reported in this chapter is that time spent with teachers is important, but that there are not definitive answers as to which activities might be most productive. The value of specific coaching activities may differ depending on the context, the needs of teachers, and students in specific schools. Moreover, we do know that there appear to be relationships between amount of time spent coaching and student learning, and between amount of time spent coaching and the extent to which teachers value it.

What we can infer from the results of the studies reported in this chapter is that time spent with teachers is important, but that there are not definitive answers as to which activities might be most productive. The value of specific coaching activities may differ depending on the context, the needs of teachers, and students in specific schools.

An important point is that literacy or reading coaches often do more than coach. They may be responsible for helping teachers assess students and then interpret results, which can be an impetus for a successful coaching relationship. They may also be involved with outreach efforts with parents or community agencies, or coordinate instructional services, making decisions about which students receive special support from reading specialists, special educators, and so on. They are often involved with curriculum development or materials selection. In other words, they are literacy leaders in the school (see Bean & Carroll, 2006, for a complete list). Figure 14.2 (page 330) provides a list of possible coaching activities, group and individual (Bean, 2009). Some of these activities can be used as a means of developing rapport and trust with teachers—locating resources for teachers or helping teachers plan. Bean et al. (2008) also found that coaches often conduct "on the fly" coaching—short, informal interactions with teachers in the hallways, outside classroom doors, or even on the way into school in the morning. Other activities such as observing and providing feedback, coteaching, or modeling require that coaches establish a more in depth relationship with teachers that enable them to coach effectively.

> An important point is that literacy or reading coaches often do more than coach. . . . They are literacy leaders in the school.

But even if coaches have time to coach, they often wonder how they can increase teacher receptivity. The comments of a university basketball coach in a television interview provide some intriguing insights; his reply to the question "What makes this team so good?" was, "They are coachable, they want to be coached, they respond to coaching." The same might be said about coaching in a school: teachers must be receptive to and willing to be coached. So, how does this happen? First, if both coach and teacher have the same goal—student learning—there is likely to be much more acceptance of coaching. In other words, any discussion about change has to do with how to help students learn more effectively. More specifically, there seems to be some evidence that talking about student data with teachers makes an important contribution to the coaching process (Marsh et al., 2008). Second, the relationship between coach and teacher should be one of collaboration or at least cooperation. The

Group Activities

- Developing, locating, or sharing resources with teachers (written or oral)

- Participating in meetings with grade-level or subject-area teams to discuss assessment, instruction, curriculum, analyzing student work, teacher assignments, and so on

- Participating in committee work (developing curriculum, preparing materials)

- Leading or participating in study groups to discuss specific materials read by the group

- Leading or participating in more traditional types of professional development workshops

- Participating in more formal lesson study (Stigler & Hiebert, 1999) with groups of teachers

- Assisting teachers with online professional development

Individual Activities

- "Coaching on the fly" (COTF)—impromptu meeting with a teacher to discuss a topic of importance to that teacher (a specific student, test scores, and so on)

- Coplanning lessons

- Having conversations with individual teachers

- Modeling

- Co-teaching

- Observing and providing feedback

- Combining activities—modeling, co-teaching, and observing while working with teachers in the classroom (generally for a block of time)

Adapted from Bean (2009). The Reading Specialist: Leadership in Classroom, School, and Community. *New York: Guilford Press, p. 12. Used with permission.*

Figure 14.2: Coaching activities.

wise coach understands that not all relationships will be equally easy to develop or maintain, and as Hasbrouck and Denton (2005) state, "*You cannot provide coaching services to someone who does not want to cooperate with you*" (italics in original, p. 3). They suggest that through effective coaching, relationships may develop from one of cooperation to one of collaboration. Finally, and most importantly, coaches must differentiate their coaching if they are to support teachers in their instructional efforts: not all teachers require or need the same type or amount of coaching.

In figure 14.3, two scenarios are described that illustrate how a coach differentiated his coaching with two teachers. In the first scenario, Ethan worked intensely with Shelley. Although Shelley lacked basic knowledge about teaching reading at a specific grade level, she was receptive to the in-depth coaching that Ethan could provide. In the second scenario, Sharice, an experienced teacher, felt little need for coaching; she exhibited what might be called a "wait and see" attitude. But when she requested support, Ethan was quick to respond. He provided the necessary resources and then found a way to continue his involvement with Sharice, indicating that he would like to know how students responded to this instruction. These scenarios illustrate the ways in which one coach varied his work based on teacher needs and preferences (Kise, 2006).

Scenario One

Shelley was transferred from teaching middle school English to a third-grade classroom position. She immediately went to Ethan, the reading coach, and asked for help, indicating that she had little experience or knowledge about how to plan for the needs of her twenty-five students during the core reading block. On two occasions, she and Ethan talked about the core reading program and her students; they reviewed data from the recent progress-monitoring test and discussed Shelley's observations. Ethan taught Shelley's class so she could observe another third-grade teacher during part of the reading block. They both agreed that they would work together on and off for two weeks. They coplanned lessons, and then Ethan did combination coaching on two consecutive days (modeling, co-teaching, and observing), with Shelley assuming more responsibility on day two. Shelley and Ethan also met to discuss the lessons and Ethan helped Shelley plan lessons for the remainder of the week. Ethan stopped by on Friday afternoon during her planning period to ask how things were going.

Figure 14.3: Coaching of two teachers. Continued →

Together they discussed and celebrated some of the "successes" of that week. They also agreed to meet the following Friday to discuss specific ideas for grouping and differentiation of instruction.

Scenario Two

During the first few months of the year, Sharice, an experienced and well-respected seventh-grade social studies teacher, had been very quiet in the grade-level meetings, listening attentively to teachers talking about their instructional plans on how to use literacy strategies in their content-area teaching. Although several teachers talked enthusiastically about the work they were doing with Ethan in the classroom, Sharice just listened. In November, however, she dropped by Ethan's office, sat down, and told him that she was starting a new unit on the Civil War. She then told him that she wanted to have the students read a related novel and whether he had any ideas. Ethan asked when it would be convenient to discuss this and promised he would search for some possible resources. They met two days later; Ethan came prepared with copies of three alternative novels and some other material that he thought would be useful. Sharice chose *1863: A House Divided—A Novel of the Civil War* by Elizabeth Massie as a novel to read to the class during the unit. She thanked Ethan and told him that she planned to think about discussion questions that she could ask after reading short segments. She wanted these questions to provoke high-level thinking and discussion. Ethan agreed that such a plan would stimulate thought and asked Sharice if she would be willing to let him know how this approach worked with her students. She smiled and suggested they meet the following week for a short time during her planning period.

Implications for coaches are as follows:

- Establish priorities—Recognize that some time each day should be spent with teachers even though another task or responsibility may not be accomplished.

- Be accessible—Walk the halls and stop in classrooms on a systematic basis to see if teachers need anything as a nonthreatening and effective means of establishing rapport with teachers and encouraging them to ask questions or request coaching support. Additionally, teachers should know how to get in touch with the coach. Some coaches post their schedules, and teachers sign up for conferences; others make certain that teachers know their email addresses and telephone numbers.

- Develop a schedule—Make it possible to work with all teachers in the school, but recognize that there will be differing degrees in the extent of coaching for specific teachers. Some coaches indicate that they work with teachers from a specific grade level for a concentrated period such as two weeks or a month. During that time, they are involved in various activities as a means of getting to know teachers, students, and the curriculum. They meet and plan with some teachers, coteach, model, observe, and provide feedback. They meet individually or in groups. In other schools, there might be a specific literacy focus, such as to improve vocabulary learning of students. Coaches might lead several miniworkshops to provide important content knowledge, introduce several research-based strategies, and provide teachers with resources they need to apply these strategies. They may also schedule time to meet with individual teachers to help them implement these strategies successfully.

- Keep a log—Indicate how time is spent, and reflect on the results. The log can also be an important tool if there is a need to discuss with the principal ways to make the coaching role more effective and efficient.

- Recognize the value of group coaching for its efficiency and effectiveness—By working with all teachers, the concept of coaching as "only for those who aren't doing the job" can be diminished. Moreover, such meetings can provide opportunities to establish relationships, build trust, and establish a sense of community. Often, this sort of coaching can provide the foundation for a more intense, in-depth relationship with individual teachers.

Final Thoughts

As evident in this chapter, creating positive coaching conditions increases the likelihood that coaching will have a positive influence on teachers and students. However, several key questions continue to be raised. The first, and the most difficult to answer, is, "Does literacy coaching work?" Those asking that question generally want to know whether coaching has an effect on student learning, and, as reported in this chapter, such evidence is difficult to obtain. So many factors affect student learning—such as a new reading program, increases in time allotted to reading instruc-

> As evident in this chapter, by creating positive conditions for coaching, there is more likelihood that coaching will have a positive influence on teachers and students.

tion in schools, reduction in class size, and so on—that it is difficult to isolate the effects of coaching. A better question might be, "What kind of coaching works, for whom, and when?"

A second question has to do with the cost efficiency of coaching, that is, "Is there a less expensive and equally effective means of providing professional development?" Again, this question may be too simplistic as stated; schools may need to think creatively in terms of what support teachers in their buildings need and how it can be provided. Perhaps a reading specialist, who has both instructional and leadership opportunities, can provide the support needed in a school.

As we learn more about coaching, that knowledge should enable school personnel to make modifications in how they select coaches, in what they *call* coaches, and even in their job descriptions. However, the research of the past few decades has provided the field with evidence that coaching does have much to contribute to teacher growth and student learning.

References

Atteberry, A., Bryk, A., Walker, L., & Biancarosa, G. (2008, March). *Variations in the amount of coaching in literacy collaborative schools.* Paper presented at the annual conference of the American Educational Research Association, New York.

Bean, R. M. (2009). *The reading specialist: Leadership for classroom, school, and community.* New York: Guilford Press.

Bean, R. M., Belcastro, E., Draper, J., Jackson, V., Jenkins, K., Kenavey, L., et al. (2008). *Literacy coaching in Reading First Schools: The blind men and the elephant.* Paper presented at the National Reading Conference Meeting, Orlando, FL.

Bean, R. M., & Carroll, K. (2006). The literacy coach as a catalyst for change. In C. Cummins (Ed.), *Understanding and implementing reading first initiatives* (pp. 139–152). Newark, DE: International Reading Association.

Bean, R. M., Draper, J. A., Hall, V., Vandermolen, J., & Zigmond, N. (2010). Coaches and coaching in Reading First schools: A reality check. *Elementary School Journal, 111*(1), 87–114.

Brown, D., Reumann-Moore, R., Hugh, R., Christman, J. B., Riffer, M., du Plessis, P., et al. (2007, October). *Making a difference: Year two report of the Pennsylvania high school coaching initiative.* Philadelphia: Research for Action. Accessed at http://pdf.researchforaction.org/rfapdf /publication/pdf_file/344/Brown_D_PAHSCI_Year_2_Report.pdf on September 20, 2009.

Camburn, E. M., Kimball, S. M., & Lowenhaupt, R. (2008). Going to scale with teacher leadership: Lessons learned from a districtwide literacy coach initiative. In M. M. Mangin & S. R. Stoelinga (Eds.), *Effective teacher leadership: Using research to inform and reform* (pp. 120–143). New York: Teachers College Press.

Carroll, K. (2007). *Conversations with coaches: Their roles in Pennsylvania Reading First schools.* Unpublished doctoral dissertation, University of Pittsburgh.

Costa, A. L., & Garmston, R. J. (2002). *Cognitive coaching: A foundation for renaissance schools* (2nd ed.). Norwood, MA: Christopher-Gordon.

Covey, S. (1989). *The seven habits of highly effective people.* New York: Simon & Schuster.

Deussen, T., Coskie, T., Robinson, L., & Autio, E. (2007). *"Coach" can mean many things: Five categories of literacy coaches in Reading First* (Issues & Answers Report, REL 2007–No. 005). Washington, DC: Regional Educational Laboratory Northwest. Accessed at http://ies.ed.gov/ncee/edlabs on September 20, 2009.

Frost, S., & Bean, R. (2006, September 27). *Qualifications for literacy coaches: Achieving the gold standard* (Brief). Urbana, IL: Literacy Coaching Clearinghouse. Accessed at www.literacycoachingonline.org/briefs /LiteracyCoaching.pdf on March 20, 2009.

Garet, M. S., Cronen, S., Eaton, M., Kurki, A., Ludwig, M., Jones, W., et al. (2008). *The impact of two professional development interventions on early reading instruction and achievement* (NCEE 2008–4030). Washington, DC: National Center for Education Evaluation and Regional Assistance.

Hasbrouck, J., & Denton, C. (2005). *The reading coach: A how-to manual for success.* Longmont, CO: Sopris West.

International Reading Association. (2004). *The role and qualifications of the reading coach in the United States: A position statement of the International Reading Association* [Brochure]. Newark, DE: Author.

International Reading Association. (2006). *Standards for middle and high school literacy coaches.* Newark, DE: Author.

Johnson, D. W., & Johnson, F. P. (2003). *Joining together: Group theory and group skills* (8th ed.). Boston: Allyn & Bacon.

Kise, J. A. G. (2006). *Differentiated coaching: A framework for helping teachers change.* Thousand Oaks, CA: Corwin Press.

L'Allier, S. K., & Elish-Piper, L. (2006, December). *An initial examination of the effects of literacy coaching on student achievement in reading in grades K–3.*

Paper presented at the fifty-sixth annual National Reading Conference, Los Angeles.

Leana, C. R., & Pil, F. K. (2006). Social capital and organizational performance: Evidence from urban public schools. *Organization Science, 17*(3), 353–366.

Leithwood, K., Louis, K. S., Anderson, S., & Wahlstrom, K. (2004). *Review of research: How leadership influences student learning.* Minneapolis: University of Minnesota, Center for Applied Research and Educational Improvement; Ontario, Canada: University of Toronto, Institute for Studies in Education.

Marsh, J. A., McCombs, J. S., Lockwood, J. R., Martorell, F., Gershwin, D., Naftel, S., et al. (2008). *Supporting literacy across the sunshine state: A study of Florida middle school reading coaches.* Santa Monica, CA: RAND Corporation.

Matsumura, L. C., Sartoris, M., DiPrima Bickel, D., & Garnier, H. E. (2009). Leadership for literacy coaching: The principal's role in launching a new coaching program. *Educational Administration Quarterly, 45*(5), 655–693.

Neuman, S., & Cunningham, L. (2009). The impact of professional development and coaching on early language and literacy instructional practices. *American Educational Research Journal, 46*(2), 532–566. Accessed at http://aerj.aera.net on May 27, 2009.

Rodgers, A., & Rodgers, E. M. (2007). *The effective literacy coach: Using inquiry to support teaching and learning.* New York: Teachers College Press.

Roller, C. M. (2006). *Reading and literacy coaches: Report on hiring requirements and duties survey.* Newark, DE: International Reading Association.

Shidler, L. (2009). The impact of time spent coaching for teacher efficacy on student achievement. *Early Childhood Education Journal, 36*, 453–460.

Taylor, J. E. (2008). Instructional coaching: The state of the art. In M. M. Mangin & S. R. Stoelinga (Eds.), *Effective teacher leadership: Using research to inform and reform* (pp. 10–35). New York: Teachers College Press.

Thibodeau, G. M. (2008). A content literacy collaborative study group: High school teachers take charge of their professional learning. *Journal of Adolescent and Adult Literacy, 52*(1), 54–84.

Toll, C. A. (2004). Separating coaching from supervising. *English Leadership Quarterly, 27*(4), 5–7.

Toll, C. A. (2007). *Lenses on literacy coaching: conceptualizations, functions, and outcomes.* Norwood, MA: Christopher-Gordon.

Walpole, S., & Beauchat, K. A. (2008, June 2). *Facilitating teacher study groups* [Brief]. Urbana, IL: Literacy Coaching Clearinghouse. Accessed at www.literacycoachingonline.org/briefs/StudyGroupsBrief.pdf on January 20, 2009.

Zigmond, N., Bean, R. M., Kloo, A., & Brydon, M. M. (2011). Policy, research, and reading first. In A. McGill-Franzen & R. L. Allington (Eds.), *Handbook of reading disability research* (pp. 464–476). New York: Routledge.

Index